ARCHBISHOP WILLIAM ALEXANDER AND THE AFRICAN ORTHODOX CHURCH

ARCHBISHOP DANIEL WILLIAM ALEXANDER AND THE AFRICAN ORTHODOX CHURCH

Morris Johnson

International Scholars Publications
Lanham • New York • Oxford

Copyright © 1999 by
Morris R. Johnson

International Scholars Publications
4720 Boston Way
Lanham, Maryland 20706

12 Hid's Copse Rd.
Cumnor Hill, Oxford OX2 9JJ

All rights reserved
Printed in the United States of America
British Library Cataloging in Publication Information Available

Library of Congress Cataloging-in-Publication Data

Johnson, Morris R. (Morris Rodney), 1944
Archbishop Daniel William Alexander and the African
Orthodox Church. / Morris Johnson
p. cm.
Includes bibliographical references and index.
1. African Orthodox Church—History. 2. Alexander, Daniel
1883-1970. I. Title
BX6194.4J65   1999   289.9'3'092—dc21   98-54996 CIP

ISBN 1-57309-337-8 (cloth: alk. ppr.)
ISBN 1-57309-341-6 (pbk: alk. ppr.)

∞™ The paper used in this publication meets the minimum
requirements of American National Standard for Information
Sciences—Permanence of Paper for Printed Library Materials,
ANSI Z39.48—1984

DEDICATION

TO ALL MY AFRICAN
WOMEN ANCESTORS, BUT ESPECIALLY TO:
Portia, Mary, Dora, Ella and Pat

ACKNOWLEDGEMENTS

Since so many individuals encouraged me along life's highways, I am not sure where to commerce the act of gratitude. The writing of this book brought me into contact with numerous individuals who offered me suggestions and advice; to them, I am deeply appreciative.

I am particularly thankful to the African Studies and Research Program at Howard University for providing me the opportunity to study and interact with some of the best minds of the African diaspora. I was always encouraged to express ideas and views that comprised the entire ideological spectrum. Such encouragement from faculty found expression in my book. It was through the exposure in many classes and seminars that my thesis took shape. Indeed, it was the extensive readings in South Africa History that provided me with the technical data necessary to write this historical-religious study. I, alone, take the full responsibility for opinions and errors presented.

My three years in residency at the African Studies and Research Program was made enjoyable because of Mrs. Ann Brown, Judith Knight and Mellenia Jones who cheered me on and became my friends. A very hearty acknowledgement is made to the past Director of African Studies, Dr. Robert J. Cummings, who helped me enter the program in 1980. To this expression of gratitude I must also add Dr. Sulayman S. Nyang, current Director, who guided me with a fatherly hand.

I am greatly indebted, as well, to Dr. Robert Edgar, who advised and supervised my dissertation. His support, patience and confidence in me brought this dissertation into fruition. Thank you, sir, for suggesting that I research the topic of Daniel William Alexander and his church.

Additionally, I wish to thank Dr. Luis Serapiao, Dr. Sulaymen Nyang and Dr. Robert Cummings for reading and offering many suggestions, for the book.

Deep appreciation are expressed to the following individuals who have played critical roles in assisting me to write this work: His Beatitude Stafford James Sweeting I, Patriarch, Welmore Cook, Dorothy Williams, Rose Robinson, Vophsie Cantave, Alvin Elkes, Russell Buffaloe, Elaine Jarvis, Joan Saldamando and Professors Phyllis Washington, Daisy Walker and Cynthia Clark.

Phyllis Washington and Daisy Walker have earned my eternal love for their patience and general support given to me. Phyllis dedicated many months in proofreading my chapters, while Daisy gave part of her life to type the many suggestions offered for the chapters.

Special thanks must go also to Jackie Ammerman, Curator of Archives manuscripts, and Jim Cooper, Assistant Curator of Archives, of the Pitts Theological Library at Emory University.

In South Africa, to the Curators of the State Archives in Pretoria and to the Curators of the Africana Library in Kimberley (especially Mrs. C. Duminy) a warm and gracious thank you.

To all my teachers at Mays Senior High, Miami-Dade Community College, North (Dr. William Primus), George Washington University and Syracuse University (Dr. Ottey Scruggs), I thank you for the time you spent, in class and privately, providing me with a solid academic foundation.

Finally, to my TEAM who typed and dissected the chapters of this book for publication, thank you for making *OUR* project a reality: Professor Joseph McNair, Sandile Situpa, Danyal Moss, Mrs. Carol Allen, Professors Lou Skillings and Josett Pete. Professor Cynthia Clark, I love you.

Again, my love to all my family members for their love and support over the years.

Morris R. Johnson

FOREWARD

Morris Johnson's impressive study of the life of Archbishop Daniel William Alexander and the history of the African Orthodox Church of South African is a welcome contribution to scholarship on African independent churches. Although, there is an abundance of literature on African independent churches, we have very few studies based on documentation generated by an independent church.

Too often we have to construct church histories based on external sources such as missionaries, government officials, and policemen whose views are unsympathetic or hostile to independence churches. Fortunately, this is not the case with Alexander and the African Orthodox Church. From the church's founding in 1925 to Alexander's death in 1970, it maintained a unique and impressive record of Alexander's leadership and church organization and activities. In the late 1980's, the church papers were transferred to the Pitts Theological Seminary at Emory University. Johnson's study is the first to make full use of them.

Alexander and his church have been of particular interest to scholars over the years because of Alexander's connections to the Marcus Garvey movement in the United States and because the African Orthodox Church carried its mission outside South African boundaries to establish branches throughout southern and eastern Africa. Johnson's study recounts these developments as well as the African Orthodox Church's battles against segregation and apartheid, its internal tensions and schisms, and its relationships with a host of other independent churches.

Morris Johnson's study is a major contribution to our understanding of African Christianity and the establishment of African independent churches. We are indebted to him for recognizing Alexander's importance and setting out to chronicle his life and the evolution of his church. With the publication of this remarkable study, scholars have a major source for understanding a critical independent church and its institutional evolution over several generations.

Robert R. Edgar
Professor of African Studies
Howard University

FOREWARD

The analysis of black and African figures is passing through several stages. Special attention has been given to reconstructing the historical figures that have been omitted from the study of ethnic communities that also have been ignored. Johnson seeks to correct this double invisibility by examining the poignant struggle of Bishop Daniel William Alexander's effort to establish the African Orthodox Church through the lens of liberation theology. Those familiar with the literature will recognize Morris Johnson's pioneering application of this methodology to the deeds and creeds of this neglected figure in African and African American religion.

Liberation theology introduces a new hermeneutics for the historical analysis of religion, riveting our attention on the reciprocal dependence between our social activity in the economic, social, and political arena and our worldview, our theology. Whether we choose to conserve and preserve the present social hierarchies or seek to correct them is determined by the concept of God we embrace. Unmasking and exposing the ideological misuse of religion and theology as an instrument of oppression, (Jose Bonio's method of "theology of suspicion"), Liberation theology rereads the deeds and creeds of religious history through the lens of "praxis verification:" "The verification principle of every theological statement is the praxis that it enables for the future. Theological statements contain as much truth as they deliver practically in transforming reality." Dorothy Soelle. *Political Theology*. Philadelphia: Fortress Press, 1974.

This interpretive and critical framework provides a fresh and attractive framework to explore still unsettled issues in the black independent and separatist churches in Africa, the "colorline" as it relates to black identity in Africa and the Diaspora, and the "not so odd couple" linkage that researchers like Carter G. Woodsen exposed between religion and the political, religion and oppression.

Applying this methodological insight to the mission school, for instance, Johnson's provocative case study confirms Carter G. Woodsen's role of mis-education in the spawning of mis-religion and the vital role that each serves in the maintenance needs of oppression. Also noteworthy is the methodological imperative, not yet acknowledged in historical research in religion, that it recommends: historical reconstructions that omit or undervalue this critical angle of analysis are highly suspect. My own research has long advocated this approach as indispensable, and I am happy to see its application growing.

The reader will find here a text that is satisfying at many levels, analytically and historically, but especially in the provocative and intriguing research hypotheses that it generates for the next generation of scholars.

William R. Jones
Florida State University
Tallahassee, FL 32306

Tables of Contents

Title Page I

Copyright Page II

Dedication III

Acknowledgements IV

Forward V

I. GIVING VOICE TO THE VOICELESS 1

    Endnotes 13

II. A CRITIQUE: South Africa, Capitalism and the African 14

    The African American Connection 21
    The Separatist Church Movement 26
    Diamond and Gold Mining 30
    Endnotes 54

III. DANIEL WILLIAM ALEXANDER: What Manner of Man? 55

    Marcus Garvey, African Redemption and South Africa 66
    South Africa 71
    Alexander in America 74
    Endnotes 86

IV. THE INSTITUTIONALIZATION OF THE AOC 87

    Mission Efforts 92
    Uganda 93
    Kenya 97
    Ecumenical Efforts 111
    Endnotes 130

V. THE EYE OF THE STORM: Apartheid and Black Resistance 131

    The Nationalism of Afrikaner Religion 139
    AOC, The Anglican Church, and the Non-European Unity
    Movement 143
    Endnotes 159

VI. AOC IN THE POST WAR YEARS: Conflict and Expansion 160

    Endnotes 172

VII. SCHISM AND INDEPENDENCE WITHIN THE AOC 173

    Endnotes 193

VIII. CONCLUSION: AOC and African American History 194

    Endnotes 199

Sources Consulted:

    The AOC Archives 200

    Government Publications 201-202
    Periodicals/Articles 203
    Books 204-214

Chapter 1
GIVING VOICE TO THE VOICELESS

This study provides a detailed analysis of the origins and institutionalization of the African Orthodox Church of South Africa, AOC. Its focus is on Archbishop Daniel William Alexander, who was the church's founder and whose life was inseparable from the rise of this urban church based in Kimberley, South Africa. His life from 1925 to 1969 reflected a intense struggle to plant African Orthodocy in a hostile environment of rigid segregation.

He was born on Christmas Day, 1833, in Port Elizabeth. As a "Colored", he enjoyed greater freedom of movement and opportunities than black Africans. He embarked early on a religious path, which took him from the Anglican Church to his long involvement with black separatist Christianity. At the time of his death in 1970, he built a church with over 10,000 followers, 50 ministers, church property worth tens of thousands of dollars, and branches scattered throughout southern Africa.

For nearly forty-five years, Alexander labored in a milieu of intense racism and oppression to establish a black religious organization free from European control. This effort coincided with some of the most profound changes that shaped the South African scene. Therefore, the following question must be noted to provide a full account of the rise of the AOC: How did the racist legislation of the Botha/Hertzog/Smuts governments, and the rise of the apartheid system produced profound consequences not only for the AOC but also personal bitterness in Alexander's life as well?

What manner of man was Alexander? Of course, the question is easy to answer of we are dealing with him as a mature adult. He seems to have been driven by an all-consuming power to establish the African Orthodox Church in South Africa. Therefore, he was constantly searching for individuals to support his goal; however, if an individual lied to him or did not fulfill a promise, he would banish them to hell. He, on the other hand, never told bold-faced lies; he never borrowed money and did not attempt to repay it; he was never unfaithful to

Mother Alexander and he always believed and practiced the old adage: "let your Word be your Bond". We do not have any clues as to the early experiences that helped shaped Alexander's stern character. The record is silent on his childhood years. Except for the names of parents and a few scant references, no material exists. Even oral history, which provides some insights into the personalities of Shaka and his mother, is voiceless as well. So we simply do not know if he enjoyed music or liked to dance, or if he dedicated many hours to his schoolwork.

Perhaps he came to the ministry as a means of providing hope and salvation for those locked out of the banquet. Beaconsfield, located on the fringes of Kimberley, was the new headquarters of the AOC. The area was bleak, and the poverty pervasive. Nevertheless, the mystery remains: why no records of his early life? The African Orthodox Church (AOC) Archives, housed at Pitts Theological Center, Emory University, in Atlanta, Georgia, is voluminous. Alexander, over the decades, collected hundreds of letters, dozens of files, numerous news clippings and travel ledgers. In fact, the late Patriarch of the AOC, South Africa was gathering data to leave an account of his church for future generations.

My South African sojourn produced no early biographical data; however, it allowed me to absorb some of the unique elements of his environment. I met His Beatitude Moran Mar James II, current Patriarch of the AOC. He is a dignified elder who provided transport for me to Alexander's grave and to the original location of the Mother Church in Beaconsfield. I was deeply moved by the sights. For me, Alexander's life became real and the problems he surmounted more worthy of respect. Of course, in the early days of his pastorate, he did not own a car. Reverend Matthews, over lunch, informed me that the Bishop walked great distances and even used a donkey cart to provide care for his church members. Alexander's granddaughter noted he was loved, but he could be stern and was quite a disciplinarian.

Equally stern was George Alexander McGuire. He was a consummate churchman and a passionate proponent of black religious nationalism. It was during the early 1920's that Alexander, in his continued search for authentic spiritually, turned to McGuire as a source of valid apostolic succession. Without McGuire's vision and creation of a black "owned" catholic church, Alexander may have been doomed to an endless quest for a "home".

McGuire was born in Sweets, Antigua, in 1866. He received his theological training at the Moravian's Nisky Theological Seminary on Saint Thomas. For a few years, he served the African Methodist Episcopal Church and in 1894 he came to the United States and was ordained a priest in the Protestant Episcopal Church. His abilities moved church officials to appoint him rector of the historic African-American Church in America, the Church of the Crucifixion in Philadelphia. Another outstanding achievement on his part was being appointed, in 1905, archdeacon of "colored work" in the diocese of Arkansas. This was the highest post that could be held by a black within the Episcopal realm.

McGuire nonetheless, was spiritual empty. He returned to Antigua (1913) and within six years he was back in the USA. That year, 1919, found him involved in Marcus Garvey's Universal Negro Improvement Association (UNIA), as his Chaplain General. The nationalist impulse of Garvey's ideas merged with McGuire's religious search for spiritual autonomy. Indeed, two years later, the African Orthodox Church was born with McGuire as it founder, first bishop and Patriarch.[1] He had been driven from the Episcopalian house due to white religious bigotry and discrimination. Now at long last the search for autonomy was complete. McGuire's desires for spiritual autonomy and the origin of the AOC was revealed in the pages of Garvey's newspaper *The Negro World*. Without this organ of international black (Pan-African) nationalism, Alexander would not have been exposed to McGuire's "Black Christian Theology." The two men were linked, until McGuire's death in 1934, in the serious mission of institutionalization of the AOC in South Africa. Garvey, on the other hand, had no direct contact with Alexander; nonetheless, all three were attacked for plotting sedition and rebellion.

Before we analyze the issue of sedition and rebellion, it must be noted that a file existed on Alexander. The South African government watched carefully all black "Native" churches, which applied for government recognition or permission to establish new churches in the various "reserves". The European officials were suspicious of all religious groups that were not under direct white supervision. As early as 1924, Alexander applied for permit to build a new church, since his departure from the African Church. Officials of the Native Affairs Department were not sympathetic to his initial request; the department wanted to be sure Alexander did not have "Ethiopian" sentiments.[2]

"Ethiopian" was a label placed upon organizations and churches deemed anti-white and rebellious by the state. As Garvey's movement gained momentum internationally, suspicion of the AOC and other separatist churches increased inside of South Africa as well. His message was lucid and provocative: Africa belonged to the black races of the world; if the white colonial masters refused to leave the continent, they must be ousted. So any association with him, real or imagined, produced fear and hysteria among the white ruling elites of South Africa.

Alexander's "crime" was not sedition or rebellion but association with McGuire, i.e., the AOC and indirectly with Garvey's UNIA. Nevertheless, South African authorities noted that Alexander denied returning to Africa to establish McGuire-type churches to stir up dissension among the "natives". It was generally understood, according to the document, that the consecration of clergymen by McGuire was part of a scheme, with Garvey's consent, to cause trouble throughout the British Empire.[3]

The Garvey matter became entangled with Alexander's passport difficulties. He left for America in 1927. The authorities, in London and New York, contacted the Department of Interior in Pretoria. It was stated plainly by the Department that the Archbishop did not approach their office for a passport.[4] The Secretary of Native Affairs also complained he was not aware that Alexander had left South Africa.[5] The French, too, were drawn into the winding discussion of the passport. Of course, their Consul-General agreed with the other European officials that a native or African should not be given a passport; however, his impression of Alexander was that he appeared to be a half-breed and perhaps of

French ancestry. Be that as it may, the Consul-General suggested that since Alexander claimed he was French and not a British subject, he could perhaps be deemed a prohibited immigrant and denied re-entry into South Africa based upon the Immigration Act of 1913.[6]

Alexander's woes would not vanish. It was suggested that the police should become involved and that more information was wanted on the Archbishop. However, his church activities in Uganda and Southern Rhodesia caught the eye of authorities. In Uganda, the Reverend Sparta, an emerging leader of the AOC in its infancy, petitioned the Provincial Commissioner of Buganda, in 1929, seeking permission for the AOC to teach its doctrine in the area.[7] The Commissioner contacted the officials in South Africa. They responded by stating that the AOC was deemed unfit to be granted any privileges.[8] Additionally, another document revealed that Sparta was interest in the UNIA. The report did not prove much information on Alexander; however, it did note that he was on the prohibited immigrant list, and that he should be kept under observation while in Dageya (site of the AOC in Uganda).[9]

The Ugandan government refused all applicants of the AOC for official recognition. The ghost of the UNIA haunted the decisions. Alexander could not erase the alleged political ties of his church with sedition. The Secretary of Native Affairs had to concede in 1932:

> "Up to the present this Department has received no reports of definitely unfavorable character regarding the activities of the African Orthodox Church nor has it been represented that Alexander and his associates have been concerned in the spread of political propaganda or doctrines of an objectionable or subversive character".[10]

The "subversive" character of the AOC was also trumpeted in Southern Rhodesia. As in Uganda, the obstacles to official recognition for the AOC were again the Garvey connection with radical laymen. The activities of John Mphamba and Dick Dube were harmless; however, given their nationalist rhetoric and union sympathies for the radical ICU, the Rhodesian authorities were convinced that the AOC was engaged in intrigue. The European response was hysterical when compared to the resources of the ICU, the AOC or the UNIA to abolish or impede colonial control.

The colonist masters took seriously any hit of a tie between communism and black activism. The false charge that Garveyism and communism were twin doctrines was pervasive in southern Africa. It was unfortunate that Josiah Gumede was elected as President-General of the African National Congress and a staunch supporter of the UNIA. He was also affiliated with the Communist Party, although membership cannot be ascertained. He proclaimed that McGuire would unite all Africans and drive out the whites. In his person, the strains of Garveyism, communism, and the AOC converge. A heady combination, indeed, to produced fears and suspicion in the white establishment. It was unfortunate that the AOC and its membership was viewed as a web of sedition; it produced for Alexander many headaches and sham hurdles to be surmounted in a sea of regulations designed to break the spirit of Blacks.

European authorities caused Alexander many moments of despair but his spirit remained indomitable. They sometimes assailed him as an ignorant native or colored who was head of a "sect". They poked fun at the Pro-Cathedral, in Beaconsfield, as a shack that looked as if it would collapse at any moment. They refused to accord him, particularly in Rhodesia, a reason for not granting his church official recognition. They even lambasted his title of Archbishop and Patriarch as if it were a joke.

Yet he survived. He possessed the tenacity of a bulldog. A document from the Native Affairs Department demonstrates this tenacity:

> In 1926 he applies for government recognition for his church it was refused by the Native Affairs Commission on the grounds of instability and unfitness. In 1927 Alexander proceeds to American on a French passport. He did not apply to this Department or to [the] Interior for a passport as he is a French subject (although born in South Africa). In November 1929 application for recognition was again refused by the Native Affairs Commission on the same grounds mentioned above. In May 1935 the Native Affairs Commission again refused to

grant government recognition to this church. No reports have been received against the activities of this church. Although one of its members was convicted and punished in 1931 for performing the functions of a marriage officer without a license. On two occasions, while Alexander was away for long periods, Likhing appointed as temporary Marriage Officer [.] [In] order that the church should not be out to any inconvenience.[11]

Inconvenience! Ten years after the first application was presented for official recognition (1934), Alexander bemoaned: "I have consistently written to the Native Affairs Commission through its Secretary, and also filled in the form 117, but the answer is always the same, your request cannot be acceded to …[12] Thus the refusal to grant recognition was not related to fitness or stability but the exercise of raw power to control the political sentiments of the black community.

The Afro Athlican Constructive Church or the House of Athly, an American-based group, experienced a similar fate to the AOC. He was in attendance, as the UNIA's representative, at the first official meeting of the AOC. Prophet Robert Athlyi Rogers founded it in Newark, New Jersey. However, in South Africa, the leadership role was in the hands of Joseph Masogha, the "Prime Comet". He applied to the Native Locations Department, in Kimberley, to become a Marriage Officer.[13] In fact both Alexander and Masogha resided in the same area of No. 2, Location in Kimberley. But the latter advocated a radical "Black Christian Theology." In time, the data gathered against the House of Athlyi was sweeping.

The prophet contacted the Secretary of the Interior to assure him that Masogha was an ordained minister of the church[14] and to please grant the privilege of Marriage Officer. As evidence mounted, the prophet's plea was never to be realized. The first report on Masogha stated he was a postman and constable but he had a drunkenness charge.

The report also noted "… He is the S. African distributing agent for the *The Negro World*, and Ethiopian publication with a large circulation in America."[15] By June 1928, all police chiefs in the Eastern Cape were alerted and provide information on the House of Athlyi. It stated the prophet's name, the location of the church in America and that the membership in Kimberley was approximately 400. The Divisional Inspector, of the Cape, went on to allege that Masogha was a "... notorious agitator at Barkly West about 8 years ago after which he came to Kimberley, where he was a very prominent member of the Native National Congress . . ."[16] The report indicated, too, that the church was refused a site and the Inspector was keen for all police branches to keep tabs on the activities of this most secretive group.

The activities of the House of Athlyi were reported to the Commissioner of Police who, in turn, shared the contents with the Secretary for Native Affairs. In essence, the report noted that diligent inquires had been made in Kimberley and in Beaconsfield to ascertain whether any black American newspaper were being circulated. Several local officials, Postmaster and Editor-in Chief, generally concluded that for months nothing was uncovered. The concern, of course, was the influence, in general, of the UNIA and, in particular, upon Masogha as he was the point man for distribution of *The Negro World*.

Then in August 1928, the Divisional Criminal Investigation Officer of Kimberley informed the Commissioner of Police in Pretoria the following:

> "I find that the House of Athlyi is a branch of Marcus Garvey's organization known as the Negro Improvement Association. The idea is to have a religious side to the Negro Improvement Association, where the Ministers can spread the doctrine of hatred to all Europeans. This Association recognizes that they will have to rely on the coming generation to oust the Europeans from this country, and thus instill into the parents at their meetings the importance of instilling into their children the one idea that the supreme enemy of the black man is the European. Their watch word is 'Oust the White man'. The organization also sells pictures depicting angels as black men and the devil as a European. They are also distributors of the Negro World. They will have nothing to do with "The Ethiopian[sic] Church, as they hold that Association are too moderate".[17]

The Kimberley official ended by saying that his informant was Doyle Modiakgotla the Provincial Secretary of the I.C.U. His hope was to provide greater details at a later date.

The authorities also launched a search for a copy of the House of Athlyi's Secret Constitution which delt, it's alleged, with teaching "native" children to hate and injure Europeans.[18] The files did not reveal a copy of this work; however, another report noted it was sending a copy of a booklet entitled *The Anthlian New Light of the World*.[19] The nature of its contents must not have been inflammatory, since it was forwarded to the Secretary for Native Affairs without commentary. A search to produce this document was in vain.

And so, too, were the endeavors of Alexander and Masogha in vain; both were refused official recognition by the government. Both were also viewed as agitators and part of Garvey's U.N.I.A. plot to unleash worldwide terror against Whites. Add to this charged social milieu the activities of the I.C.U. and the Communist Party, white officials rigorously dissected church applications and expanded their surveillance tactics. However, Alexander, McGuire, Masogha and, to a lesser extent, Garvey were unaware of the international synchronized efforts to track their movements and, if possible, employ operatives to gather data on their activities.

The above review of the police and American church groups was taken from documents collected, in South Africa, several years after the book was completed. Since the House of Athlyi was located in Newark, there may be a connection with the Moorish Science Temple founded by Noble Drew Ali. Prophet Ali's message was one of nationalism and spiritual reawakening through Islam. The information provided, I think, will enhance our appreciation of the universal influence of Garvey and the importance of the role of black religious nationalism in the drive for liberation.

Chapter Two is broad and theoretical in scope. It discusses the importance of the European missionary educational effort on the mission-trained African elite. It is this writer's contention that the African struggle for liberation was retarded by the African's adherence to the "theology of submission" preached by European missionaries. Therefore, a definition of this concept will be explored.

Since the AOC is an American church, attention must be given to the social/political conditions that shaped black America in general and there religious experiences in particular. We must try to discern the effects of racism and segregation to see why these forces produced concern for Africa, emigration, and notions of redemption and the desire to spread the Christian message to their brethren in South Africa. This concern for Africa was deeply rooted in Bishop Henry N. Turner's conviction to redeem Africa. An assessment of his visit to South Africa is in order.

A sub-theme of this chapter is to trace the origins of black independent church movement and relate how the rise of a capitalist economy produced a fertile environment for the growth of black separatist Christianity. Some background information, therefore, on the rise of the diamond and gold industries must be presented. The grist for the industrial mills of South Africa was plenty of cheap black labor. These black workers were maltreated; most were a part of a vast system of migratory exploitation. How this peasant/proletariat responded to their inhumane treatment must be critically analyzed.

What manner of man was Alexander? This is the key question in Chapter Three. Since biographical data about him is limited, the writer, nonetheless, has tried to provide a glimpse into his personally and development into adulthood. Alexander's departure from the Anglican Church, his entrance into the independent church movement and his encounter with the AOC in America are presented in detail. What must also be explained is how Alexander became aware of the AOC, what his experiences in America were and how Marcus Garvey influenced black independent church movement in South Africa and America.

The institutionalization of the AOC in Africa was due to the character and tenacity of Alexander. Chapter Four reveals his work with the clergy to ensure the survival of the AOC, how money matters served as a disruptive force within the church and the quality of his leadership and the character expectations he had for his clergy. This process to ensure the survival of the church was rooted in a theology of submission. Within the Afrikaner community during the same year, a theology of "power" emerged. The question becomes why no such theology emerged from the mission-educated black elite. A comparative analysis of the Afrikaner experience is presented.

At the same time, the institutionalization process was linked to missionary and ecumenical efforts by the AOC. This book explores Alexander's involvement in missionary ventures in southern and east Africa and the problems or difficulties he faced as he extended his hand of fellowship. This chapter will also present a critical account of his ecumenical efforts to unify other independent churches with the AOC.

Chapter Five discusses how apartheid came into fruition and how the AOC responded to the apartheid challenge. What was the official position of the Aoc's Synod to the mandates of apartheid? Apartheid put into place a flood of racist legislation. The Population Registration Act of 1950 in particular created a crisis in Alexander's life. Attention will be given to the general coloured response to the constitutional crisis over voting rights and the Population Registration Act. Resistance to white domination intensified from 1945 onward and Africans leaving the Anglican Church exemplified the new rise in militancy.

Chapter Six provides an even closer look at Alexander and his relationship with his priests. As has been the case from the inception of the AOC, money issues and respect for the archbishop's authority still produced conflict within the church. The "love/hate" relationship between Alexander and James Mdatyulwa (Secretary of the AOC) is fully revealed; also treated is in sensitive account of Alexander against his better judgement, allowing another clergyman to borrow money from the church, which was not repaid. No issue so vexed Alexander as the Masiko affair.

The schism that occurred within the AOC in 1960-61 is the heart of Chapter Seven. Background information to the conflict is provided. This chapter looks at the attempts of Alexander's bishops to oust him, the role of American Prelates during the initial stage of the conflict, and the tactics used by Alexander to secure his position as head of the new AOC in South Africa. The conflict within the AOC led to government involvement and the creation of a new AOC. The efforts of the government and those of Alexander are discussed to show how their cooperation led to the establishment of an independent AOC in South Africa.

END NOTES

1. Robert Hill (ed.) *The Marcus Garvey and Universal Negro Improvement Association papers*. Vol.II. 27 August 1919 to August 1920. (Berkeley, Los Angeles, London: University of California Press, 1983) pp. 508-509. Robert G. Weisbord, Ebony Kinship: Africa, Africans, and the Afro-American (Westport, Connecticut and London, England: Greenwood Press, Inc. 1973). See chapter 2.

2. State Archives, Pretoria, Nationalists, 11/214 (Hereafter known as SAP, NTS) Document to Director of Native Labour (Johannesburg). From Official of Barkley West 24/12/1924 " . . . I have issued instructions to the Police that no Location Permit is to be issued to any Native Preacher who is not under the direct European supervision of some recognized European Mission Church or Society . . . My principle object in issuing this instruction is as far as possible to keep the Ethiopian out of the defines locations."

3. SAP, NTS, 295, 111/214. Document to the British Consulate General, New York. From H.M.'s Principal Secretary of State (Foreign Affairs) London; 10/5/1927.

4. SAP, NTS, 111/124. See the following: Document to the Secretary for Native Affairs (Pretoria). From Secretary for the Interior, 5/12/1927.

5. SAP, NTS, 111/214. Document to the Magistrate, Kimberley. From Secretary for Native Affairs, 9/1/1928. SAP, NTS, 111/214.

6. SAP, NTS, 111/124. Document to Secretary for Native Affairs. From the Magistrate, 12/1/1928.

7. SAP, NTS, 111/124. Document to the Chief Secretary, Entebbe. From R.S.S. Mukasa Sparta, AOC Uganda, 17/1/1929.

8. SAP, NTS, 111/214. Document to Chief Secretary, Entebbe. From Secretary for Native Affairs, 27/3/1929.

9. SAP, NTS, 111/214. Document to: Not clearly marked. From W. Younger, Superintendent, 13/10/1931.

10. SAP, NTS, 111/214. Document to the Chief Secretary, Entebbe. From the Secretary for Native Affairs, 3/5/1932.

11. SAP, NTS, 111/214. Document to Native Affairs Department Stationary; however, it look duplicated. In fact this *Memo* is typed but hand written. K.M. seems to be the bottom of the page; the date 30/8.

12. SAP, NTS, 111/214. Document to Senator F.C. Thompson of the Cape Province. From DWA who is seeking support for his cause in gaining recognition for the AOC, 23/8/38.

13. Kimberley Public Library, Housed/Africana Library, (Hereafter known as KPL, H/AL). Document to the Magistrate of Kimberley. From the Secretary for Native Affairs, 9/4/1926.

14. KPL, H/AL. Document to Secretary of the Interior. From Shepherd R. A. Rogers (Newark, U.S.A.). No date was provided; however it must have the year of 1926.

15. KPL, H/AL. Document to the Magistrate of Kimberley. From Protector of Natives, 22/4/1926.

16. KPL, H/AL. Document to all District Commandents, South African Police (Eastern Cape Division). From the Headquarters of the Deputy Commissioner, Divisional Inspector, 16/6/1928.

17. KPL, H/AL. Document to Divisional Criminal Investigation Department (Kimberley). From the Divisional C. I. Officer (Kimberley), 8/9/1928.

18. KPL, H/AL. Document to Officer of the Deputy Commissioner (Transvaal Division) Pretoria. From Deputy Commissioner, Transvaal Division, 22/9/1928.

19. *Ibid.*

CHAPTER 2
A CRITIQUE: SOUTH AFRICA, CAPITALISM AND THE AFRICAN AMERICAN CONNECTION

The nature of the missionary movement into Africa determined many of Alexander's spiritual responses in the early twentieth century. The Portuguese began the movement to bring Christian "enlightenment," salvation and hope to Africans in 1505. However, it was the landing of Jan Van Riebeeck in 1652 that produced a permanent European settlement at the Cape and paved the way for sustained Christian contacts. Van Riebeeck declared his profound concern for the spiritual uplift of the indigenous people of the area, the *Khoisan*. As the tiny enclave grew and absorbed more members, particularly slaves from Angola and Madagascar, concern for their intellectual and moral welfare was met by religious instruction. These instructions were made more attractive by providing brandy and tobacco to the reluctant "converts" of Christianity. However, most slaves who converted to any religion converted to Islam.[1]

Eventually, the Dutch came into conflict with the Khoikhoi, who accused the Dutch of physical maltreatment, stealing their sheep and cattle, and encroaching upon their lands. Van Riebeeck's response was that the khoikhoi had lost the war, so they were in no position to make demands. He stated:

> In answer to this, they (Khoikhoi) were reminded of the many exemplary, punishments meted out by us to those against whom they had brought in charges of such molestation. If they were not satisfied with that, but preferred every time to take their revenge by means of robberies and thefts such as those mentioned, peace could never be maintained between us, and then right of conquest we should take still more of their land from them, unless they were able to drive us off . . . . [2]

This clash of cultures and economic systems established a precedent for future contacts between Africans and Europeans. The superiority of European arms, not justice or religion determined who would be the new masters.

In 1795, the Boers made plain their position that any Khoisan they captured would become their property for life and that this condition would be perpetuated from generation to generation. The Boers also held that escaping individuals would be pursued and properly punished.[3] The London Missionary Society's (LMS) appointment of Dr. Van der Kemp in 1799 did not substantially change black/white relationships. Van der Kemp spent a good deal of his time with the mushrooming Coloured community and established mission stations for them. His marriage to an ex-slave only aroused the deeply held prejudices of Europeans against such mixing.

The appointment of Dr. John Philip to the Cape in 1820 did not set well with the majority of Europeans who were opposed to having a cleric hostile to their interests in their midst. Philip declared that he was against the maltreatment of anyone and he labored for nearly a decade to institute a fair and "liberal" policy on race relations. It must be noted that Philip enjoyed the backing of friends in London, particularly Farwell Buxton (successor to Wilberforce), who applied continual pressure on Cape officials to produce change.

On July 17, 1828, the "Ordinance of improving the condition of Hottentots and other free persons of colour", or Ordinance 50, became law. It repealed previous proclamations that were designed to bind people of "colour" to their masters. It lifted restrictions on freedom of movement and granted equality before the law between whites and Coloureds. One important consequence of the ordinance was that it contributed to the Afrikaners' Great Trek of the 1830's. They moved into the interior, taking their "property" with them, partly to avoid the harmful influence of a few radical missionaries.

However, missionary activities and influence increased during the 1840's and 1850's. Many activities were focused around the mission stations, which were composed of a church, a school and small dwellings for Christian converts. Some mission communities became paragons of Western "civilization" because they consumed Western goods and built European-styled homes. By the 1870's, many African societies had experienced increasing contacts from missionaries. During the 1890's, missionary activity exploded with new fervor and excitement due to the African-American connection and the rise of the notion of the "White Man's Burden."[4] The combination of overt white racism and black American Christian nationalism provoked many European missionaries to look upon separatist/independent church movement as a Black "curse." In order to comprehend missionary fears and contempt of this movement, it is important to examine in detail the missionary "weltanschauung" concerning Africa.

The notion of the inferiority of the black man was part of the missionary mind set. Dr. Albert Schweitzer's attitude typified the missionary view of the African's moral and mental capabilities.

> The Negro is a child, and with children nothing can be done without the use of authority, we must, therefore, so arrange the circumstances of daily life that natural authority can find expression. With regard to Negroes, then, I have coined the formula: "I am your brother, it is true, but your older brother."[5]

Africans were also considered heathens and savages. The image of Africa was of a "Dark Continent" inhabited by hordes of "uncivilized" people who were devoid of culture and religion and who existed in such a base condition that they needed the light and salvation of Christianity. The traveler, H. M. Stanley, remarked that "The missionary discovers the barbarian, almost stupefied, with brutish ignorance, with the instincts of a man in him, but yet living the life of a beast."[6] The subhuman essence of the African was grimly expressed by another missionary: "When I carry my torch into the caves of Africa, I meet only filthy birds of darkness."[7]

Missionaries also attacked African customs as heathenous practices that African converts had to discard. Polygamy was one issue that irrationally obsessed the vast majority of missionaries; they argued polygamy was anti-Christian and tantamount to concubinage. They extended their attacks to all facets of African traditional life. They condemned lobola (which the Europeans termed brideprice) as an act of female slavery; they viewed clitoridectomy as evil; they saw revering ancestors and sacrificial offerings as "devil" worship. According to them, what Africans termed religion was "organized superstition" devoid of knowing the true God. But traditional African beliefs, contrary to European opinion, expressed an authentic world view:

> The African attitude towards God is contrary to what intellectual gossip would have you believe. He believes that everything done for the good of society originates with his God. There is no such word as "sin" in his vocabulary, though there is a strong sense of right and wrong which is founded not on the changeable laws of man, but on the dictates of the conscience. He believes that when he makes mistakes he is not in harmony; that when he gets ill that he is making sacrifices for his failings. Sickness is a gentle reminder that he is out of harmony with his creator, Since all in harmony are strong of mind of body. Accepting this, the African does not hesitate to offer sacrifices to the creator; not because he is supposed to be full of superstition as he has foolishly been accused, reverence and deep humility and sorrow to the creator . . . [8]

African music and dance did not escape Eurocentric righteousness. Traditional dances were labeled savage and obscene. Music which did not glorify the Lord or which did not produce severity of spirit had to be rejected. Traditional music (particularly drumming) was a prime example of vulgarity in sound.

Almost all educated Africans were products of mission schools. This institution ripped Africans out of their cultural framework and created a "new" black person with a desire for a Western lifestyle.[9] This was achieved through a curriculum with a heavy Eurocentric bias. The schools placed great emphasis on the fundamentals of reading and writing as well as on developing a proper Christian character. Included in such a character was the belief in literacy: good Christians had to be able to read the Bible. Reading opened the entire world of western civilization to the educated black elite and was the main avenue for absorbing European culture. Africans who possessed the magic of reading and writing were considered civilized and progressive by many Africans.[10]

Another sign of character was that a Christian life must be dedicated to personal salvation so that the elect would be able to receive their reward in heaven. Their lives had to reflect piety, decency and hard work. They had to avoid violence and radicalism at all cost. This theology of submission[11] was designed to create an African who did not call into question the colonial state's authority, who respected missionary control, and who viewed resistance and radicalism as anti-Christian or evil.

The theology of submission was rooted in an activist notion of individualism.[12] Each person was not only expected to obtain his salvation but also to seek economic gain. This helped to rupture further the traditional society's communal base. The concepts of Christian brotherhood and equality were constantly discussed in mission circles; however, any attempt by Africans to assert true Christian brotherhood and meaningful equality was met with hostility and a lecture on the real meaning of these concepts. Individualism permeated mission education. Personal self-improvement was necessary for the ego. If society benefited from one's endeavors, that was good; but if not, the poor masses had to suffer the consequences of their moral delinquency. This hunger for Western culture drove mission school students to read Shakespeare dutifully, to listen to Mozart or form thespian societies to perform plays, preferably by English and French dramatists. In Kimberley and Cape Town during the 1890's, the newly educated, male and female, produced a beehive of activity, organizing "progressive" and "civilized" events within the black Christian communities.[13]

Education and theology had racist foundations in colonial South Africa, and both were almost natural outcomes of an age drunk with industrial expansion and black exploitation. What many missionaries taught as Christianity was simply ethnocentric religious twaddle. Missionary education smashed the African's concept of himself; and, in wake of the attack, there came an identity crisis. Because of education and familiarity with European ways, the educated black elite demanded to be treated as a civilized individual. Many were of the opinion that "raw natives" who were ignorant and superstitious could not be accorded the same amenities as whites. They were rooted in a dying culture that was backward and inferior to Western culture. However, educated Africans were different; they demanded respect.[14]

Some of the educated African elite rejected nearly all of their ethnic ways. In fact, they were more European than the Europeans, condemning their own music, dance, art and languages. Like their African cousins, a few rejected the blackness of their skin and erected a great barrier between themselves and the exploited black masses. But fate dealt most of them many harsh blows. They were forced to live in locations with other Africans. They were employed in menial jobs. Insults and ugly discrimination constantly reminded them that with all their education, they were never as good as the poorest white. Sadly, a few of the newly educated steeped themselves even further in European ways and hoped in vain for acceptance. But some stopped hoping for acceptance and initiated their own separatist churches.

Some missionaries were also agents of the capitalist penetration of South Africa. Although occasionally they were at odds with the colonial rule because it meant a challenge to their own authority. John Booth was the only white to advocate a program of 'Africa for Africans."[15] European missionaries in southern Africa found Booth's idea anathema. Their program of stripping the African of his cultural identity and replacing it with a weak bourgeois notion of Christian morality and individualism, served well the industrial needs of capitalism by creating wage earning workers and peasants who desired European goods.

The missionary was a key agent in the conquest of southern Africa. As one scholar has suggested:

> The conversion of the native population represents, even if only symbolically, its incorporation into the mental and cultural universe of the white...Christianity in colonial areas is a domestication of the indigenous population: Objectively, it breaks the Africans into European thought and mores; subjectively, it frees the European of his terrors of the African by including him within the same canon

as himself...A colonial system needs a subject population with a certain minimal level of Europeanization, for the purpose of order and exploitation...[16]

However, meaningful exploitation could not be achieved until African resistance was broken, their land and cattle taken away, and their desire for European goods instilled. The missionary wanted Africans to wear pants and shoes as proof of being civilized; the traders were of the same mind in order to make a profit. The end result for the African was the same: he had to become a wage earner in order to purchase capitalist goods.

As Bernard Magubane has noted, the Natal "Kaffir Commission" of 1852-1853 and subsequent colonial policies achieved important economic results. Whether the issue was nudity or idleness, the colonial authority deemed it necessary to bring Africans into "civilized ways" and to consume Western goods.

> The need to make Africans consumers of British manufacturers was a recurring preoccupation. Sir George Grey's opening address to the Colonial Parliament in 1855 underlined the importance . . . of British goods. "The Natives were" he said, "to become a part of ourselves, with a common faith and common interests, useful servants, consumers of our goods, contributors to our revenue . . . such as Providence designed them to be" . . .[17]

Missionaries and colonial officials had a meeting of the mind on many points concerning the African becoming civilized. The African's rejection of his traditional food, clothing and housing was a dismal introduction to capitalistic exploitation. Only a few Africans during the 1890's comprehend these cultural economic changes. The *Kholwa* communities of the Eastern Cape and Natal were progressive; a small segment of the African population was truly becoming western. Norman Etherington viewed this progress as incorporation into a new economic system:

> The clothing which missionaries recommended for the sake of modesty was for many of their converts an introduction to a new system of production and

exchange. Whether a convert earned his new clothes by wage labor or fabricated them with European looms and needles, [s]he was entering new kinds of economic relationships. The "upright houses" which rose in all mission stations embodied materials and demanded the use of tools unknown in the precolonial period.[18]

Western capitalistic Christianity was alien to the continent. This narrow religious perspective created massive conflict with indigenous values. Many missionaries refused to adapt their ideas and concepts to the African milieu. Moreover, the ideological and political content of their gospel and educational programs aimed to destroy African independence internally; externally, European military might ended black autonomy. Meanwhile, missionaries, traders and politicians all joined ranks to exploit the African economically and politically.

In America, white Christian hypocrisy and the exploitation of African Americans were also important in the rise of the independent black church movement in America. The history of the AOC, however, cannot be fully understood without a review of events in America that encouraged African Americans to take up the cause of African redemption and African colonization.

THE AFRICAN AMERICAN CONNECTION

When Alexander visited the U.S.A. in 1927 for his ordination, he expressed his pride over the achievements of his black American brothers and sisters. But despite some success, African Americans in the mid 1920's were not far removed from the horrors of the late nineteenth century. With the "emancipation" of four million slaves in 1865, their real bondage started in earnest. They were left without savings, property, literacy and citizenship. However, they longed to be Americans and the optimistic days of early Reconstruction provided them with citizenship and opportunities for economic gain. The years between 1867 and 1877 saw unprecedented numbers of American Blacks participating in the political arena and making substantial gains in higher education. Indeed, many of the newly emancipated felt that America was finally their home.[19]

With the collapse of Reconstruction (1877), a nightmare of terror, violence and murder engulfed the black community. The limited gains of reconstruction were short-lived and illusory; signs of black maltreatment were everywhere. The Ku Klux Klan and other white supremacist organizations attacked the black community with such ferocity that many African Americans called into question the value of their citizenship and began to contend that America could never be home. The Compromise of 1877 signaled a downward turn. Economic slumps and recessions produced extremely hard economic times for the masses of blacks and whites.[20] It has been suggested that Booker T. Washington's famous, or infamous, Atlanta Speech in 1895[21] and the United States Supreme Court decision of Plessy vs Ferguson (1896)[22] also contributed to the deterioration of the African American's social status. Greater stress, however, ought to be given to the growing racist literature, which viciously attacked Blacks as being degraded and subhuman. These attacks brutally charged Blacks as being stupid, criminally inclined, and animalistic in their sexual behavior.[23] In this bitter atmosphere, charged with viperous racism, grinding poverty and the blatant murder or lynching of hundreds of black folk, the search for a new home in Africa generated great emotion and interest.

Although many literate Blacks initially rejected emigration proposals[24] from 1850 onwards, the schemes eventually gained ground among black workers and a tiny strata of the black middle class. The Compromise of 1850, which seemed to many Blacks a license to reduce free people of color to slavery,[25] helped spark the initial discussion of emigration, Black Nationalism and the separatism. Martin Delany's perspectives rejected timid salvation and the philosophy of integration. His affirmation that Black Americans were a separate nation in need of their own territory, gave increased legitimacy to emigration.[26] The Civil War cooled many of the passions for emigration and black separatism, but with the collapse of Reconstruction and the South under white Democratic control, the smoldering embers of black nationalism and emigration gained new life. Veteran fighters such as Edward W. Blyden and Alexander Crummell never doubted the efficacy of emigration, even as others lost heart.

In his *Christianity, Islam and the Negro Race*, Blyden argued that the redemption of Africa was the special mission of Blacks "exiled" in America, and he urged them to build a new future in Africa.[27] He also developed a form of pan-black nationalist theology which stressed the salvation and redemption of Africa, which meant the political and economic well being of people of African descent everywhere. Like Blyden, Crummell gave an international perspective to the resolution of the Black man's predicament in America. To him, African redemption and salvation also included commercial ideas and business ventures between Africa and the Americas – with an activist leadership role being assigned to the American black elite to provide race uplift.[28] To be sure, there was a strand of black nationalist thinking which advocated an identical program but emphasized that black destiny and advancement must take place within the United States. Some prominent middle class Blacks such as Thomas Fortune used their wealth and control over the black press to battle emigrationist schemes.[29] Their efforts failed because increasing white terror and bitter economic times produces greater interest in African redemption and emigration. The 1890's personified the themes of Africa, salvation and redemption personified in one man, Henry McNeil Turner, AME bishop from 1880 to 1915.

Bishop Turner was unshakable in his opinion that due to the racist nature of America, blacks would never be accorded justice or true citizenship; their lot was one of continual abuse and economic exploitation. After many years of witnessing the brutal maltreatment of blacks, Turner began advocating "a return to the land of their fathers."[30] To him, leaving America was not an act of cowardice or an escapist fantasy, but a hard-headed recognition of the historical and economic realities which had prevailed since the British intrusion into North America. Indeed, he used the official organ of the AME Church, the *Voice of Missions*, to propagandize church members and others on the need for black nationalism, emigration, African redemption and resistance to white terror.[31]

Turner, Crummell and Blyden elaborated upon two themes that struck a responsive chord on the African continent: redemption and race solidarity.[32] Redemption meant that God, in His infinite wisdom and mercy, would save the African continent from death, disease, war and sin. Redemption also contained a strong message of social justice. But some Blacks advocated a strong social justice element as being authentic Christianity. Critics of European Christianity such as Turner, Blyden, Chilembwe and Kimbangu understood redemption as liberation and salvation from exploitation, illiteracy and white domination. Redemption, from a black perspective, did not distinguish between religious, social, political and economic life.[33]

Race solidarity openly stated that only Blacks were capable of ministering to black spiritual needs because European racial prejudices negated the Gospel's true meaning. Pigmentation solidarity linked all of African birth and ancestry in a common history of racial oppression and capitalism exploitation. Visual identification by color meant that an automatic Christian brotherhood existed which excluded many whites. The notion also asserted a pervasively held idea that God and Jesus were black. Turner in the US and Matswa, in South Africa, helped to popularize the belief of blackness of Christian deities. Finally, the pigmentation issue was linked to Ethiopianism and to the past glories of ancient African civilization. Psalm 68:31 reads: "Ethiopia shall stretch forth her hands into God." This is the classic verse that fed an attachment to Ethiopia all over the black world.[34]

Ethiopianism in the South African context signified spiritual emancipation from European clergy. It held that Africans could minister better to the needs of Africans. Ethiopianism was not a reactionary but a futuristic doctrine. It claimed God had given a promise of salvation and the greatness of things to come. The old glories of Africa would be achieved again and the continent would become a paragon of progress, Christian commitment and humane treatment of all ethnic groups.

During the last quarter of the nineteenth century, the Ethiopian impulse was most evident in the rise of the independent black church movement. In 1883, an early breakaway was led by Mangena Mokone, who resented Wesleyan Methodist authority. European leaders, both secular and religious, condemned these churches as hot beds of paganism, sedition and hatred. The South African government also viewed Ethiopianism with hostility and as an alien doctrine introduced by mischief-making American Blacks. To be sure, substantial missionary and student exchanges had begun to occur between black Americans and black South Africans. However, the primary proof of the malevolent aims of American Blacks was Bishop Turner's arrival in 1898 for a six week tour of the Cape Colony and theTransvaal that received much publicity in the South African press. He came to South Africa to organize formally the AMEC in southern Africa. His visit produced no revolution in the political or social spheres, but it helped to give birth to the novel idea that American Blacks would be liberators of their oppressed cousins in South Africa. Notions of black liberators and black nationalist churches created a response from white officials which bordered on hysteria.

It should be noted that both in the United States and South Africa, Blacks were subjected to increasingly restrictive controls. The widespread terror in the South and the ruthlessness of capitalistic exploitation in the South African mining compound[35] intensified the black search for strategies to relieve their pain, shame and degradation.

For a number of Blacks in America, Africa became the "city upon the hill", pure and open to all from the ebony diaspora. Without Mother Africa and redemption, they were forever trapped in a white world without relief. The search should not be misconstrued as a program put forth by lunatics and con-artists. Thousands left for Africa and many more supported the black separatist impulse because of genuine sentiments.[36] Their search was anchored in the economic and political realities of the day and in a Christian hope for liberation. It was a religious search stemming from the power of religion to attract the black masses and to mobilize their nationalist/racist tendencies for authentic struggle.

Africans in South Africa were impressed with the limited achievements of their American cousins. The churches, schools, universities, newspapers, businesses and homes that African Americans had established, created a hope among black south Africans that they could duplicate these achievements. At the same time, the search in South Africa was not outer-directed as in America, but focused on internal redemption since they had become strangers in their own land.

The two religious nationalism of the United States and South Africa reinforced each other. The African American fostered, particularly with Bishop Turner, increase in the black membership of the separatist church movement and a greater desire for redemption. In the rise of the AOC in South Africa, the spirit of nationalism was evident. In order to appreciate fully the rise of the AOC, it is important to explore the origins of the separatist church movement in South Africa.

THE SEPARATIST CHURCH MOVEMENT

"Black Separatist Christianity" in South Africa was of two strains: radical and reform. The African Orthodox Church fell within the latter category, meaning those churches that wanted spiritual emancipation but wished to retain European liturgical and doctrinal forms. Radical separatist churches were set apart by their militant anti-white attitude and their adamant rejection of European secular authority.[37]

However, many European officials tended to perceive all separatist groups as dangerous and incompatible with white rule. As the numbers of separatist churches increased during the late nineteenth century, Africans found themselves increasingly exploited as cheap labor and under greater European control in the mines and urban areas. One of the most dramatic expressions of dissatisfaction with white subjugation was the schisms leading to separatist churches. Both radical and reform elements participated in schisms.

These churches were similar to early Christian diversity in the third century A. D. There could be no meaningful Christianity in Africa until the Church was rooted in African philosophy, mythology, customs and mores. Schisms were not the workings of an infantile people who were unable to cope with the sophistication of Western religion. For centuries, Blacks developed a form of Christianity in Egypt and Ethiopia. The key problem was with the introduction of modern Christianity by the missionaries of western Europe.

The ideology of the European missionary helped to weaken African traditional society, already shattered by the onslaught of capitalist development. R. V. Selope Thema, a newspaper editor, noted that:

> early Missionaries taught the Africans to look upon all things African as wrong and ungodly . . . The result has been that our dances were all tabooed, our games stopped, our customs and laws discarded . . .It is perhaps not an exaggeration to aver that the early Missionaries, did not and do not, concern themselves with the material welfare of the Africans. The whole object of the evangelization of the Africans seems to have been the saving of their souls . . . . The saving of the soul in heaven is a very good thing indeed; but to save the soul it seems to me one has to save the body from all manner of evils.[38]

Daniel Thwaite, in his provocative study, *The Seething African Pot: A Study of Black Nationalism, 1882-1935*, also suggested a negative role for the European missionary. He noted:

> In their disregard for every aspect of native life, the white men carelessly took no account of the fundamental difference separating the Christian from the Bantu philosophy . . . [39] They tackled problems that they were not prepared to solve, they taught precepts they often could not put into practice themselves: They condemned customs they could not understand; lightly, and without reflecting converts in excess of their real merits, careless that in consequence these native would regard themselves as superior to their pagan brethren . . . .[40]

Thwaite's views were applied to whites in general and to missionaries in particular. The *Report of Native Churches Commission* (1925), which was the official response to black separatist development, interviewed hundreds of Africans along with many European authorities and put forth the following thesis on African spirituality and the rise of separatist sentiments:

> The reasons for the rapid spread of Christianity among the natives are not hard to find; not only were [the early missionaries among the ablest and most earnest of men], but the native mind was a field ready to receive the sowings of the gospel. Here were a people with no established and clearly defined religion like Confucianism, Brahmanism or Shintoism. . . . [41]

In the course of its investigations, the Commission received numerous complaints from Africans regarding the attitude of European missionaries:

> It is quite certain that one of the causes of the separatist activity of the natives has been the conviction on the part of many natives that the colour bar feeling has entered the domain of religion. . . .[42] A further and inevitable cause for dissatisfaction with European missions arose from the spread of education . . . a dangerous thing . . .as well as the individual interpretation of the scripture in the protestant churches . . . disillusionment in the Christianity of many Europeans, European example and (later) the [influence of the Negro Church in America], all led to separation in church matters. Further, when it is found that separatism was not only opposed by the authorities but that separatist native clergymen shared in the government privileges accorded to non-separatists the movement received an added momentum.[43]

The report held that the color bar of European clergy and the influence of the "Black American Church" fermented separatist tendencies. The report's position was that the "old" clergy was more progressive than the "new" clergy. The former was said to be more sensitive to the needs of Africans, but that position must be rejected. The economic exploitation and spiritual bondage of the African produced separatist sentiments that aided in the rise of the independent black church movement.

One of the first recorded South African churches was the Tembu Church or Tembu Catholic Church, founded in 1884 when Nehemiah Tile seceded from the Weslyan Methodist Church and organized a new religious body. His former church superiors praised him as eloquent, hard-working and of good racial stock.[44] However, he had become impatient with European control and commenced advocating separation from the parent church. One source argued that Tile left the Wesleyan church over some petty incident and started an association that "quickly fizzled out."[45] The Native Church Commission suggested that his leaving was due to "bad living there"[46] "[but], it is clear that he had been infected with the political aspirations of Ngangelizwe and Dalindyebo."[47] This "infection" allowed Ngangelizwe, a member of the Tembu royal house, to become head of this new religious group. European church officials viewed the break and the installation of Hgangelizwe as nationalistic and anti-white. A more in-depth analysis of political/social conditions of Tembuland revealed the hostile moves by whites to acquire land and labor. The African nobility resisted these encroachments, and Tile sided with then in their struggle. Tile reasoned that if Queen Victoria was the head of the Church of England, why could Ngangelizwe not be head of the Tembu Church.[48]

Tile's church has been described as "tribal." Tribal in the Western context conveys an image of barbarism and reaction. Consequently, Western scholarship on separatist churches has viewed Tile's church as flawed and lacking the "universal" outlook of Western Christianity. There was nothing illiberal or backward-looking about Tile's theology. He clearly understood that the Gospel message was one of liberation from bondage; in order to achieve this end, he felt an African must be in the leadership position to interpret scripture and to enhance the economic and political needs of Blacks. Of course, the argument may be made that Tile's membership was confined to the Tembu, but that was dictated by geography and not by his ontological precepts. Later advocates of Black Theology shared Tile's stance: that in the existential moments of struggle and abuse, a true Christian theology empowers the oppressed. They vigorously contested any suggestion that the "wretched" of the earth must suffer maltreatment and exploitation because God has preordained it. Tile's theology of resistance was similar to that which led to the formation of the AME in the United States.

The AME Church was born in the 1780's because of the maltreatment and abuse of slaves and "free" Blacks. Similar to South Africa context, white Americans dominated Blacks in their various denominations. Richard Allen and Absolom Jones left St. George Methodist Episcopal Church when they were asked to take communion after whites and were relegated to "nigger" pews.[49] In 1789 Allen and other like-minded brethren formed the African Free Society, which later blossomed into the AMEC. By the end of the nineteenth century, this black independent church movement also included the African Methodist Episcopal Zion Church (AMEZ), the Colored Methodist Episcopal Church (CME) and many Baptist churches.

DIAMOND AND GOLD MINING

As powerfully as Bishop Turner fought to further the black Christian movement in South Africa, it was another development that sustained the movement: the discovery of gold on the Witwatersrand in 1886. Before discussing the gold revolution, a brief description of Kimberley is in order to demonstrate how the diamond industry transformed the rural mining environment.

The name Kimberley came into existence because one of the original camps, Vooruitzigt, was too difficult to pronounce and the name of another camp, New Rush, was also considered too undignified to be associated with the Queen's dominions; the several camps were consolidated and named Kimberley in June, 1873. As a town, then, Kimberley was a vast sea of tents with many gambling "hells." By the end of the 1870's, there were bars, canteens, a few hotels and several "Kaffir" eating dens. It was noted that in 1875, the only brick house in Kimberley belonged to a diamond buyer, Joseph Robinson. In fact, it was expensive to live in this emerging town because all commodities had to be imported by oxen drawn wagons from the coast that was more than five hundred miles away.[50]

The mass of humanity that converged on Kimberley was drawn to the diamond fields. Europeans from all over the world and Blacks from throughout southern Africa trekked to the fields. Of course, Europeans controlled the new wealth of Guiqualand West. Africans were needed to unearth the diamonds and were therefore recruited. Many of them, however, would travel over a thousand miles, covered with filth and sores, to earn money for guns and other European goods. By the early 1880's, thousands of Black were a permanent feature of the Kimberley landscape.

One of the greatest problems associated with the diamond industry was the trade in illicit diamond buying (IDB). Since it was alleged that Africans were incorrigible thieves, they were constantly monitored in compounds where they lived. However, Africans were not alone in IDB business. "Among these illicit buyers were 'respectable persons': churchgoers, clubmen, loud denunciators of IDB and its associated evils."[51] It must be noted that white workers were neither subjected to stringent searchers or to a required pass system as were African workers. These developments were also in keeping with the nearly universal trend in South Africa to control Africans in order to have a large black labor reserve.

By 1900 Kimberley had become an impressive city. Some of the most extravagant structures belonged to the giant diamond concern, De Beers. In fact, the growth of Kimberley was inseparable from De Beers because it was the key company that produced wealth, power and influence on the southern tip of the continent. Gone were the days of flies, drought and dust like a plague from hell. Kimberley was now an affluent though racially divided city with Africans and Coloureds at the lowest rungs of status. Nonetheless, it was in Kimberley that Alexander commenced his life's work as Archbishop of the AOC. Over the years, he also asked for donations from De Beers to sustain his church in South Africa. But the late 1920's, Kimberley was overshadowed by Johannesburg as the new economic center of South Africa.

However, it was the massive capital generated from the diamond mines of Kimberley that fueled the gold revolution in Transvaal. Johannesburg or Egoli (its African name) came into existence almost overnight. From this new financial capital, the Transvaal Republic was incorporated into the international capitalist order. Gold mining capital stabilized the country as a whole by expanding foreign trade and generating revenues.[52]

The gold rush commenced with the opening up of the Barberton Fields in 1885. The bonanza finds of the Rand were not yet discovered, but the news of gold traveled like wildfire not only throughout southern Africa, but internationally. Thousands of *uitlanders* or foreigners poured into South Africa hoping to make their fortunes. The Afrikaner population resented the skills and English culture of these newcomers. But these aliens were the vanguard of capitalist development, and their capital and skills, along with the Kimberley resources, provided new markets, vastly expanded opportunities for export goods and created new opportunities in the areas of agriculture and manufacturing.[53] By the end of 1886, the Rand reefs were yielding thousands of tons of ore[54] and the capitalist transformation of southern Africa had accelerated in earnest.

By 1888 there were forty-four gold mines in operation. Two years later, over 100,000 men were employed on the Rand. This increased economic activity spawned a host of problems. First, the Kimberley experience was transplanted to Transvaal. Segregation in work, residence, play and education became the norm. African laborers lived in enclosed tightly regimented compounds,[55] and the pass system monitored their movements. Second, the African proletarian/peasant, who was the linchpin of economic development, was in short supply, but the mines' need for African labor resulted in unscrupulous practices by recruiting agents and some African chiefs to meet manpower demands.[56] The Transvaal State, controlled by European farming, was the crucial element necessary to put into operation a comprehensive plan to coerce black labor into the expanding economy of capitalist South Africa. Third, notions of white supremacy pervaded all aspects of societal development and infused the Christian message with a crude religious social Darwinism. Its anti-black core aided the political and economic status quo by providing a rationale for European authority, thereby negating the African's quest for spiritual autonomy.[57]

Although profound changes occurred because of the mining revolution, by 1899 the struggling South African economy was in a deep crisis and was no longer able to provide for itself such essential items as meat, eggs, wheat and milk.[58] The irony of the bleak economic situation was that the increase in population and the creation of new rail lines that fostered industrialization and urbanization, were the very means by which the economy experienced recession. The population explosion placed a serious strain on agriculture production. At the same time, the rails were used to import foreign products. Some goods came from as far away as Australia. Purveyors of these goods competed so successfully that they worked to the detriment of the indigenous market.[59] In addition, drought and rinderpest imposed an additional burden upon the black peasant/proletariat masses. In this climate of increasing industrialization and urbanization, black Christian groups sought spiritual emancipation from their European masters. More and more of these groups militantly demanded racial separation and ecclesiastical autonomy. The loss of African independence, the brutal maltreatment of Blacks at the mines, and the traumatic general encounter with European culture sparked widespread protest, with Africans seeking "salvation" from white control and capitalist exploitation. Liberation, quite simply, meant salvation from the evils of white control and exploitation.

Alexander's religious heritage was rooted in the economic and social turmoil of the late nineteenth century. Increased urbanization provided greater social contacts with Europeans and more opportunities for mission education. The greater exposure of Africans to European culture in the cities meant the Blacks were subjected to a barrage of criticism that they were primitive, savage, inferior and repugnant. This helped to foster their resentment of whites. Missions education of respectability, love, brotherhood and civilization became a tool in the hands of some literate Blacks to demand better treatment and limited political involvement in the affairs of the nation.

To be sure, many peasants were satisfied with their traditional life-styles and did not see any pressing need to work for Europeans. But with the growth of mines, industry and agriculture, tremendous pressure was placed on African societies to provide labor. Coercive measures and systematic acts of manipulation were used to push Africans off the land and into the cities. The cities and towns were for exclusive European use and blacks were "aliens" without recourse to political rights. With the imposition of taxes on traditional societies, few Africans remained outside the cash economy. Nevertheless, the tax policy brought most black workers under white control. European control over the mines was shameful due to the subhuman living conditions on the compounds. Mine officials justified the conditions by contending that since Africans were given meals and lodgings free, they should not complain. Disease took its heavy toll on the mine population and epidemics erupted periodically, taking many lives.

Conditions in the city were no better. The "kaffir" quarters were dens of disease, misery and congestion. At first, little attention was given to the presence of Africans; however, when their numbers increased substantially, there was a great outcry for recognition of a serious problem. The European press (1880-1910) called for action against the "Native Social Pest" and suggested the need for more vigorous segregation measures against Africans because they were carriers of sickness and death.[60]

In the press and pulpit, Europeans hammered away at the corrupting influences of city life upon African peasants. Civilization was an indispensable element for uplifting "degraded" black people. However, many believed that Blacks had absorbed the worst features of European behavioral patterns since African crime, prostitution, and alcohol consumption were on the increase in the urban areas.

The educated Africans and concerned Europeans offered remedies: Christian social clubs, abstinence from spirits and harsh segregation measures. The single most important function of the Christian clubs was to inculcate morality and docility in the general black population. Worse yet, were the vile and gross depictions by Europeans of Africans as "stinking raw Kaffirs." Because of the African appearance and alleged behavior, it was suggested that Europeans, particularly white women, must be shielded from the spectacle of half naked "savages."[61] Of course, this tendency to treat Africans as subhumans led directly to gross exploitation of them in economic and political relms. Many of the ordinances and policies of the mining and agricultural interests denied Africans control over their wages, their homes and their manhood.

In order to reduce the trauma of their encounters with Europeans, Africans utilized various forms of resistance. First came armed conflict. For instance, in Rhodesia, the rising of Ndedele and Shona people in 1896-1897 proved a vain effort to repel European political authority. Such events were repeated in Southwest Africa where the Ovambo, Nama and Herero clashed with German settlers and imperial troops. The powerful Xhosa and Zulu peoples of South Africa fought courageous battles; however, their political autonomy was destroyed. As the nineteenth century neared its end, great political/military leaders such as Cetshwayo,[62] Lobengula,[63] Sekhukhune[64] and Moshoeshoe[65] had left the scene. This leadership vacuum created a crisis of profound magnitude for black people. Since African military strength was now broken, some Africans began to explore how mission education and Christianity might be of service to reduce, if not eradicate, European dominance, and negate European control over spiritual, economic and political affairs.

Another area of resistance was labor protest. As capitalist development incorporated more land resources, the demands for more labor increased. European mining interests created recruiting agencies to increase the African labor pool. The Chamber of Mines (1889)[66] established the Native Labour Association (1877), which became the Witwatersand Native Labour Association (WNLA) (1901)[67] and The Native Recruiting Organization (NRC) (1912). Mining interests used measures, fair and foul, to coordinate capitalist interests to produce the manpower necessary to perform the menial jobs in the mines. Since conditions in the mines and locations were hellish, dissatisfaction was rampant. It should be noted that food, drugs, and prostitution were manipulated to ensure peace and obedience to the rules and regulations of the mines.

This environment of intimidation and maltreatment led to various forms of resistance. One of the most common acts was desertion. African workers, knowing that they were in violation of contractual agreements, simply walked away from camps and contracts by the hundreds. Not quite as successful was the technique of haggling over wages. If the labor supply reached a critical shortage point, many black workers moved from the mines to white-owned farms and back to the mines in order to increase their negotiating power. In a few notable exceptions some African workers were able to receive higher wages; however, most of the time the majority of black workers were powerless to make any such demands.

The strike was the weapon most feared by mining interests. The few strikes by the budding African proletariat in the late nineteenth and early twentieth centuries were the beginnings of class-consciousness. These early efforts were at best feeble, but the larger strikes of the 1920's, 1930's and 1940's attested to the growing political savvy of African workers.[68] Due to the potential of any major strike to cripple an industrial society, the capitalist state of South Africa responded brutally to crush worker resistance. One basic element in the early days of resistance in the mines was religion, which was the cement which joined Blacks together in defiance against mining interests and aided mission educated Africans in their struggle to achieve equality under bourgeois democracy.

Religion in southern Africa functioned both as primary and secondary forms of resistance.[69] In the former, armed conflict was an attempt to repel European dominance and capitalist exploitation. In the latter, resistance was nonviolent and followed a reformist pattern: petitions, deputations and civil disobedience. A prime example of religious resistance was the Xhosa cattle-killing episode (1850).[70] Although it has been argued that this event brought starvation and death, nonetheless, it was an attempt at marshalling the religious energy to dramatically reverse the vassal relationship between Africans and Europeans. The millenarian nature of rebellion should not obscure the objective that Nongqause hoped to achieve: authentic liberation for the Xhosa people.[71]

During the Shona-Ndebele rising (1896), the religious mediums were used as messengers between two societies, historically suspicious of each other, to coordinate military efforts against Europeans. The prophets of both groups were active in these wars of resistance. By the 1896, these wars ceased. Black separatist or Ethiopian Churches, however, continued the struggle but on another level.[72] The whole of Southern Africa was permeated with religious agitation by African Christians seeking autonomy from European mission-controlled churches. Their protest against white authority in the spiritual realm led some Blacks to extend their protest to economics and politics.

Nearly all European denominations frowned upon the budding black nationalism and sought to inculcate acquiescence to colonial authority. As the separatist impulse broadened its appeal, religion merged with nationalism to create even greater resistance. Bishop Turner's dramatic visit to South Africa in 1898 reinforced the belief among South African Blacks that Africans were capable of spiritual autonomy and that they could call upon their American kinfolk for moral support. Indeed, the independent church movement produced actors who played minor roles in the Bambata Rebellion[73] (1906) and major roles in the Chilembwe Rising[74] (1915).

Rural areas, too, expressed the separatist norm of rejecting European control. The Watch Tower Movement rejected all forms of earthly authority.[75] This rural radicalism, which emanated from the mines and villages of the countryside, merged with urban discontent and helped to escalate racial animosities between Africans and Europeans. The period between 1880 and 1930 produced an intense search for avenues to end white domination and exploitation. As Latenari suggested, "promontory religious movements of revival and transformation usually lie at the origin of every political or military uprising among native peoples and take the form of messianic cults promising liberation."[76] The mode most often used was the religious one, which some writers have harshly analyzed as chialistic, escapist, primitive and superstitious. Africans, at best, were portrayed as simple-minded souls who struggled in vain to comprehend societal transformations that could not be properly understood within the African conceptual framework. Opinions such as these came from a rigid Eurocentric perspective. For example, European missionaries and colonial authorities condemned Simon Kimbangu,[77] Andre Matswa,[78] Zaccharias Bonzo,[79] and Nehanda.[80] They alleged that the religious leaders' actions were not only criminal but anti-Christian as well. All of these freedom-fighters demanded an end to white rule. The vast majority, too, wanted to abolish European taxation. A few were desirous of seizing white property and sharing it with other Blacks. These interactions with colonial authority and missionaries heightened their religious consciousness and gave way to new biblical interpretations. The most profound of these interpretations was that God was on the side of the oppressed and that He would deliver the Black Man from the evils of white domination and exploitation.

The pain, hardship, broken hopes and setbacks of Africans in South Africa were due to the rising levels of economic exploitation. Separatist churches provided comfort from a hostile capitalist world and, at the same time, a channel to mount an offensive for spiritual emancipation. Although black traditional political and economic systems were under assault, the strong religious bond adjusted itself to the new conditions of Western education, urbanization and capitalist exploitation. To be sure, as Temu and Swai make plain, the traditional religious leadership wanted nothing to do with Europeans or capitalism.[81] They struggled to eradicate every vestige of European rule. Therefore, much of the separatist church movement, including the AOC, was a protest phenomenon and not a revolutionary attempt to overthrow the new order. It was, nonetheless, the separatist religious ethos that provided tens of thousands of proletariat peasants with a coherent body of moral and ethnical principles that gave them faith and discipline to struggle against capitalist exploitation.[82]

By the end of the nineteenth century, the independent black church movement had been institutionalized. Some of Tile's followers, who had left for the goldfields, carried with them their rebellious ideas and attempted to bring others into the separatist vineyard. The records are silent on the matter of Tile's followers establishing new churches. The separatist impulse, however, produced such churches as the Ethiopian Church (1891), the African Christian Union (1896), the African Presbyterian Church (1898), the African Coloured Baptists (1899-1901) and the Zulu Congregational Church (1896-97), all of which gave the movement an impressive appearance and caused alarm in the European community.[83] Indeed, the Ethiopian Church, founded by Rev. M. M. Mokone, sought affiliation with the AME Church in 1896. A merger was achieved within that year. In 1897, the Rev. James Dwane visited the U.S. and returned with the title of General Superintendent in South Africa for the AME Church.

Unfortunately, this unification between Africa and America received a setback when Dwane became disillusioned with the AME over its failure to provide $10,000 to build a vocational school and over his title of General Superintendent. Seemingly, he wanted the honor of being a bishop. But Dwane never regretted the merger. To him, it was part of his dream for a Universal African Church in communion with African brethren throughout the diaspora. He later organized another group, the Order of Ethiopia, which brought him back into a European-controlled denomination.[84]

Bishop Turner left an indelible mark upon the South African terrain. His tour in 1898 lasted almost six weeks. He visited the Transvaal and the Cape Colony that contained several large well established communities of African and Coloured Christians. AME ministers were seen as "missionary raiders."[85] European missionaries not only feared their competition, but also were very aware of the emotional and theological soundness of the perspective that argued that Blacks could minister better to the spiritual needs of other Blacks.[86] Of course, many whites denied this viewpoint, but the rising numbers of separatist churches forced many Europeans to confront the issue of black displeasure with white missions. Turner posed a great threat because he ordained dozens of ministers and deacons and baptized hundreds of souls. Such a bold proselytizing thrust could not escape the attention of European officials who were aware of the political consequences of Turner's actions.

On his trip, Bishop Turner met several prominent white leaders, including President Paul Kruger of the Transvaal Republic. Turner always chose words to flatter them and to ease their fears concerning black Christianity. It goes without saying that Turner could also be brutal in his critique of white society. He had called the American Constitution a dirty lie that should be spat upon by every Black; the American flags a rag.[87] When the bishop was attacked in the *Christian*

Express as the archmischief-maker who poisoned black minds with his speeches against whites, it was correct. What the editor failed to acknowledge was the horrible economic and social conditions that made Africans receptive to Turner's ideas. John Tengo Jabavu, a conservative newspaper editor who supported the status quo, attacked Turner for importing racist doctrines into South Africa. Given Jabavu's loyalty to missions, he was a most willing participant in casting aspersions upon Turner's views. Although Jabavu was not hostile to the independent church movement and wished it well, he nevertheless felt that the movement was composed of ignorant and "raw natives" who needed European supervision.[88] But Turner remained undaunted by the uproar created in the press.

Circulation of the AME newspaper, *Voice of Missions*, within South Africa was the major mode of disseminating black nationalist Christianity. The importance of *Voice of Missions* must be ranked with Marcus Garvey's *The Negro World*, in the 1920's, since many literate black South Africans read both. *The Voice of Missions* featured articles on segregation and lynching and the maltreatment of Blacks in the United States. It also included stories on the acquisition of property, the building of Churches and the founding of schools. A very important function of all black religious news organs was the educational thrust for liberation. The general theme sounded was that redemption, nationalism and education were all linked in the struggle to "make the world safe" for Blacks. The African American religious press, therefore, was one of the critical factors in fostering black nationalism within a small circle of literate Africans during the late nineteenth century.

The European press rarely discussed the exploitation of Africans by European missionaries. *The Voice of Missions* featured remarks accusing the European clergy of living in luxury off the sweat of Blacks and maintaining rigid segregation between themselves and their black congregations.[89] But this segregation was not maintained on the labor front. Ostensibly, white missionaries needed "boys" to carry their luggage, to dig their bathrooms, to cook their meals and to build their missions stations. Some European clergy went so far as to suggest that Africans in pursing religious training should receive no wages since personalized attention provided by missionaries was of greater compensatory value than money.

Whatever Turner may have stated privately to South African officials, his nationalist/anti-white stance was made clear before he left South Africa. A more aggressive black religious nationalism could not take hold in America or, more importantly, in South Africa because of the general support given by the AME Church to the British Empire. Of course, Turner found these views to be anathema; nonetheless, support of such views mitigated against a black nationalist view and wasted Turner's energies in fruitless debates concerning the graciousness of British rule. One historian noted that:

> Both African and Afro-American were almost naively loyal to the British crown. The AMEC viewed the advent of British sovereignty over the two republics of Transvaal and Orange Free State, as the precondition for racial justice and equality throughout South Africa. There were a number of African propagandists in the United States who wrote articles that were printed in AME newspapers and who gave speeches that were delivered from AME podiums, all extolling the superiority of British over Boer rule.[90]

Clearly African and American Black nationalism were flawed. Few held the beliefs of Rev. George Washington Woodbey, a black socialist, who advocated social ownership of the means of production and that the teachings of Christ were compatible with socialism.[91] To appeal to one oppressor over another as being benign and just was lunacy. The AMEC's adoration of the British in the political sphere mirrored their "slave" mentality in their preference for the Anglican Church over the Dutch Reformed Church. Turner's point was that the black nationalist view must be critical of all things European. Because this fundamental point was not comprehended, Africans were duped time and again about "white friends."[92]

In sum, the Black American missionary involvement on the South African landscape was reformist. According to Carol Page:

> AME missionaries entered South Africa at a time when Black American Missionaries viewed Africa as their special domain. The AMEC, which was the best organized in mission activities, took a leading role in what one scholar has called the Evangelical Pan-Africanist movement. Although accused by the colonial authorities as being the 'parent of Ethiopianism' and of importing racialist doctrines into the country, the fact is that the AMEC entered South Africa more than two decades after South Africans began their exodus from the established churches. The AMEC's first emissaries were 'impeccably gradualist' as one historian has described them. What they imported into the country was Booker T. Washington's philosophy of thrift, capital accumulation, and character building, in short, all the middle class values inherent in the AMEC.[93]

A line of demarcation must be drawn between Bishop Turner and the AMEC in general. In the church's two-hundred-year history, no bishop had combined redemption and nationalism as thoroughly as Turner did. His love of Africa and his desire for the liberation of his people generated total dedication to his vision and to their elevation. The orientation Turner deemed appropriate for his church was a Pan-African one. The point was that the bishop was radical due to his message of no compromise with the evils of lynching, the white man's burden, Anglo-Saxon superiority and religious imperialism.

The dawn of the twentieth century did not lessen the African-American's influence upon religious developments on the African continent. In South Africa, the Bambatha Rebellion of 1906 triggered violence. It is important to note that although a few of the separatist Christians played a minor role in the rebellion, some of them were members of P. J. Mzimba's African Presbyterian Church. The rebellion that took its name from a minor Zulu chief, Bambatha, ended with the death of 3,000 Africans and 30 whites.[94] The separatist impulse emphasized suspicion of whites and resistance to European rule. Given this climate of opinion, the imposition of poll taxes led to the violent encounter with officials.

Another important religious confrontation involved the Israelite movement led by Enoch Mgijima. His organization's roots were partly in the Black American Church of God and Saints of Christ. Mgijima's visions, which brought him into conflict with American church officials, revealed a "battle between two white governments and [that] a baboon came and crushed these governments.[95] The vision's meaning was not hard to grasp. Africans would crush whites. The American Church of God and Saints of Christ "discommunicated" Mgujima, but he sustained his Israelite group and moved his members onto Crown land. The police were called in to evict these African "squatters." They "believed that the end of the world was coming and . . . . refused to leave their holy village of Ntabelanga."[96] In May 1921 a massacre occurred. Police bullets murdered at least 163 at the Bullhoek location, and scores more were injured.

This Old Testament identification with the Israelites was a point of radical departure for this tiny group. Blacks scattered throughout the diaspora would make similar claims of being the true heirs of the Biblical Hebrews. Although most of these claims have been denied by the academic community in western Europe and America, mounting evidence has confirmed the blackness of many ancient peoples previously presumed to have been Caucasian. The African American connection again did not cause the bloody confrontation; however, on a secondary level, it fostered resistance, race consciousness and religious self-reliance.

In no other event were race, resistance and religion so intertwined as in the Nyasaland Rising of 1915. George Shepperson has provided valuable insights into the American experience that Chilembwe encountered during the late 1890's.[97] It was more precisely the southern U.S. black experience of violence and segregation that radically sensitized him to the abuses of colonial origins. In January 1915, Chilembwe's rising left three whites dead, three wounded and scores of Blacks dead and incarcerated. Chilembwe was not the Sambo of the American South, the neurotic weakling, who as a child was overly dependent upon his mother.[98] Most assuredly, he was not a crazed lunatic who loathed whites.

The African American connection introduced Chilembwe to Jim Crow laws and Black American history. Chilembwe wanted to "strike a blow for freedom" and liberate his people; this was the sentiment of Nat Tuner and John Brown. The pressing need to be free from white rule was embodied in the separatist impulse that was pervasive throughout southern Africa. This "spirit" aided Chilembwe in taking a Kierkegardian leap; having the "courage to be", he attacked whites. This act of violence authenticated his person and conferred psychic wholeness. He did not indulge in the glorification of violence as some ideal, but rather, as a tool used by to smash the entire range of taboos designed to render Africans castrated and docile. It was a tortuous road that led Chilembwe to such violence. He had to free himself of the "demons" of not having mass black support or European approval. He had to contemplate death and dying. In some very lonely existential moments, Chilembwe, like Nat Turner, resolved to do the unthinkable: take up arms. Chilembwe and Bishop Turner agreed that Blacks should not participate in white folks' wars that were exploitive and deplorable. The First World War which was then consuming black lives, coupled with the resentment of whites "eating" the land, charged the atmosphere with the need to "strike a blow for freedom."

The drive for freedom became more intense as Blacks sought to control their destinies; however, the efforts to reduce their uprootedness was not entirely in their hands. South Africa's entry into the world market economy sealed the fate of the institutionalization of black Christian separatism. In the early 1880's, only a few separatist churches existed. With the gold revolution in the Transvaal at the end of the nineteenth century, dozens of these churches came into existence. Gold mining produced the need for huge quantities of cheap black labor recruited from throughout southern Africa. Labor recruiting set in motion a vast system of migratory labor in which Africans, who were introduced to separatist ideas in South Africa, carried them back to their homes. Moreover, the concentration of Africans in developing urban/industrial environments meant that coercive legislative measures magnified racial tensions. Africans expressed their discontent by joining trade unions and establishing separatist churches. Capitalism, therefore, was critical in fostering black religious separatism

By 1925, separatist churches were common throughout southern Africa. In that same year, Daniel William Alexander became head of a new separatist group, the African Orthodox Church. It is the story of Alexander's early life, his visit to America and the institutionalization of the AOC in South Africa that will be explored in the next several chapters.

ENDNOTES

1. For a look at early missionary efforts in South Africa, see J. A. DuPlesis, *A History of Christian Missions in South Africa* (London: Longmans, Green, and Co., 1911). See also Richard Elphphick and Herman Gillomee, *The Shaping of South African Society, 1652-1800* (London: Longman, 1979).

2. Jan Van Riebeeck, *Journal of Jan Van Riebeeck*, Vol. 3, 1659-1661, (ed.) H. B. Thom (Cape Town: A. A. Balkana, 1958), p. 196.

3. Stephen Neill, *Colonialism and Christian Missions* (New York and Toronto: McGraw-Hill Books, 1966), p. 30.

4. This notion of the "white man's burden" was developed by Rudyard Kipling. He suggested that the European, particularly the Anglo-Saxon, was destined by wealth and power to bring "civilization" to the backward "colored" peoples of the world.

5. Ran Desai (ed.), *Christianity in Africa as seen by Africans* (Denver: Alan Swallow, 1962), p. 13.

6. *Ibid.*, p. 14.

7. *Ibid.*, p. 14.

8. *Ibid.*, p. 36.

9. The mission-educated Blacks acquired many cultural manifestations of European life. Of course, they felt more keenly the daggers of European rejection than did Africans who maintained traditional ways and values, because absorption of European culture by Africans produced alienation. However, arising out of this condition of alienation were the seeds of nationalism and revolutionary struggle.

10. Although many of the educated African elite considered themselves "progressive" and "civilized", none argued with more consistency than D. T. T. Jabavu that Africans steeped in European ways should be granted amenities, i.e. exemption from harsh segregation laws not extended to "raw" natives.

11. European missionaries used this theology of submission throughout the world to make Africans and others more responsive to European rule. A theology of submission attacked violence and militant struggle as anti-Christian, identified the status quo and adherence to its rule as "good" and negated all interpretations of Christianity developed a theological critique to attack the missionary notion of

submission. James Cone, however, provides an excellent historical analysis of the limitations of modern Western theological thought in *God of the Oppressed* (Maryknoll, N. Y.: Seabury Press, 1975).

12. Individualism (the personal to become Westernized) was the offering of capitalism which reached its maturity in the nineteenth century. This narrow position of self advancement was an economic concern for profit and greed. In the African milieu, the important bonds of mutual group love and support were negated, respect for elders was diminished, and societal sharing of economic, social and political links within traditional black society were destroyed.

13. See Brian William's *Sol Plaatie South African Nationalist, 1876-1932* (Berkeley and Los Angeles: University of California Press, 1984), pp. 28-57.

14. *Ibid.*, p. 48. S. Mankazana was a respectable member of the black community and the lead person in the case of R. V. Mankazana (1998). The case was fought because many of the educated black elites felt they were unduly harassed and maltreated. Of course, if these activities had been confined to "raw native," this court probably would not have emerged at all.

15. Joseph Booth in his pamphlet, *Africa for the African*, advocated complete political autonomy for African rule.

16. Perry Anderson, "Portugal and End of Ultra Colonialism." Part 2. *New Left Review* 16 (1962), pp. 102-3.

17. Bernard M. Magubane, *The Political Economy of Race and Class in South Africa* (New York and London: Monthly Review Press, 1979), p.61

18. Norman Etherington, "African Economic Experiments I Colonial Natal, 1845-1880's", *African Economic History* (Spring, 1978), pp. 1-15. This article demonstrates that acquisition of European culture by Africans meant their economic "enslavement". See also Louis B. Wright's *Religion and Empire: The Alliance Between Piety and Commerce in English Expansion 1558-1625* (Chapel Hill: The University of North Carolina Press, 1943). Wright's study demonstrated that the alliance between economic exploitation and religion in the West has a long history.

19. John Hope Franklin, *Reconstruction: After the Civil War* (Chicago and London: The University of Chicago Press, 1961); Kenneth M. Stampp, *The Era of Reconstruction, 1865-1877* (New York: Vintage Books, 1965); Forrest G. Wood, *Black Scare: The Racist Response to Emancipation and Reconstruction* (Berkeley and Los Angeles: The University of California Press, 1970); and Winthrop D. Jordan and Leon F. Litwack, *The United States*, combined edition, seventh edition (Englwood Cliffs, New Jersey: Prentice Hall, 1991).

20. Florette Hennri, *Black Migration: Movement North, 1900-1910)* Garden City, New York: Anchor Books, 1976). For an excellent overview of the social, political and economic conditions faced by Blacks, see chapter 1, pp. 1-48.

21. John Hope Franklin, *From Slavery to Freedom: A History of Negro Americans*, 6th ed. (New York: Alfred A. Knopf, Publisher, 1988), pp. 246-249. See also August Meier's *Negro Thought in America, 1880-1915: Racial Ideologies in the Age of Booker T. Washington* (Ann Arbor: The University of Michigan Press, 1963), chapter 2.

22. Benjamin Quarles, *The Negro in the Making of America* (New York: Collier Books, Macmillan Publishing, 1987), pp. 142-144.

23. George M. Frederickson, *The Black Image in the White Mind: The Debate on the Afro-American Character and Destiny, 1817-1914* (New York: Harper Torchbooks, 1972), chapter 9: "The Negro as Beast: Southern Negrophobia at the Turn of the Century", in C. Vann Woodward's *Origins of the New South, 1877-1913* (Louisiana State University Press and the Littlefield Fund for Southern History of the State of Texas, 1951).

24. Howard Brotz, (ed.) *Negro Social and Political thought, 1850-1920* (New York and London: Basic Books, Inc. Publishers, 1966), p. 2. This volume contains excellent selections from the work of major African American intellectuals of this period.

25. Martin R. Delany, *The Condition, Elevation, Emigration and Destiny of the Colored People of the United States* (New York: Arno Press and the New York Times, 1968). See chapter 16, especially pages 153-158. See also Alfonso Pinkney's *Red Black and Green: Black Nationalism in the United States*, (Cambridge University Press, 1976), pp. 23-27. Rodney Carlisle, *The Roots of Black Nationalism* (Port Washington, N. Y. and London: National University Publications, Kennikat Press, 1975), chapter 7.

26. *Ibid.,* pp. 67-68.

27. Charlise, *op. cit.,* pp. 78-82. For a critical examination of Blyden's ideas, see V. Y. Mudimbe's *The Invention of Africa: Gnosis, Philosophy and the Order of Knowledge* (Bloomington: Indiana University Press, 1988), pp. 98-134. Edward W. Blyden, *Christianity, Islam and the Negro Race*, Reprint, (Edinburgh: Edinburgh University Press, 1967).

28. For an introduction to Crummell's ideas in detail, read his *Africa and America, Addresses and Discourses* (Miami, Fl: Mnemosyne Publishing Inc., 1969), chapters 14-15.

29. T. Thomas Fortune, *Black and White: Land, Labor and Politics in the South* (Chicago: Ebony Classics, Johnson Publishing Company, Inc., 1970). He argued that the future of Blacks was in America and that the political solution to the race problem was assimilation.

30. There exists no full-scale biographical account of Turner's life; however, Redkey's study provides many insights into Turner's character and career. See Edwin S. Redkey, *Black Exodus: Black Nationalists and Back to Africa Movements, 1890-1910* (New Haven and London: Yale University Press, (1969).

31. During the presidential election of 1896, Turner gave the following advice to Blacks: "What time has the fool Negro to bother with the gold or silver side either, while he is lynched, burnt, flayed . . . two-thirds of the time . . . vote any way in your power to overthrow, destroy, ruin . . . wreck, consume, demolish . . . subvert, smash . . . expunge, and fragmentize this nation, until it learns to deal justly with the black man . . ." Robert G. Weisbord, *Ebony Kinship: Africa, Africans and the Afro-Americans* (Westport, Connecticut: Greenwood Press Inc., 1973), p. 33.

32. Most Europeans and American missionaries agreed that Blacks could minister better to their kind; however, Bishop Turner scandalized the southern religious community by stating that God was a "Negro". This powerful but short articles is in John H. Bracey, Jr., August Meier and Elliott Rudwick (eds.), *Black Nationalism in America* (Indianapolis and New York: the Bobbs-Merrill Company, Inc. 1970), pp. 154-155.

33. For an able discussion of redemption and black religion, see Olin P. Moyd, *Redemption in Black Theology* (Valley Forge: Judson Press, 1979); St. Clair Drake, *The Redemption of Africa and Black Religion* (Chicago: Third World Press, 1970), and James Cone, *My Soul Looks Back* (Maryknoll, New York: Orbis Books, 1986). Cone, in chapter 4, provides a concise analysis of Black theology and Third World theologies' thrust for eradication of human bondage – i.e. redemption.

34. In 1880, Blyden gave an address before the American Colonization Society entitled 'Ethiopia Stretching Out Her Hands Unto God or Africa's Service to the World". Of course, the attachment to this biblical verse to the nation of Ethiopia itself was extension; however, nowhere was this attachment so great, as noted by many scholars, as in Jamaica. Horace Campbell's *Rasta and Resistance: From Marcus Garvey to Walter Rodney* (Trenton, New Jersey: African World Press, Inc., 1987) makes the point that Ethiopianism was not always escapism as so often assumed but has an active element in lives of the poor to destroy claims, poverty and white culture domination.

35. The conditions in the mines of Southern Africa are graphically detailed in Charles Van Onselen's *Chibaro: African Mine labour in Southern Rhodesia. 1900-1933* (London: Pluto Press, 1976).

36. Theodore Draper's *The Rediscovery of Black Nationalism* (New York: The Viking Press, 1970). Draper views Black Nationalism as a crippled action of African Americans in a "superior" Western society. Draper states: "Delany, Bishop Turner, Edward N. Blyden, Hiford Douglas, the Reverend Henry Highland Garnet, and a few others have become the heores and prophets of today's black nationalism. Even Frederick Douglas is being denigrated as a kind of Uncle Tom because he opposed this trend. In their own time, however, relatively few Negroes took Delany or Turner very seriously and even fewer acted on their advice. *The historical problem is not merely why they advocated going back to Africa but why their efforts came to so little*", [my underlining] p. 47. See also Robert G. Athearn's *In Search of Canaan: Black Migration to Kansas, 1879-80* (Lawrence: The Regents Press of Kansas, 1978). Athearn pointed out that the move by Blacks to Kansas was a sign of displeasure with their economic and political condition in the Old South. This black exodus was part of the large movement to leave America.

37. The Watch Tower or the Kitawala Movement rejected all earthly authority and therefore was a threat to European political dominance. The Mgijima Massacre, however, was the most "extreme" incident of Africans rejecting European authority. For a brief introduction to separatist religious manifestations, see George Shepperson's 'Ethiopianism: Past and Present" in C. G. Baeta, (ed.) *Christianity in Tropical Africa* (London: Oxford University Press, 1968), pp. 249-264.

38. See R. V. Selope Thelma's "Social Conditions of the Africans" in J. Dexter Taylor (ed.), *Christianity and the Native of South Africa: A Year Book of South African Missions* (Lovedale: Constable and Co. Ltd., 1935), p. 13.

39. Daniel Thwaite, *The Seething African Pot: A Study of Black Nationalism 1930-1935* (London: Constable and Co. ltd., 1935), p. 13.

40. Ibid.

41. *Report of Native Churches Commission* (Cape Town: Cape Times Limited, Government Printers, 1925), p. 19.

42. *Ibid.*, p. 21

43. *Ibid.*, p. 23

44. Taylor, *op. cit.*, p. 74.

45. Thwaite, *op. cit.,* p. 27

46. Native Church Commission, *op. cit.,* p. 23

47. *Ibid.,* p. 23

48. See Edward Roux's *Time Longer Than Rope: A History of the Black Man's Struggle For Freedom in South Africa* (Madison: University of Wisconsin Press, 1964), pp. 77-86.

49. James H. Cone, *Speaking the Truth: Ecumenism, Liberation, Black Theology* (Grand Rapids, Michigan: William B. Eerdmans Publishing Company, 1986), pp. 91-96.

50. Oswald Doughty, *Early Diamond Days: The Opening of the Diamond Fields of South Africa* (London: Longmans, 1963), p. 133.

51. *Ibid.,* p. 145

52. The following volumes are important in showing the impact and transformation of the South African economy due to gold: Duncan Innes, *Anglo America and the Rise of Modern South Africa* (New York: Monthly Review Press, 1984), chapter 2 and 4; Selim Gool, *Mining Capitalism and Black Labour in the Early Industrial Period in South Africa: A Critique of the New Historiography* (Stockholm: Lund, 1983); Robin Palmer and Neil Parsons, (eds.) *The Roots of Rural Poverty in Central and Southern Africa* (Berkeley and Los Angeles: University of California Press, 1977). (See, in particular, Legassick's chapter 7.); F. A. Johnstone's *Class, Race and Gold* (London: Routledge and Kegan Paul, 1976); Sheila T. Van der Horst, *Native Labour in South Africa* (London: Frank Cass and Co. LTD., 1971); Monica Wilson and Leonard Thompson, (eds.) *The Oxford History of South Africa*, Vol II, (New York and Oxford: Oxford University Press, 1971); and Francis Wilson, *Labour in the South African Gold Mines, 1911-1969* (Cambridge: University Press, 1972).

53. Palmer and Parsons, *op, cit.,* pp. 181-186.

54. Van der Horst, *op, cit.,* pp. 126-127.

55. Van Onselen, *op, cit.,* pp. 48-57. Van Onselen's analysis is critical of the mine officials. Data provided in Gardner F. William's *The Diamond Mines of South Africa* (London: Macmillan & Company, 1902) present mine officials as caring employers who were concerned about the welfare of their "natives." See chapter XIV.

56. See Alan Jeeves, *Migrant Labour in South Africa's Mining Economy: The Struggle for Gold Mines' Labour Supply, 1890-1920* (Kingston, Ontario: McGill-Queen's University Press, 1985).

57. Ernie Regehr, *Perception of Apartheid: The Churches and Political Change in South Africa* (Scottsdale, Pennsylvania and Kitchener, Ontario: Herald Press and Between The Lines, 1979). Regehr makes plain the role of white Dutch Reformed Churches in establishing Afrikaner nationalism and Afrikanerdon is presented in a brilliant analysis in T. Dunbar Moodie, *The Rise of Afrikanerdom: Power, Apartheid, and the Afrikaner Civil Religion* (Berkeley, Los Angeles and London: University of California Press, 1975) and Pierre L. Van der Berghe, *Race and Racism: A Comparative Perspective* (New York: Wiley, 1967). In a similar vein, two American scholars have produced detailed studies on white supremacy and racism: George F. Fredrickson, *White Supremacy: A Comparative Study in American and South African History* (New York and Oxford: Oxford University Press, 1981) and John W. Cell, *The Highest Stage of White Supremacy: The Origins of segregation in South Africa and The American South* (Cambridge and New York: Cambridge University Press, 1982).

58. Wilson, *op, cit.,* p. 114.

59. Although traditional African farmers suffered setbacks from the environment, they nonetheless, competed successfully in the expanding South African "economy." See Van der Horst, *op, cit.,* pp. 104-109.

60. Maynard Swanson, "The Sanitation Syndrome: Bubonic Plague and Urban Native Policy in the Cape Colony, 1900-0," *Journal of African History*, 3 (1977), pp. 387-410.

61. Ray E. Phillips, *The Bantu in the City: A Study of Cultural Adjustment on the Witwatersrand* (New York: Ams Press, 1977) Phillips' work provides much data concerning health, education, crime, racial attitudes, income and even views concerning censorship of western movies for Africans.

62. Christopher Saunders (ed.) *Black Leaders in Southern African History* (London: Heinemann, 1979). See chapter 5 for an excellent introduction to Cetshwayo's life.

63. Brian Roberts, *The Zulu Kings* (New York: Alfred A. Knoff, 1978). This sordid affair to defraud Lobengula of Ndebele land is revealed on pages 99-112. See also Terrence O. Ranger's classic work, *Revolt in Southern Rhodesia, 1896-97: A Study in African Resistance* (Evanston, Ill.: Northwestern University Press, 1967).

64. See Peter Delius, *The Land Belongs to Us: Pedi Polity, the Boers, and the British in the Nineteenth-Century Transvaal* (Johannesburg: Ravan Press, 1983).

65. See Leonard Thompson, *Survival in Two Worlds: Moshoeshoe of Lesotho, 1786-1870* (Oxford: Clarendon Press, 1975).

66. Simon E. Katzenellenbongen, *South Africa and Southern Mozambique: Labour, Railways and Trade in the Making of a Relationship* (Manchester: Manchester University Press, 1982), pp. 36-39.

67. For a good introduction to WNLA, see Alan Jeeves' "The Control of Migratory Labour on the South African Gold Mines in the Era of Kruger and Milner", in Martin J. Murray, *op, cit.,* pp. 137-171. Also see Frederick A. Johnstone and Selim Gool, *op, cit.*

68. See Martin J. Murray's "The Development of Non-European Political Consciousness, 1910-1948", pp. 327-359; and Dan O'Meara's "The 1946 African Mine Workers' Strike and the Political Economy of South Africa", pp. 361-396, in Murray, *op, cit.*

69. See A. Temu and B. Swai, *Historians and Africanist History: A Critique* (London: Zed Press, 1981), pp. 23-29 and pp. 39-42.

70. Jeffrey B. Peires, *The Dead Will Arise: Nongqawuse and the Great Xhosa Cattle-Killing Movement of 1856-7* (Johannesburg: Ravan Press, 1989).

71. Peires sees the cattle-killing incident as a tragedy. Of course, it was, but it was also a religious/spiritual thrust to end expanding European power. The extreme nature of the cattle-killing movement suggests how desperate the Xhosa people were in trying to retain their autonomy.

72. The chief flaw of the separatist church struggle was its blind trust in British or liberal good will in aiding Blacks to redress their grievances. Many of the educated black elite frowned upon any militant action by the black masses as harmful to the advancement of African people.

73. Shula Marks, *Reluctant Rebellion* (Oxford: Oxford University Press/Clarendon Press, 1970). Her ideas dealing with the Bambata Rebellion are almost definitive; however, I am convinced that the separatist Christian ideas created a climate that helped to produce the rebellion.

74. George Shepperson and Thomas Price, *Independent Africa: John Chilembwe and the Origins, Setting and Significance of the Origins Native Rising of 1915* (Edinburgh: Edinburgh University Press, 1958). See in particular the last chapter on the relationship between Chilembwe and African American History.

75. T. O. Ranger, *The African Voice in Southern Rhodesia, 1898-1930* (Evanston: Northwestern University, 1970). For an introduction to the Watch Tower Movement and its ideas, see pages 200-222.

76. Vittorio Lantenari, *The Religious of the Oppressed: A Study of Modern Messianic Cults* (New York: Alfred A. Knopf, 1963), p. 3.

77. George Balandier, *The Sociology of Black Africa: Social Dynamics in Central Africa* (New York and Washington: Preager Publishers, 1963), p. 3.

78. Ibid., pp. 389-409.

79. Lantenari, *op, cit.,* pp. 13-20.

80. No full-scale study exists on the life of Nehanda. She combined the drive to liberate her people with traditional spiritual values; this was and is the key quality, organized violent resistance that is missing among African Separatist Christians as they seek emancipation today.

81. Temu and Swai, *op, cit.,* p. 110.

82. Marxist scholarship has been critical of the role of separatist churches in bringing about the liberation of South African society. Yet, some scholars have noted the "religious" nature of Marxism. Kenelm Burridge in *New Heaven, New Earth: A Study of Millenarian Activities* (Oxford, Blackwell, 1969) argues that Marxism is a relatively young millenarian movement.

83. Taylor, *op, cit.,* pp. 86-95. Also read Rev. Lea's expanded study, *The Native Separatist Church Movement in South Africa* (Cape Town and Johannesburg: Junta and Co., Ltd., 1926).

84. Gayraud S. Wilmore, *Black Religion and Black Radicalism* (Garden City, New York: Anchor Press/ Doubleday, 1973). In Atlanta, in 1896, Dwane informed Bishop Turner that Africans would not allow Europeans to push them around and that given time, black Africans would produce great governments. But a decade later, Dwane was in almost the same spiritual predicament as in 1892 – under European church control. See page 175.

85. Carol A. Page, "Colonial Reaction to AME Missionaries in South Africa, 1891-1910" in Sylvia M. Jacobs (ed.), *Black America and the Missionary Movement in Africa* (Westport, Connecticut: Greenwood Press, 1982), p. 178.

86. Europeans conceded that Blacks were better suited to minister to the needs of other Blacks. In addition to this, they noted ". . . that 'native' pastors would be better able to overcome the obstacles of distance, expense, and climate inherent in

Chapter 3

DANIEL WILLIAM ALEXANDER:
WHAT MANNER OF MAN?

Eighteen-eighty four was a year of great significance because it marked the rise of the first recorded black separatist church in South Africa. The previous year, Daniel William Alexander was born on the 25th of December in Port Elizabeth, Cape Province.[1] These two events intersected three decades later in the person of Alexander, who was not only a leading actor in the creation of the AOC, but also one of the major figures in the institutionalization of the Black Independent Church movement throughout West, South and East Africa.

Alexander's parents were Henry David Alexander and Isabella Demilton. The only additional information revealed about his parentage was that his father was Roman Catholic and a "native" of the French colony, Martinique; his mother was of Cuban and Javanese extraction.[2] According to Alexander, he was their second son. He was baptized at St. Peter's Catholic Church by Father Leo Smith. At an early age, Alexander left Port Elizabeth with his mother for six months to visit his maternal grandmother in Kimberley. Upon his return home, he commenced his education at the Roman Catholic Sisters of Mercy school and at St. Peter's with the Marist Brothers "until he passed the first year of civil service."[3] His formal training was augmented by an apprenticeship in boat building, a practice that was not uncommon for young African, European and Coloured males.

Although Alexander provided few insights into his early life, it must be noted that Africans and Coloureds set his growing up against a backdrop of increasing urbanization, strict segregation laws and a new search for a group identity. Of course, Coloureds saw themselves racially and culturally different from Africans, but the European community rigidly maintained the economic and political subordination of both groups. This important question of race and identity had major significance for Alexander over the next sixty years.

The race question intruded upon young Alexander with the outbreak of the Anglo-Boer War in 1899. At the age of sixteen, he was commandeered[4] into service as a cook for Boer troops while living in Johannesburg with his grandmother. Along with five others. He received orders to proceed to the Natal front; eventually, they were attached to a Boer regiment under the leadership of General Ben Viljoean.

During the war, Alexander witnessed the battle of Dundee and the 16th Lancer's charge of the Boers at Elandslaagte, but he did not participate in any fighting. Nonetheless, he was still arrested for being a British spy and imprisoned in Pretoria. There he found many other Coloured men incarcerated. Near the end of the war, he was freed from confinement as Lord Roberts entered the city.

According to Alexander, his release from the military in 1900 signalled a new beginning for him in Pretoria. During the war, he was separated from his wife, Maria Horsley, because she moved to another city with her Afrikaner employer and died six months later. Alexander noted that it was most painful for him not knowing if their short union had produced a child.[5] He found employment as a baker, and he took his first steps on his path to a new religious career.

In 1900, the death of Mrs. Neale, an elderly Coloured woman, brought about an encounter between Alexander and Father Godfrey, who was the only Anglican priest left in Pretoria because the Boers had expelled almost all English ministers. Godfrey asked Alexander whether he was familiar with the Anglican order of service since Alexander's English was flawless, and whether Alexander could assist Godfrey with Mrs. Neale's funeral. After the burial, Godfrey asked him to provide religious instruction for Pretoria's Coloured community. Alexander consented to his request and took charge of the work at St. Cuthbert about 1902. A year later, he went off to Shenwell to study for the ministry. He stayed in Pretoria for a while; then he moved to Vernwelen and planted the seeds of the Church of the Good Shepherd.[6] Before the end of 1903, he was ordained an

Anglican priest and had married his second wife, Elizabeth Koster (Mother Alexander).[7]

At this point, Alexander was not involved in the black Christian separatist movement. In fact, his consciousness was "colouredcentric." He did not consider himself Black or African. Although Alexander was quite comfortable with being labeled Black, his acceptance of an African identity was another matter. The Corfield Report alleged that Alexander used a passport claiming Mauritian ancestry.[8] Many individuals of this ethnic category were classified as Europeans in South Africa. The desire to be considered European was very dear to many Coloureds. Alexander fitted comfortably into this universe of "colouredness"; however, due to the massive social dislocation and the increasing level of interracial contacts between Coloureds and Africans, Alexander's spiritual development broadened to embrace the religious needs of Africans who were the most exploited of all in southern Africa.

The first decade of the twentieth century, however, found Alexander not only concerned with spiritual emancipation but also with the social and political well-being of the Coloured community in Pretoria. He joined the African Political Organization (APO) founded by Dr. A. E. Abdurahman in 1902. The APO was composed primarily of Coloureds[9] and was dedicated to advancing the political rights of non-Europeans. It must be noted that in Cape Province, some Africans and Coloureds were able to vote, obtain education and own property. But in the Orange Free States, Natal, and the Transvaal, these opportunities were virtually nonexistent. Alexander's involvement with political issues may have provided the backdrop for his expanding social consciousness.

Alexander's social consciousness must have undergone a major change after he left Pretoria and the Anglican Church in 1914. His reasons for breaking from the Anglican Church were not presented in concrete terms; however, they were likely tied to his search for spiritual emancipation. Later that same year, he took a job with the African Life Assurance Society in Johannesburg. The years between 1914 and 1924 must have critical for his spiritual development, although surviving records provide almost no insights into this period of his life. In

Johannesburg he had contacts with Africans and was introduced to "African Separatist Christianity." He joined the Ethiopian Catholic Church in Zion (ECC) and was ordained Deacon and priest by S. J. Brander. It should be noted that Brander was one of the following trail blazers of the separatist church movement. Many looked upon the ECC in Zion as a prestigious organization.[10] In 1924, Alexander left Johannesburg for new religious duties in Kimberley.[11]

Alexander's relocation to Kimberley was in response to a group of poor Coloureds asking him to help them find a minister. He noted that since he could not find a suitable candidate to work in the slums, he decided to go himself. Presumably, he terminated his official relationship with the ECC to start a new church group. He stated:

> [I] started to preach, as we had no churches, on a vacant lot in Broadway, later I hired a house, and converted it into a Mission Chapel. Sunday afternoons I devoted to instructing the young, Of whom we have close to 50 on the roll. We also started a Penny Bank to learn them thrift . . . .[12]

Thus, Alexander commenced his work among the poorest Coloureds. Without any assistance, he struggled to provide spiritual and educational care for his fragile flock. Within six months, his tiny congregation also attracted an African following. It was this African element that helped lead him to the AOC and the institutionalization of orthodox Christianity in South Africa.

The metropolis of Kimberley was the financial and spiritual center of his new church. One of the most developed urban areas in southern Africa; Kimberley was also a racially divided city.[13] Political and economic power was firmly in the hands of whites; Coloureds enjoyed a greater degree of acceptance and mobility from white local authorities than Africans who were relegated to the bottom of society. Over the years, Alexander tackled the poverty of Coloureds by soliciting from the diamond company, DeBeers. This powerful capitalist mining interest owned the land that Alexander negotiated to purchase soon after his arrival in Kimberley in 1924. The long and amicable relationship between

Alexander and De Beers lasted for over forty years as De Beers honored many of the AOC's requests for donations.[14]

De Beers's political/economic importance was a central element in the emergence of the Industrial Revolution that shaped capitalist South Africa. By the time Alexander arrived in Kimberley, two other cities, Johannesburg and Pretoria, had become centers of political and economic power. Although the headquarters of the AOC was located in Kimberley, the city itself played no significant role in the development or dissemination of separatist Christianity. A year after establishing the AOC in 1925, it was the Rand that simmered with separatist Christianity (see Chapter Two). Kimberley's importance for the AOC resided solely in the fact that since Alexander was Archbishop, all AOC Synods were held in that city until 1963.

Another important feature of Kimberley was its "wild" frontier existence of mud huts and prostitutes.[15] However, by the time Alexander arrived in that city, Kimberley had achieved a reputation for being part of the Cape's liberal tradition of "fair play" and African political and social advancement. But one historian writes of the extraordinary high rates of arrests and convictions of Africans. William Worger notes:

> By the mid to late 1880's, black mineworkers were, for all intents and purposes, ascriptive criminals, subject to laws restricting every aspect of their behavior and incarcerated within a series of institutions- jail, convict stations, and company compounds – for the duration of their stay in the industrial city.[16]

Worger's observations undermine the notion of liberalism and expose the stark reality of a harsh Kimberley environment that was intact as Alexander put his meager resources into the founding of the AOC.

The harshness of Kimberley was also reflected in the social problem of alcoholism. Throughout Alexander's long life, he railed against this social disease. Another important Kimberley personality, Sol Plaatje, on his return from America (ca 1924), expressed shock at the "orgy of drunkenness" that was pervasive in Johannesburg.[17] Plaatje was a member of the Independent Order of True Templar (IOTT), which advocated abstinence from all forms of strong spirits. He assigned the blame for African moral degeneracy of the African's traditional life to cope with the "evils" of alcohol.[18]

Alexander must have also witnessed this "orgy" on the Rand. Like Plaatje, he became a member of IOTT and urged Blacks not to call upon the government to support their efforts to abolish alcohol because the government was chief benefactor of profits derived from the beer halls (although it was on a smaller scale in Kimberley). Alexander believed that the surest method of defeating alcoholism was abstinence.

In July 1924, Alexander commenced his church work in Kimberley, but he had already initiated contact with American Blacks while still in Johannesburg, possibly as early as 1923. In a letter dated October, 1924, Patriarch McGuire informed Alexander that he, too, had once been an Anglican priest and that he was ready to aid his brethren overseas in the AOC.[19] He set forth the procedures for establishing an autonomous church in South Africa:

> We are not believers in foreign Missionary work . . . you in Africa must be Independent of outside support, control, and Supremacy. . . . hence instead of being a Department of AOC ... My advice is to call your Priests and Laity together and organize The South African Orthodox Church. . . Prepare your Canons, Declare your purpose to be in communion with A.O.C. after your First synod for a constitutional program. Hold later a second to Elect the first Bishop and Primate, send him with a request for Consecration to our General Synod in September, 1925, we over here could not, or would not be expected to finance his coming, But we are certain that we could finance his return...[20]

Nearly, forty years later, Alexander cited this document as proof of his legal and spiritual right to operate independently from the "control" of the American church.[21] What attracted Alexander initially to the AOC was this matter of being independent of Anglican control and finding a church with legitimate apostolic orders.

Alexander moved purposefully to establish the AOC in South Africa once McGuire granted him the status of Vicar Apostolic with the power to establish a local branch of the AOC.[22] Alexander revealed to McGuire that in the first meeting of the Kimberley/Beaconsfield Synod (September, 1925), a resolution was passed seeking communion with the Holy African Orthodox Church of America. Alexander went on to explain to the Patriarch that:

> it is our second that we are holding to pass all matters discussed at our first meeting, so that your Grace is aware that we need only pass my attendance to the General Synod in America, and I am herewith forwarding to your Grace, the Formal Deed of Election we also thank your Grace for the offer to pay my return to South Africa, after attending the General Synod, in September 1925. .[23]

At the same time as Alexander was establishing contact with the American AOC, he was, as early as 1922, contacts with Bishop J. M. Kanyane Separatist African Church. But Alexander broke with Kanyane's church due to Kanyane's "mismanagement" of funds and because he was seeking a viable organization to advance his career.

The linkage to the AOC was formally established in October, 1924, during a Provisional Synod with 400 people in attendance. At that time, the AOC of South Africa was instituted.[24] On a motion by Rev. Ezekiel Leagise:

> The Synod voted to elect Alexander bishop, to seek affiliation with the AOC in America, and to ask McGuire for credentials authorizing Alexander to administer the diocese and to deal with the South African government on behalf of the church ....[25]

The initial relations between McGuire and the new Bishop-elect proceeded smoothly and the stage was set for the first General Synod of the AOC, South Africa in September, 1925. Indeed, Alexander contemplated his consecration in September of the same year, and he looked forward to going to America for his election. The foundation forged between the two men was anchored in Alexander's belief that people of African descent must be aroused from spiritual slavery within the Anglican Church, to reject the crumbs from their master's table and seek ecclesiastical emancipation.[26]

Ecclesiastical union was realized at the first Provincial Synod held on Thursday, January, 1925 at the Church of St. Augustine of Hippo-Beaconsfield. The Synod commenced at 10:00 am with a High Mass attended by many friends and influential citizens of Kimberley. The celebrant of the service was the Right Rev. Daniel William Alexander, Vicar-Apostolic, assisted by Rev. Michael Moncho and Rev. James Monroe. In keeping with the Orthodox doctrines, the filioque clause, for the first time, was omitted from the Nicene Creed.[27] Alexander based his sermon on the Gospel of St. Luke, Chapter 10, verses one through nine, which begins: "Behold I send you forth as lambs among wolves . . . ."[28] Before the closing of the morning session at 1:00 p. m., the Synod chose two important officers of the church: John Balston as secretary and Charles Sweetwater as treasurer.[29]

The remaining four days of the Synod proved to be equally important in stabilizing the church's internal structure. The Synod established a finance committee, a church extension fund committee and a committee on Episcopate Fund. Suggestions were also put forward to establish Christian societies to commence educational work among young men and women. A group that was dear to Alexander's heart was the Children's Christian Fund. Alexander implored all members and clergy to support the various funds to guarantee their success. Within a short span of time, The Guild of St. Monica, temperance societies and a seminary were added to the AOC and provided a fullness to the spiritual life of this charge to the Provincial Synod. He spoke glowingly of the occasion:

> this is an historic gathering which in years to come to our children's children will have cause to bless. This gathering brings to mind the Assembly in the upper room where the twelve Apostles and those assembled with them gathered, to await the promise of their Master . . .[30]

He then stated the specific purpose for the synodic gathering:

> You will called upon . . . to Sanction and pass, as passed by the Committee on October the 6th 1924, that we secede from the African Church under [the] Reverend J. Kanyane Napo, an affiliate to the African Orthodox Church, established in New York under the most Rev. Leo Alexander McGuire . . .[31]

Alexander spoke about the qualities of men and women whom he desired to become servants in the church. His views were ones that he stressed repeatedly over the next forty years. Clergy members should be honest, faithful, courteous, sincere, and unselfish since the welfare of the church came first. In a mild Pan Africanist vein, he contended that for their race to advance, the AOC's motto should be "All for one, and one for all." Otherwise, Black people would be unable to organize massive movements for their own upliftment.

Uplift was indeed the "universal" theme that solidified the spiritual alliance between McGuire and Alexander. In their correspondence, McGuire reinforced the need for Alexander to attend the Fifth General Synod in America in September, 1925 and to forward all transactions ratified by South Africa's Provincial Synod.[32] On the important issue of whether to grant Alexander the status of Archbishop, McGuire maintained that:

> While there is no discussion in the minds of our brethren concerning consecration, the matter of your title as Archbishop will cause difference of opinion. But "Primate" is taken for granted. You will have to show to the satisfaction of Gen. Synod the reason you desire this title at once. It was three years we in America got the Episcopate that we were in a position to use the title and elect an Archbishop from three bishops . . .[33]

In March 1925, however, McGuire was of the opinion "that our Conclave or House of Bishops will be given by the Gen. Synod the authority to consecrate, but with a recommendation that such consecration be deferred . . .[34] The reason for the deferral was to provide ample time for the AOC in America to confirm all of the information provided by Alexander. McGuire appointed Isaiah P. Samuel of Cape Town[35] as his official South African emissary to "represent us in gathering all the information General Synod may need and as our Vicar Apostolic until your consecration . . . I shall hope that you will cooperate with him . . ."[36]

The selection of Samuel did not meet Alexander's approval. He wrote McGuire: "your Grace will see that your grace's brother Mr. I. Samuels has become a Congregational minister . . now can a Protestant be fair to a catholic [sic]."[37] Although Alexander was not pleased with the Patriarch's choice, he maintained he would remain faithful to the AOC.

Because Alexander had requested a loan of L25.0.0 and the church in America had agreed to pay Alexander's return expenses from the United States, McGuire deemed that a closer inspection of Alexander's finances and other church connections were in order. He stated:

> Their judgement [church officials] is that your own work, which they understand to be independent, and not missionary . . . This request has made them curious as to the stability of your work, and it is now quite clear to me that much probing into its status, and your own, will be made before consent is given to your consecration. Particular information is needed concerning your past
> ministerial connection with other religious bodies and the reasons for their termination, also concerning your education. The same facts are needed from your clergy, which should be given in their own handwriting . . .[38]

McGuire hoped Alexander would not resent the investigation. Indeed, McGuire opined that a probe was mandatory to protect the most precious gift of the "Apostolic Episcopate." He encouraged Alexander to work, save funds and await the action of the General Synod, which would deliberate upon his case.[39]

The conferring of apostolic succession upon Alexander through prayers and the laying on of hands of three bishops would grant him complete spiritual equality with the AOC Patriarch. The AOC was willing to grant the leadership of the church to its adherents in South Africa and not send bishops from the West as was traditionally done by most denominations. This indigenous leadership would have the complete authority "to develop the details of . . . work, along such lins as are best suited to the condition and needs of . . . [the] people . . ."[40] The AOC in

America, according to Bishop Grant of Long Island, would assist the AOC in South Africa with advice and supervision to aid its development and growth. But in matters of internal control, Alexander was free from American "interference".[41] This last point must be stressed: McGuire and AOC officials in America gave Alexander the authority to establish a fully independent church.

The bills introduced by Prime Minister Hertzog to curtail black rights marked the AOC's early years. The legislation was so obnoxious that Alexander devoted attention to these measures in his Bishop's charge of 1926 to his Synod. He blasted white superiority by stating that it was unworthy and that the white race had a "low estimate of their own superiority, when it has to be hedged around with the color bar bill . . ."[42] He went on to say that "our women must carry passes, but we thank God that the case has been won."[43] He forcefully told the Synod gathering that contentment with the current political situation was not acceptable. With a prophetic note, he warned the audience that their troubles had only commenced and they would have to suffer, sacrifice and even be incarcerated to gain their freedom.[44]

A year later at the Third Synod, Alexander sounded the alarm again against segregationist legislation:

> For Parliament is in session, and the Premier's Four Bills, are to be made law, separating us who are blood kin from each other, robbing you my Bantu brother to give me at your expense a little more . . . I say rather let us fight together for our rights politically as well as spiritually, and we who are assembled together let us fight in the spirit, asking God continually to put our oppressors to confusion. . .[45]

Hertzog's bills were designed to cripple African and Coloured social and political rights. Three of the bills were concerned with African control of land, African voting rights and African housing accommodations in the urban areas. The fourth bill was designed to "review" Coloured political rights. The bills had been first introduced in 1926. Although they did not become the laws of the land for another decade, by 1927 Alexander and others understood the severe implications of Hertzog's political goals.

Alexander ended his charge with three important announcements. First, he stated that all who wished to become Marriage Officers should complete their applications. Indeed, he insisted the clergy should not blame him for government standards because the clergy that passed the government requirements would become marriage officers. He remarked that he desired more officers so that he would be free for more important administrative tasks. Second, Alexander proclaimed that the AOC was not "a little sect . . .[,]"[46] but was part of a long history with St. Peter as the first bishop of the AOC. To him, a sect was an organization with one-man rule, where the leader viewed himself as the alpha and omega of the church's existence. Third, Alexander noted that during his trip to America, no Synod would be held. Nevertheless, he expected the church to appoint a Vicar-General or Council to oversee matters until his return and for all archdeacons to convene their District Conferences. Finally, Alexander made a special request for the assembled body to take care of Mother Alexander during his absence and to " . . . see that she is not in want, do not let me hear on my return that you have starved her . . ."[47] The Synod ended on the note of Alexander's voyage to America.

MARCUS GARVEY, AFRICAN REDEMPTION AND SOUTH AFRICA

America was the place where the key strands of diasporic black nationalist Christianity converged. Alexander was from Africa; he advocated a reformist brand of black nationalist Christianity. However, McGuire and Garvey, both from the Caribbean, advocated a more militant strain of black Christianity. Garvey's Christian Nationalist message was more radical and contained revolutionary implications for church developments in America. Without the ubiquitous presence of Garvey, the AOC in South Africa would not have emerged. The minutes of the preliminary meeting held on 6 October 1924 to bring the AOC into existence announced:

> At this juncture Mr. Joseph Masaga, the local agent of the Negro World, and organizer of the Afro-Construction Church of the House of Athlyi was introduced with his secretary, Mr. Mabusa, and was welcome with a few appropriate remarks by the chairman; in reply Mr. Masaga said he was glad to be present on this auspicious occasion, and wished the Dean [Rev. Daniel W. Alexander] and Brethren of the Clergy and Laity every success in the great work they are about to engage; the Dean as elected head in South Africa, must remember that he was going to carry a heavy load on his back, but with patience and forbearance, he will ultimately succeed and what he had witnessed this day will be published in the Negro World, and when the minute of this
> gathering is published, I will be witness, and as the Dean goes further he will know the Orthodox as I know it.[48]

Garvey's *The Negro World* was a vital link throughout the diaspora in spreading the message of liberation from European bondage. Critical to the message of *The Negro World* was salvation and redemption of the race and Africa by Blacks themselves. Alexander and McGuire understood salvation/redemption in spiritual terms and they put into operation their respective views of black Christian nationalism. Masoga, then, fitted into this Pan-African theme of salvation/redemption. Of course, he was pleased that Alexander now walked the path of spiritual upliftment. For Masoga, recording these events was a small measure to demonstrate his appreciation of Alexander's courage and to provide international publicity for the importance of Garvey's ideas in the general rise of the AOC.

The Garvey connection with the AOC had existed since the founding of the AOC in 1921. Garvey, a Jamaican who immigrated to America in 1916, was the first Black of African descent to organize a global mass movement for the "redemption" of Africa. His ideas on race consciousness and group solidarity influenced ideological developments throughout the dispora—in Cuba, South

Africa, the United States, Trinidad and England. His motto of "One aim, One God, One destiny" struck a responsive chord throughout the black world.[49]

In the religious realm, Garvey's Universal Negro Improvement Association (UNIA) had far-reaching consequences for black Christian nationalism. Garvey's mass meetings in Harlem took on the appearance of "old fashioned" Baptist revivals. Hymns and prayers were part of the general program. Garvey fostered the religious ethos to advance his movement's political and economic aims. Like some of his black separatist counterparts in South Africa, Garvey viewed religion as a tool for emancipation. This idea matured to its fullest with the rise of the AOC in America under the leadership of George Alexander McGuire.[50]

The liberation themes of Garvey's theology have not been adequately explored. Much of Garvey's "God-talk" was anti-colonial and anti-racist. To him, God was the creator of the universe who endowed the human family with equality. Garvey was hostile to the stereotype of biblical characters as blond, blue-eyed Europeans. He directed even more hostility against a "theology of submission", which lulled Blacks into accepting their brutalization and exploitation. Religion had to empower the oppressed to arm themselves against whites. Because of the stridency of Garvey's analysis, he has criticized for being anti-white and racist. He certainly could be brutal, but his acid diatribe against America in general and the white religious community in particular could (or should) not obscure the soundness of his black nationalist Christian perspective. Garvey, like Bishop Turner and James Cone, was aware that whites were heirs of wealth, power, and privilege; therefore, their theology and religious values interpreted the Gospel to perpetuate white political and economic interests. Their presentation of the Gospel preserved the status quo and stigmatized militant opposition to the established order as dangerous and unchristian.

Garvey understood that for black people to achieve significant advances, they must first break the chains of religious bondage and marshall their energy to generate sustained support for their political/economic interest.[51] Black political and economic condition shaped Garvey's ideas of African redemption. During the 1920's, most of Africa was still under foreign domination. The land, people and natural resources were exploited for the benefit of European colonizers; the African masses were poor, illiterate, malnourished and had few allies. To Garvey, African redemption meant a reversal of these terrible conditions. God in His infinite wisdom promised that "Ethiopia" would bring about the continent's salvation from all social ills, including white people. Thus, redemption was both sacred and secular; it necessitated Africa's spiritual and moral upliftment and the economic development of Africa for Africans. Once this regenerative process occurred, Garvey could then move to develop an international position of respect and fair treatment for Africans.[52]

Related to the idea of redemption and nationalism was Garvey's conception of a "black" God. The religious imperialism of Western Europe was a crucial factor in producing social disorientation among African peoples in the diaspora, thereby facilitating their enslavement. Garvey simply fought fire with fire by posing a black God in contradiction to a white God. On a mundane level, Garvey wanted Christ and the Virgin Mary physically portrayed as ebony. African suffering and maltreatment in the Americans made such a physical identification crucial for his program of moral and economic upliftment on the African continent. On the metaphysical plane, however, Garvey was content to worship God in spirit, devoid of all anthropomorphic characteristics.[53]

One might conclude that Garvey's religious views, like those of Turner and Blyden, were grafted onto black nationalism. This was not the case. It was the black preacher who first voiced the religious-politico message of solidarity, mission and redemption. Black nationalism was in essence a Christian/moral stance against American violence and capitalist exploitation. Pan-Africanism, the highest theoretical expression of black nationalism, became the twentieth century secular component of the religious message of solidarity and unity. Garvey, McGuire, Blyden and Turner all stressed the three cardinal elements of solidarity, mission and redemption. These key elements were important in constructing black Christian nationalistic thought and they benefitted Garvey in the 1920's.

African Americans were aware of the fact that they were part of the African race. They had been brought to the New World against their wills, and the majority of their number had been enslaved. Their bitter oppression and pigmentation were that foundation of black consciousness and solidarity. In the face of white hostility and the consolidation of white power, Blacks attempted to organize to combat white aggression. Organization was necessary for their physical and spiritual salvation. Black American solidarity, then, grew out of their common heritage, their old struggles to end slavery and to escape from brutal racism, and their Christian belief in a future mission for Africa.

This notion of mission was part of a general American belief that God had entrusted Americans with the special duty of spreading Christianity and democracy to the "benighted" world. Black Christians, too, accepted the dictum "Go ye into all the world and preach the gospel, teaching all nations . . . ."[54] Because Africans on the continent were worthy of their missionary efforts, Black Americans believed that social uplift would benefit the future prosperity and glory of Africa. Africa could then stem the tide of white aggression and the "rape" of the land. Education, too, could become a weapon because it freed the people from ignorance, poverty, sickness and disease. African Americans, then, could share in the great Christian endeavor of the alleviation of human suffering. Mission was not simply a matter of whim, but was sacred and ordained by God.[55] Providence was beyond doubt at work within the black community since ". . . God's destiny for Black Americans was graphically revealed in his 'providence'. Blacks had been brought to America for a training fitting them for the work of civilization and evangelizing Africa."[56]

The concept of redemption was the key element for Garvey and most early nationalists; it was perceived as an eschatological hope of salvation. Redemption was salvation from the states and circumstances, which destroyed the value of human existence or human existence itself. Redemption was salvation from sin and guilt. It is a term which describes what God has done, is doing, and will do, historically, in relationship with humankind and the universe.[57] The this-world orientation of redemption makes it a Christian responsibility to challenge oppressive political systems. This critical feature of redemption was closely related to the Old Testament Hebrews' usage of the term as opposed to the traditional Christian usage which was personal-sin directed. Scripture is rich in references to redemption from bondage. Deuteronomy 7:8 reads as follows: "But it is because the Lord loves you, and is keeping the oath which he swore to your fathers, that the Lord has brought you out with a mighty hand, and redeemed you from the house of bondage, from the hand of Pharaoh King of Egypt."[58] The oppressors, on the other hand, need redemption from the guilt of dehumanizing Blacks, but Blacks needed "redemption from oppression. They need an Exodus out of the state of circumstances of dehumanization."[59]

Marcus Garvey provided an exodus out of the dehumanizing environment of "Jim Crow" laws, racism, exploitation, lynching and economic stagnation. Garvey fused mission, solidarity and redemption into a platform, providing an attractive alternative for the black masses to express their discontent and to participate in an attractive alternative for the black masses to express their discontent and to participate in their social and economic elevation. African redemption was the cement that bonded Africans and their kin across the ocean through the centuries and enabled them to withstand the tribulations of time.

SOUTH AFRICA

Nowhere was the ridicule and domination of African folk so blatantly maintained as in South Africa. The influence of Garvey's message introduced thousands in southern Africa to the ideas of mission, solidarity and racial redemption. The U. N. I. A.'s organ, *The Negro World*, disseminated Garveyism and general information concerning the black diaspora. Garvey's greated triumph has been his legacy of race consciousness to those people of Africa who insisted that any resolution of the continent's pressing problems include, at least in part, a nationalist perspective. At the same time, the black Christian nationalism of

Garvey aided in the rise of the AOC of South Africa, under the leadership of Daniel William Alexander.

The social climate of South Africa made fertile soil for the growth of Garveyism. The enthusiasm with which the message of Africa for Africans was received attests to the power of Garvey's ideas. Many were already advocating some of these ideas from the pulpits of separatist churches. South Africa, like the United States between 1880 to 1920, experienced profound industrial expansion, intensified segregation, and a growing awareness of race consciousness to combat black exploitation. Thousands of Africans were still alive in the 1920's who had engaged in armed struggles against European domination throughout southern Africa. Many of them were not actual supporters of Garvey, but they identified with him and shared his sentiments on black domination and expelling Europeans from the continent.[60]

During the 1920's, there were some firm indications that supporters of Garvey or his ideas were part of the South African separatist milieu. For instance, the acting Postmaster-General in June 1924 informed the Secretary of the Interior: "That Post Master of Kimberley has reported that thousands of copies of the American paper *The Negro World* . . . are being received every week addressed to a native in the Kimberley location . . ."[61]

These incoming newspapers and the expanding influence of Garvey's ideas caused misgivings within the European community. "After observing Garvey's propaganda," according to the *Cape Argus* in 1923, produced "an effect (among the natives), and is beginning to cause anxiety among the white people who have worked for the good of the natives, and among educated natives, who foresee danger in the present situation. . . ."[62] Even in the rural areas, Garvey's influence was manifested in the motto: Ama Melikaa ayeza (The Americans are coming.)[63] Garvey's ideas therefore produced among many Africans a heightened awareness of race consciousness; whereas, Europeans viewed them, as increasing racial animosity.

The charge of "embittering racial feeling" had also been leveled against Bishop Turner in 1898 and now against Garvey. John Tengo Jabavu had led the attack against Bishop Turner, and his son, Don Davidson Tengo Jabavu, figured prominently in African press criticism against Garvey. Other Garvey opponents—M. Mokote Manoedi, Josiah T. Gumede, and James E. K. Aggrey— viewed Garveyism as a "pie-in-the-sky dream" that had harsh consequences for the black masses. Reflecting the European sentiment, the *Cape Argus* featured an article entitled, "Poisoning the Native Mind", alleging that Garvey's propaganda was being distributed by Bolshevik agents. The article concluded by stating:

> There is now a wide organization in South Africa, and money is sent regularly every month to America. There are about 200 American Negroes in Cape Town alone, and as they cannot speak the Bantu languages their propaganda work is confined to the semi-educated native, who generally is an eager recipient for the fairy tales of these people.[64]

Semi-educated Blacks and illiterate peasants comprised the bulk of Garvey's nationalist "army;" however, some middle class Africans were also in his camp, James Thaele was one who became an ardent advocate of Garvey's views. In his newspaper, *The African World*, a twin of Garvey's propaganda organ, Thaele sounded the theme of the importance of Garveyism for South Africa. His audacity earned him the wrath of the *Sunday Times* (1925) of Jahannesburg:

> A more treacherous, inflammatory, deluded and deluding publication it is difficult to imagine. In any but a British country those responsible for its publication would instantly be dealt with in swift and certain fashion. The avowed aim of the African World is to 'free Africa from the incubus of European control' and 'to install the psychology and traits of Zaghbul Pasha in the Africa race'. In its third issue, published on June 13, it had the barefaced impudence to refer to 'the imperishable message of his Highness, Marcus Garvey-Potentate of the Universal Negro Improvement Association'. Every well-informed native knows Marcus Garvey to be an unprincipled rogue and swindler who is now serving five years in prison for cheating Negroes of the United States out of huge sums of money.[65]

The race consciousness introduced by Garvey and Bishop Turner heightened political activity for emancipation. In the religious sphere, Garvey's influence helped to launch the rise of the AOC of South Africa. Alexander became acquainted with the AOC by reading *The Negro World* in 1924. In America, the Garvey movement was at its apex; and in southern Africa, at least thirty branches of the U.N.I.A. had been established. There is no recorded evidence to suggest that Alexander was a member of the U.N.I.A. What linked Garvey, Alexander and McGuire into a black separatist union was the notion that spiritual liberation and African redemption were inseparable. Alexander, however, never equalled the militancy of Garvey or McGuire in nationalism or anti-European sentiments, though he labored for over four decades to make black spiritual emancipation a reality and to institutionalize African Orthodoxy.

ALEXANDER IN AMERICA

In July 1927, Daniel William Alexander embarked upon his journey to the United States. Ironically, several months before his arrival, Marcus Garvey was deported from the United States. As the future Primate of South Africa boarded the R.M.S. Balmoral Castle in Cape Town for Southampton, England, he stood on the deck after the good byes and sang "Te Deum." His thoughts were with those whom he left in Beaconsfield. He hoped this would be the first of many trips to America, but this was to be his only trip away from the continent.[66]

The voyage to England took seventeen days, and Alexander noted how monotonous the whole journey was. Although he was the only black passenger aboard, he felt he was given extremely good treatment. As the liner entered Southampton harbor, he was amazed at the hub of activity in the port. From Southampton, he took the "Boat Train ninety-six miles to London to feast upon greater amusements."[67] He was pleased with the fact that no "colour bar" existed in public places as it did in South Africa and the United States. A white passenger asked him about the replacement of the Union Jack in South Africa by another flag. Alexander responded tactfully that he was not a statesman; however, from his own personal perspective he was "fairly certain that the British Emblem will never be removed from the flag of South Africa..."[68]

Some Blacks still praised Britain's benevolent rule. Even Alexander boasted:

> There is no individual born in any overseas possession of the British Empire, West Indies, South and West Africa or elsewhere, who does not experience a feeling of achievement when he reaches London and visits the various ecclesiastical buildings of which he had read so much.[69]

The sights of the Church of St. Clement's Danes, St. Paul's Cathedral and Westminister Abbey made a deep impression on him.[70] Early the next morning he boarded the Olympia for the United States.

He arrived in New York City on 23 August, 1927. Harlem was sill in "vogue" and all the greats were there: A. Philip Randolph, W.E.B. Dubois, Cluade McKay and others of the Harlem Renaissance. Alexander, too, must have felt the excitement of being in the Black Mecca of the World. His coming to America had been publicized for months and created quite a stir in the local black orthodox community. *The Negro Churchman*, the newspaper of the AOC in America, editorialized in July, 1927 that:

> From the Homeland comes a Native Son to receive Episcopal
> Consecration from an African Archbishop 'abroad', assisted by two other Bishops of African descent. Blessed are the eyes which see the things which we shall see at synod, for many have desired to see them and yet have not seen them![71]

Patriarch McGuire's address on the importance of Alexander's arrival sounded a similar theme:

> The outstanding feature of this Seventh General Synod is the presence in our midst of a Native Son of our Motherland, a living witness of the growth, the purpose and the appeal of this Church to the African at home and abroad. At our First Synod in 1921, as Leader of this movement, we outlined Our 'vision
> of a branch of the Holy Catholic Church controlled by Colored Churchmen, gathering people of African descent in all quarters of the globe'.
>
> At our Third Synod in 1923 we further called attention to the fact that the valid and historic episcopate that we have received is to be safe guarded by us, transmitted to our sons, not only in the West, but ultimately to those awaiting us in the Motherland. The vision is about to be fulfilled. On the approaching Sunday you shall be witnesses of the consecration of a native African by Bishops of his own Race, whose ancestors were forcibly removed from their Motherland.[72]

McGuire also clarified the relationship of the Mother Church, Holy Cross, with the emerging South African province:

> The Provincial Synod of the African Orthodox Church in South Africa is self-governing in every respect, and has set forth its own constitution and Canons, not conflicting with ours in any essentials. Its faith and orders are those of the whole African Orthodox Church. Its primate and future Bishops are to be members of a Pan-African orthodox conclave, holding themselves in obedience to the Supreme Ecclesiastical Head in all spiritual matters, and consecrating no Bishop without the written consent and commission of said Supreme Authority.
>
> Over both provinces, however, and over future Provinces to be established, there must be a 'Patriarch' who shall be the Supreme Ecclesiastical Head of the entire church, while exercising also the office of Archbishop and Primate of his own Province.[73]

The above statement was to be critical in resolving a schism nearly forty years later when Alexander established a new "orthodox" church. There was no discord, however, during his stay in America.

Alexander met Patriarch McGuire and other church dignitaries in August 1927. His schedule included several appearances before the General Synod. In addition, he traveled o Chicago, Boston and Washington, D.C. for speaking engagements. One of his talks occurred in an U.N.I.A. Hall in New York City.[74] The black orthodox community rolled out the red carpet for Alexander and he was very much in demand. The tightness of his schedule did not permit him to travel to Florida as he wished, and he expressed regret to that congregation for his absence.

The consecration of Alexander as elected Archbishop and Primate of the Province of South Africa took place on Sunday, 11 September, 1927 at 11 a.m. The High Mass and regal vestments of the clergy were awe-inspring. No less sublime was the beautiful music produced by three choirs at St. Michael's (Boston, MA). Kneeling before the consecrator, the Bishop Elect recited the Oath of obedience:

> I, Daniel William Alexander, elected to the church in the Province of South Africa, from this hour henceforth will be obedient to the Holy Africa Orthodox Church and to our Eminent Father Alexander, Patriarch and his successors canonically elected. I will assist them to retain and defend African Orthodox without detriment to my order . . . . I shall receive humbly the Patriarchal mandated and execute them as diligently as possible. But if I shall be detained by legitimate impediment, I shall fulfill all the aforesaid things through a designated delegate . . . . So help me God and these Holy Gospels of God which I touch with both my hands.[75]

The movement finally arrived when the "Keys of Peter" became part of Alexander's persona:

> At the very moment when the consecrator and his two assistants laid their hands upon the head of the Bishops -Elect, and uttered the words, 'receive the Holy Ghost', nature seemed to join with men in the solemn act, for a peal of thunder instantly broke forth, followed at once by a copious shower . . .[76]

According to the Patriarch, blessed were the eyes that witnessed Alexander's elevation.

Equally as impressive was Alexander's address as Bishop-Elect. He recounted how he became acquainted with the AOC through *The Negro World* and how he immediately wrote Primate McGuire for more information. Before that information arrived, Alexander had been consecrated in the Ethiopian Catholic Church. On his return from the Transvaal, he found AOC documents and rejoiced at knowing that McGuire had obtained valid Apostolic Orders.

Alexander then proceeded to provide an accounting of the probation of the Province of South Africa and general church information. He stated that:

> When in 1925 the General Synod in America placed us under probation for two years, and His Grace appointed Prof. Isaiah Samuels as his emissary, we resented the selection of the gentlemen as not being a proper person for his post, nevertheless we were obedient, and set ourselves to the task of proving ourselves worthy . . . . We also thank the General Synod for his provision to bear our expenses back to Africa. We pray that your kindness to us will be fruitful of much good, for the homeland is awaiting your great act of love by means of which we shall be inheritors with you of the Great Gift of the Apostolic Succession . . .[77]

Dramatic as the consecration service was, the sermon preached by Bishop Arthur Stanley at Alexander's enthronement, was prophetic of the future tensions between the Mother church and the African Province. Stanley's sermon dealt with the affliction of schism. A dissenting group within the AOC, according to him, had not heeded the advice of the Patriarch or Synod and had created an independent body with an alien Archbishop who later consecrated two other bishops. This body, he noted, retained a similar name, but Stanley adamantly maintained that there was only one African Orthodox Church. Bishop Stanley predicted doom for this group of malcontents:

> These schismatics may be comforting themselves because they have created an organization with a similar name, but Solomon wisely stated that whatever is born in vanity must end in vanity. If a man builds a house, forms a party, makes a gift, or seeks an office from vanity, then as certainly as the bite of an asp will poison the body, will the expected good be turned into bitter disappointment . .[78]

Stanley inquired whether the other Bishops would warn future priests of the evil of schism and asked them not to allow schismatics to undermine the AOC's valid authority. He directed his concluding remarks at Alexander:

> And now my Brother, today you are elevated from the priesthood to be a ruler and a teacher of the church. The Master Himself has chosen you to be an overseer and pillar to truth, to govern, and to instruct the clergy and people committed to your charge. Like Saul, after he had been anointed king, step forth as a man of a new spirit to guide, guard and defend that which is instructed to your keeping. And may you prove yourself a faithful overseer of the Flock of Christ![79]

After his whirlwind tour of several cities, many speaking engagements and banquets in his honor, Alexander's sojourn neared an end. Although most of his presentations were not recorded, he must have imbibed from the black orthodox community ideas about race solidarity, consciousness and economic development. He had not expected the sensitive and brotherly reception accorded him; indeed, his American experience left him with indelible impressions of Harlem and, of course, the Patriarch.

Patriarch McGuire was a man of determined character and great spiritual vision. Unlike Alexander, he was a zealous supporter and defender of Marcus Garvey. McGuire's unshakable faith in Garvey's movement led him to direct his flock to achieve economic and spiritual autonomy. His moving address on Garvey appeared in the March and July, 1923 issues of *The Negro Churchman*. It was a brilliant exposition of the spiritual/nationalistic ethos of the Africa for Africans movement.[80] McGuire argued that those who claimed that the U.N.I.A. was not a spiritual movement were in error, and that in operation "the movement shall be spiritualized."[81] He noted that Garvey's detractors had treated the movement with levity, contempt and prejudicial criticism.[82] He also made it clear that while he had disagreed with Garvey on the "management of some of the affairs of his institution",[83] he believed Garvey was a great prophet who had touched the black masses and instilled in them mighty truth of race consciousness and gave them a profound hope for achieving their own salvation.

McGuire noted that the AOC clergy had preached "back to Africa" from their pulpits, not in a belligerent manner but as the only solution to the vexing race problem in America.[84] He maintained that those who talked of 'unconditional surrender' of rights gained by hard work or military service needed to understand that simple acceptance of "such rights and privileges, even if there were promise of their attainment in a hundred years, marks us as lacking in the vision of Racial independence and development." He added:

> The demand that 'Garvey must go' has been vociferously made by a certain group among us . . . . But whether he goes or not, the soul of the movement which he has fanned into flame, the spiritual yearnings of his legions of converts will not perish. We know where we speak. The 'spirit' may shed its physical habiliments, but it will be reincarnated. What appears to be dissolution may be only the gateway to true life. The grain of corn that dies to live; death often proves the stepping-stone to victory. 'So when this corruptible shall have put on incorruption, and this mortal shall have put on immortality, then shall be brought to pass the saying that is written, death is swallowed up in victory . . . . But we do not hesitate to warn those who desire to crush his movement, that while for the present they may harass the 'body' thereof, no human power can kill its soul'.[85]

If this were the editorial that Alexander read in 1924, we can now comprehend McGuire's compelling influence on Alexander whose departure from the Anglican Church (1914) had set him adrift in a spiritual search for authenticity and a spiritual home. This led him finally to the door of the AOC, and he savored his elevation as Archbishop.

As Alexander left America aboard the "Olympia:, he must have been concerned about Mother Alexander and the members of St. Augustine of Hippo. In Chapter Four, we will view Alexander as he struggled to institutionalize his church, repay the loan that brought him to America, and expand his missionary efforts.

ENDNOTES

1. This information is taken from a handwritten autobiographical account by Alexander. There are, in fact, two versions consisting of six pages. I have used information from both. However, there is no way to distinguish one from the other. Since both are undated, they should be used together, (Box-1, Folder-5). The archive of the AOC is housed at Pitts Theological Library, Emory University, in Atlanta, Georgia. Daniel William Alexander is referred to hereafter as DWA in citations.

2. *Ibid.* It is odd that a man of Alexander's passion for documents would provide such scant autobiographical insights into his own childhood and his early adult life.

3. I am of the opinion that Alexander wrote this account in the 1960's because the document reflects minor errors. Information in one of the documents is confusing. For instance, Alexander drew lines through some of the information concerning his early childhood and education.

4. See Autobiographical Accounts, (Box-1, Folder-5, DWA Papers).

5. *Ibid.*

6. *Ibid.*

7. Several pictures of Alexander and friends are contained in the church archive (Box-1, Folder-5, DWA Papers). The only picture of Elizabeth Koster reveals a beautiful young woman of 19.

8. See Richard Newman, "Archbishop Daniel William Alexander and the African Orthodox Church", *International Journal of African Historical Studies*, Vol. 16, no. 4 (1983), p. 615.

9. Gavin Lewis, *Between the Wire and the Wall: A History of South African Coloured Politics* (New York: St. Martin's Press, 1987), chapters 1 and 2.

10. Bengt Sundkler, *Zulu Zion and Some Swazi Zionist* (London: Oxford University Press, 1976), p. 110.

11. Letter from DWA to Mr. E. F. Raynham (Secretary of DeBeer's). 14 July 1926 (Box-10, Folder-125, DWA Papers).

12. *Ibid.*

13. Urban segregation in South Africa and the southern United States are very

similar. What is not generally conceded is that most cities in America outside of the south were also highly segregated.

14. Letter from E. F. Raynham to DWA, 4 August 1926, (Box-10, Folder-125, DWA Papers). Raynham stated in part: ". . . I beg to say that my Board have [sic] agreed to contribute on the L [pounds] for L [pounds] principle, up to a maximum of L [pounds] 80, towards the cost of L [pounds] 160 of the building which you are to purchase for use of a church . . ." This request was typical of many made by Alexander over the years.

15. C.W. De Kiewiet, *A Hsitory of South Africa, Social and Economic* (London, Oxford University Press, 1957), p. 96.

16. William Worger, "Workers As Criminals: The Rule of Law In Early Kimberley, 1870-1885" in *Struggle for the City: Migrant Labor, Capital and State in Urban Africa* (ed.), Frederick Cooper (Beverly Hills: Sage Publications, 1983), p. 54.

17. Brian Willan, *Sol Platje: South African Nationalist 1876-1932* (Berkeley and Los Angeles: University of California Press, 1984), p. 318.

18. Ibid., pp. 326-327.

19. Letter from Patriarch McGuire to DWA, 24 October 1924 (Box-9, Folder-108, DWA Papers).

20. Ibid., p. 1.

21. Ibid.

22. Newman, *op. cit.*, p. 620.

23. Letter from DWA to Patriarch McGuire, 8 December 1924 (Box-9, Folder 108, DWA Papers).

24. Newman, *op. cit.*, p. 620.

25. *Ibid.*

26. *Ibid.*

27. A. C. Terry-Thompson, *The History of the African Orthodox Church* (New York: Published by the AOC, 1956).

28. Synod Minutes, 1925-1933 (Box-2, Folder-34, DWA Papers), p. 1.

29. *Ibid.*

30. First Synod Charge 1925 (Box-3, Folder-36, DWA Papers), p. 1.

31. *Ibid.*, pp. 1-2.

32. Letter from Patriarch McGuire to DWA, 24 October 1924 (Box-9, Folder-108, DWA Papers).

33. Letter from Patriarch McGuire to DWA, 7 February 1925 (Box-9, Fokder 108, DWA Papers).

34. Letter from Patriarch McGuire to DWA, 17 March 1925 (Box-9, Folder-108, DWA Papers).

35. *Ibid.*

36. *Ibid.*

37. Letter from DWA to Patriarch McGuire, 24 March 1925 (Box-9, Folder-108, DWA Papers).

38. Letter from DWA to Patriarch McGuire, 17 April 1925 (Box-9, Folder-108, DWA Papers).

39. *Ibid.*

40. Letter from Reginald Grant (Bishop of Long Island), 26 February 1926 (Box-9, Folder-109, DWA Papers).

41. *Ibid.*

42. Bishop's Charge 1926 (Box-3, Folder-36, DWA Papers).

43. *Ibid.*

44. *Ibid.*

45. Bishop's Charge 1927 (Box-3, Folder-36, DWA Papers).

46. *Ibid.*, p. 4.

47. *Ibid.*, p. 4.

48. Minutes of the Organizational Meeting of 1924 (Box-2, Folder-30, DWA Papers).

49. Bernard M. Magubane, *The Ties That Bind: African-American Consciousness of Africa* (Trenton, New Jersey: Africa World Press, Inc., 1987), see Chapter 5.

50. An excellent but introductory account of McGuire's life and career is found in Gavin White. "Patriarch McGuire and the Episcopal Church", *Historical Magazine of the Protestant Episcopal Church*, 38 (1969), pp. 109-141.

51. Garvey's point about the necessity of religion as a force for liberation is made in Molefe kete Asante, *Afrocentricity* (Trenton, New Jersey: Africa World Press, Inc., 1988). See, in particular, Asante's discusion of the Black Christian Church, pp. 71-78.

52. See Tony Martin's *The Pan-American Connection: From Slavery to Garvey and Beyond* and *Race First: The Ideological and Organizational Struggles of Marcus Garvey and the Universal Negro Improvement Association* (Westport, Connecticut and London: Greenwood, Press, 1976). The literature on Garvey is now very extensive. The following were very useful: Robert A. Hill (editor), *The Marcus Garvey and Universal Negro Improvement Association Papers* (Berkeley and London: University of California Press, 1983) Volumes I and II; Amy Jacques Garvey, *Garvey and Garveyism* (London: Collier-MacMillam, Collier Books, 1970); Marcus Garvey, *Philosophy and Opinions of Marcus Garvey* (ed. By Amy J. Garvey), 2 volumes, (New York: Atheneum, 1969); Randell K. Burkett, *Garveyism as a Religion Movement: The Institutionalization of a Black Civil Religion* (Metuchen, N. J. and London: the Scarecrow Press, Inc. and The American Theological Library Association, 1978); Wilson Jeremiah Moses, *The Golden Age of Black Nationalism, 1850-1925* (New York and Oxford: Oxford University Press, 1988); Harold Cruse, *The Crisis of the Negro Intellectual* (New York: Quill, 1984); Rupert Lewis, *Marcus Garvey: Anti-Colonial Champion* (London: Karia Press, 1987); Theodore G. Vincent, *Black Power and the Garvey Movement* (Berkeley: Ramparts, 1971); and Randall K. Burkett, *Black Redemption: Churchmen Speak For the Garvey Movement* (Philadelphia: Temple University Press, 1978).

53. Barbara Bair and Robert A. Hill (ed.), *Marcus Garvey, Life and Lessons: A CentennialCompanion to the Marcus Garvey and Universal Negro Improvement Association Papers* (Berkeley and London: University of California Press, 1987). See, in particular, pp. 221-224.

54. Many Black Christians shared similar degrading views concerning their brothers in Africa. See Edwin S. Redkey, "The Meaning of Africa to Afro-Americans, 1890-1914," *Black Academy Review* (Spring-Summer 1972), pp. 5-33 and Walter L. Williams' "Black Journalism's Opinion About Africa During the Late Nineteenth Century", *Phylon* Vol. XXXIV, No. 3, (September 1973), pp. 224-235. Two other excellent studies that detail the African American religious experience in Africa are: J. M. Chirenje, *Ethioptanism and Afro-Americans in*

Southern Africa, 1883-1916 (Baton Rouge: Louisiana State University Press, 1987) and Walter L. Williams, *Black Americans and the Evangelizatiob of Africa, 1877-1900* (Madison: The University of Wisconsin Press, 1981).

55. Leonard I. Sweet, *Black Images of America, 1784-1870* (New York: W. W. Norton and Company, Inc., 1976), pp. 75-77.

56. *Ibid.*, p. 122.

57. Olin P. Moyd, *Redemption in Black Theology* (Valley Forge: Judson Press, 1979). See, in particular, chapter 2.

58. *Ibid.*, p. 42.

59. *Ibid.*, p. 54.

60. Robert A. Hill and Gregory A. Pirio, " 'Africa for the Africans': The Garvey movement in South Africa, 1920-1940," in Shula Marks and Stanley Trapido (eds.), *The Politics of Race, Class and Nationalism in Twentieth Century South Africa* (London and New York: Longman Inc., 1987), p. 229.

61. See Robert A. Hill's "African for Africans: Marcus Garvey, the UNIA, and the Struggle of American Nationalism in South Africa in the 1920's," (presented at the SSRC Joint Committee of African Studies, New York, New York, 1982), p.59. This published paper is the basis of his co-authored article with Pirio cited in endnote 60. I recommend that all scholars read the account because it is a detailed analysis of the influence of Garvey's ideas in South Africa.

62. Hill and Pirio, *op. cit.*, p. 219.

63. *Ibid.*, p. 222.

64. Hill, unpublished paper, p. 48.

65. Lewis, *op. cit.*, pp. 162-163.

66. *The Negro Churchman: The Official Organ of the African Orthodox Church*, Vols. 5-9,

67. 1927-1931 (Milwood, New York: Kraus Reprint Col, 1977). "A South African Abroad: Travelogue I", Vol. V, No. 10, November 1927, p. 1.

68. *Ibid.*, p. 2.

69. " A South African Abroad: Travelogue II", *The Negro Churchman*, Vol. V,

No. 11, December 1927, p. 6.

70. *Ibid.*, p. 6.

71. *Ibid.*

72. "O African Awaken! The Morning is at Hand", *The Negro Churchman*, Vol. V, No. 7, July 1927, p. 1.

73. "The Patriarch's Address," *The Negro Churchman*, Vol. V, No. 9, October 1927, p.3.

74. *Ibid.*

75. "S. Matthew's Church Chicago", *The Negro Churchman*, Vol. VI, No. 2, February 1928, p. 7.

76. "Consecration Service", *The Negro Churchman*, Vol. V, No. 9, October 1927, p. 7.

77. *Ibid.*, p. 8.

78. "Address of the Bishop-Elect of South Africa", *The Negro Churchman*, Vol. V, No. 9, October 1927, p. 5.

79. Sermon by Bishop Arthur Stanley (Abbreviated), Preached at the Consecration of Archbishop Daniel William", *The Negro Churchman*, Vol. V, No. 10, November 1927, pp. 3-4.

80. *Ibid.*, p. 4.

81. Patrick McGuire, "A Spiritual Movement", *The Negro Churchman*, Vol. I, No. &, July 1923, pp. 1-3.

82. *Ibid.*, p. 1.

83. Patriarch McGuire, " 'Back to Africa' The Other Side", *The Negro Churchman*, Vol. I, No. 3, March 1923, p. 1.

84. *Ibid.*

85. *Ibid.*

86. *Ibid.*, pp. 1-2.

CHAPTER 4
THE INSTITUTIONALIZATION OF THE AOC

The institutionalization of the AOC in southern Africa presented Alexander with many challenges in the 1920's and 1930's. Because he was of the opinion that formal education was a requisite for representative clergy and for the stability of the AOC, Alexander constantly searched for qualified leaders to head the various churches. Indeed, he also wanted an educated clergy to help further his missionary efforts in Uganda, Kenya, Pondoland, as well as Basutoland, to fortify established churches and missions, establish new churches and encourage new members. He viewed education as an element necessary to serve the spiritual needs of the congregation. He contended that an educated leader commanded the respect of his critics and followers and served as a role model to his congregation.

Related to this issue of education was Alexander's concern for the ministers' conduct. Because of their prominent positions, individuals representing the AOC had to be dependable and of good moral character. Over the years, he admonished ministers to be honest, respectful of the Bishop's authority, and men of their word. Hence, moral conduct meant fair and judicial treatment in handling individual and church affairs. It was Important to him, too, to practice ecumenical efforts with other churches. Key among them was interaction with the African Lutheran Church.

These concerns, of course, were not given Alexander's immediate attention. When the Archbishop returned to South Africa in late March, 1928, his wife and church members honored him with a banquet. But his pleasure was short-lived, as he soon resumed his busy schedule. With his clergy, Alexander emphasized the need to do more than simply pass motions and resolutions which were rarely acted upon. Equally distressing to him was the lack of education of AOC priests whom he believed must achieve a standard six level before entering seminary. He challenged his clergy to endure hardship :

> At this initial stage we must lay the foundations firm and true, we may have to suffer for a time, but the results will show in the end that we were right; there is not a sight so awful as to see an incompetent Priest at the altar....[2]

Since the AOC in Africa had obtained the valid apostolic succession, Alexander suggested the need for greater appreciation of that trust. He noted that in some separatist churches

> You find many men being called Archbishop, and Bishops who would not make a respectable Reader .... Our clergy wants their congregations to respect and be obedient to them, whilst they themselves do not give that respect to those that are put in authority over them.....[3]

This question of dealing with the respect and discipline of the AOC clergy would, over the years, tax Alexander to the breaking point. Clergymen such as R. P. Damane, James Monare and Moses Dithebe posed numerous problems for him. All were eventually expelled from the church. In some instances, Alexander became aware of his clergymen's behavior from outside sources. For example, a Mr. Wallace wrote Alexander seeking his support to collect a debt that Rev. T. Godlo owed his firm. Alexander wrote Godlo to make arrangements to pay the debt, warning him that if he did not, he would most certainly be taken to court. Rev. D.P. Morgan, the Archdeacon of Transveal, turned out to be a criminal who
had been convicted under two aliases, Phillip Thompson and Daniel Makroma.[5] Even Rev. J. S. Likhing, who was with Alexander almost from the inception of the AOC, was excommunicated in 1933 for absconding with church funds.[6]

According to Alexander, the church needed disciplined men who would make sacrifices for the race and remain firm. If those who had been disciplined left the church, then others would come forward to take their places. He believed that only qualified and good men should become leaders of the church. He wanted men of the caliber of the A.M.E. Church [7] men, no matter in what portion of the Masters Vineyard they are situated they, if they can help will roll up their sleeves and get busy, will be able to get these men, I say yes, they will come and that soon, did it not take the church in America seven years after the consecration of His Eminence, to attract Educated and Cultured men to enter the ranks of the A,O,C, [sic] . . . we will get our disappointments, our drawbacks, but when we who lead will remain faithful and the flood tide comes, we will forget all our troubles and headaches, and rejoice that we have been spared to see this day....[8]

The issue of leadership was a recurring one in his life. During the late 1920's and the early 1930's, he projected a hard attitude which bordered at times on being cruel. For example, Rev. D. F. Brown, a semi-literate clergyman, informed him that he was ill and therefore unable to collect certain church funds. Brown wrote him:

> my Lord I se [see] that you don't think nothing of me that is why you went away . . . there is no money from me if you are a father to look after your children But I se [see] you through [throw] them away the same as the whites do....[9]

Alexander's response was cold. He stated he was perplexed by Brown's allegation that he did not look after his sheep, and he charged that the problem was clearly Brown's. Alexander blasted him by saying Brown had been given the responsibility for the Transvaal church, but he had not once attended Synod, the District Conference or prepared any reports concerning church matters. Alexander went on to say ". . . you want to stay in Johannesburg, when I wanted to change you to the colony; you asked what about your children ? What about mine ?"[10] He also informed Brown that he, too, left his wife and went to Phokeng and then to Kimberly in service of the church. He scolded Brown by telling him he could not sit down and expect things to happen or others to look after his well being. Brown had "thrown" himself away and wanted, according to Alexander, to be a law unto himself :

> In everything those who obey the Law is helped by the Law, you say that I am only after money; if I had to look to you ministers for money I would never have been in America . . . I am still paying the money that was lent, and how much did you put by, not a penny, and yet you speak of that I am only after money . . . I am struggling harder than you, because I have to carry the Burden of the church, and you ministers sit at your houses, not caring anything of what happens, and when things does not go right with you, you want to blame the Bishop....[11]

In a similar vein, Alexander took J. R. Damane to task for not being a man of his word. Damane had promised Alexander that he would attend District Conference while Alexander was in America. However, Damane did not and Alexander accused him of insincerity and the desire to be a bishop by almost any means. Damane could never be a true orthodox bishop, Alexander insisted, no matter how much he used the name because of his lack of proper consecration. Alexander noted "I came from America I had to re-ordain all my clergy, because . . .[of] the ordination given me by Rev. Mcanyangwa....."[12] Alexander was, therefore, convinced he had not faltered as a bishop, but Damane had failed the church as a man and as a priest.

Almost as distressing as the behavioral problems of the clergy was the matter of church finance, and, in particular, how to pay off the outstanding debt of Alexander's American trip. The American AOC paid for Alexander's return trip to South Africa, but the journey to America remained unpaid. Alexander appealed to Rev. Poyah in 1930 :

> I am writing to you . . . because we are in great difficulty, and we need the assistance of all members . . . when I went to America we had to borrow 200,0,0 from a gentleman . . . we have paid him back 134,0,0 . . . now due . . .66,0,0. . . I am writing to all clergy to get them to send us at least 5,0,0 . . . and liquidate the debt, for I did not go to America for myself....[13]

The debt was not paid in full until several years later, and much of it came from the Archbishop's purse.

> He also borrowed money for Rev. Likhing to attend the District Conference or Synod. Alexander informed Likhing that he borrowed the money for his train fare and that a big congregation such as his should be able to pay ten shillings per month to erase the debt. Money issues plagued Alexander over the years, but it was in the 1950's that debts incurred by one clergy-member endangered the whole church.

The church was also "endangered" during these critical years, 1928 to 1938, by a leanness, a lack of funds and a small membership which the infant AOC struggled, for its existence and for greater direction. Alexander concentrated on several themes which he had wrestled with before going to America, and now he took them up again to hammer out a program to ensure his church's institutionalization.

One of his most important problems was educating the clergy. A literate clergy was absolutely necessary for conducting business with a hostile government and in helping church members survive in a highly urbanized/industrial society. His attachment to the idea of his clergy attaining a standard six education was not vain worship at the altar of European culture, but a response to a government mandate on the matter. By the 1950's, the government's requirement for clergy had risen to standard seven. All clergymen, whether African or European, had to apply to the government for licenses to perform marriages. Marriages performed by "unauthorized" clergy had profound economic consequences for black communities. When the government declared a marriage invalid, it meant that on the death of a spouse, the widows or children of the deceased lost pensions or other monetary benefits. The marriage officer in black churches could be the critical link between minimum economic well being or dismal penury.[14]

Closely related to the issue of an educated clergy was the conduct of the clergy. Alexander held men in the church to an exacting standard of behavior. Such virtues as honesty, trustworthiness, decency and sobriety were traits the Archbishop expected his clergymen to possess. He repeatedly asked that all money they collected be channeled to proper sources. He believed that the clergy should live exemplary lives which would enable them to command the respect of their congregations.[15]

Respect for the Archbishop was another pivotal theme which Alexander was forced to address continually. To be sure, without it, the AOC's entire hierarchy would have collapsed into a free-for-all of petty wants. The heart of canonical obedience was respect for the authority of the bishop, priests obeying any demands imposed upon them, and a general willingness to do all within one's power to promote the social welfare of the church. It would not be an exaggeration to state that far too many of Alexander's clergy were impertinent and hedonistic. On balance, these clergy hindered the growth of the church with their lack of spiritual vision.[16]

Another concern of Alexander was the need for the AOC to expand and attract new membership. He suggested that a newspaper and printing press were critical in spreading the views of the AOC. In addition, he also recommended that religious literature should be printed in African languages. His keen comprehension of the nuts and bolts of church operations may be viewed as a "practical", spiritual vision. He invariably asked the members of his church and the clergy to do more in building the young struggling organization.

MISSION EFFORTS

Alexander's initial missionary efforts were centered in Kimberley. His intense desire to spread the AOC's message was hampered only by his lack of personnel and dollars. At the same time, black members of European-controlled churches in Africa were agitating for greater autonomy with increased black clergy. Alexander received many requests from disaffected church members who wished to affiliate with his church. For instance, Rev. Burns informed Alexander of a Mr. Davids, of the Congregational Church, who was interested in becoming part of the AOC.[17]

Similar pleas encouraged Alexander to pursue his missionary thrust. If he had the staff and the monetary resources, AOC's growth and impact on the southern African religious scene could have been a source of considerable strength in the African community. However, an undisciplined clergy and paltry funds stymied his drive for separatist church expansion in southern Africa.

UGANDA

One of the AOC's brightest missionary efforts occurred in Uganda. R. S. S. Mukasa Sparta, a disenchanted Anglican, became aware of the AOC through reading Garvey's *The Negro World* in 1925. His quest for spiritual emancipation led Sparta to proclaim boldly that he would go to jail, hell or die for the redemption of Africa. His interest in the AOC in 1927 set in motion a flurry of correspondence between himself, McGuire and Alexander. Sparta informed Alexander in October 1928 that he had been receiving new converts into the AOC.

Sparta declared that the AOC was the local church to which right thinking Africans ought to belong, and he was equally sure where the African See of the AOC should be located. In an article entitled *"The Patriarchal See In Africa"*, he argued for relocating the See to the African continent :

> To my knowledge every church has its Patriarch where they unanimously want him to dwell, I think I am not wrong nor am I mistaken to say that our Patriarch of the African Orthodox Church should dwell and reside in Africa.

There are many good, healthy, splendid places in this continent fit for any dweller. And, as a scientist once said, "The Paradise is within Africa, especially in 'Uganda',". So if there be some fear to which is the best, healthiest place where we may build a palace for our Patriarch, think of Uganda first which is the central continent of the world. Uganda is truly 'a land flowing with milk and honey'.[18]

Sparta wanted Alexander to send a priest to Uganda as soon as possible to baptize converts and provide some church-related books. The following month, Alexander mentioned to Sparta that he expected him to attend the next District Conference, but it seemed that Sparta changed his mind about attending. On the matter of being ordained a priest, Alexander suggested that Sparta would have to come to South Africa and enter the AOC's seminary.[19] Alexander communicated that he could not send a priest to Uganda at the time. However, he desired Sparta to become the first AOC priest in that area.[20]

In a letter dated 10 January 1929, Sparta reported on his work in Uganda :

> The people who gathered and who are adhering to our church have lot [sic] of children who are unbaptized yet. But they are very anscious [sic] to have them baptized. Therefore, your grace, we earnestly pray your grace's favorable and sympathetical [sic] consecration you may as soon as possible send a Priest to come up here to fulfill and enter these people of God into His folk, and in One Holy Apostolic Catholic Church. Please deal with this as soon he may probably reach here in middle of February. And we absolutely believe that by that time he will surely find some adults who are ready for the Holy Baptism, and some who are ready for Holy confirmation. These three classes are eagerly waiting his arrival by that time.[21]

He also expressed regret that Alexander had not visited his country. He wanted Alexander to come to Uganda as soon as possible after the March Synod. Sparta ended his letter by adding, "I earnestly pray God that my time for ordination may be of very short time! Can this be willingly done!"[22] Alexander did not grant Sparta his wish immediately. However, the seed of African Orthodoxy was now planted on Ugandan soil. To Sparta, the AOC was a church in which "all right thinking Africans, men who wish to be free in their own house, not always being thought of as boys."[23]

In August, 1929 Alexander responded in an article, *"The African Orthodox Churchman*, which announced the first publication of the AOC's newspaper in South Africa and appeared in *The Negro Churchman*. The article's last paragraph provided some insight into the relocation of the Patriarch's See :

> His Grace Daniel William considers Mr. S.S. Mukasa Sparta's plea for the Patriarchal See to be placed in Africa as (very good in theory, but very bad in practice). He believes it to be 'premature' and that 'we still have a long way to go even before we can plan to get our Patriarch to visit us'.[24]

Another article appearing in the same magazine in 1930 noted how well Sparta's efforts had developed and that he had even provided the King of Uganda [25], with several pamphlets outlining Apostolic succession. The article reported that the King was very pleased to know that the AOC was headed by an African.[26]

Alexander did not establish direct contact with Sparta for several more years; then, after months of negotiation and conflicts over dates, Alexander arrived in Uganda on 2 October 1931. He stated that he found "Our people was still very deep in protestantism....."[27] He immediately embarked on the task of building an altar, sewing vestments and acquiring candlesticks. His busy schedule was interrupted three weeks later by an illness, which left his legs covered with large blisters. He credited the medicine of a Buganda herbalist for his cure.[28]

The first orthodox mass was held in Uganda at 9:30 A.M., Sunday, 11 October 1931 at the Church of Degeya. The church was dedicated to the Sacred Heart of Jesus. During the mass, Alexander confirmed the following readers: S. S. R. M. Sparta, Semioni K. Pasha and Obadiah K. Basajjakitalo. Erisa M.

Sebbowa was also given the orders of Sub-Deacon. On 25 October, Sparta was given the orders of Sub-deacon.

During the same week, another dedication service took place on Advent Sunday consecrating the church at Kyaggwe. An AOC school with 50 students was located there. At Kabonge, about three and one-half miles from Degeya, the church of St. Mary the Virgin opened. Alexander noted that St. Mary had a large congregation and if supervised correctly, would be able to accomplish many endeavors. He also indicated that without the support of many contributors, the building of additional churches seemed bleak. In addition, he blessed the Kabaka, head of the Buganda Nation, wishing him a long life, and gave a special thanks to Ebalium Masike for providing the land for a church and the Anonya School.

Alexander informed the newly constituted diocese of several important church-related issues. First, he made it clear that education for his clergy was a major priority. He wanted men of good character and of good education to enter the AOC seminary. In America, he told them, only candidates who had passed their matriculation were chosen, whereas in South Africa, the incoming students had to achieve junior matriculation before entering seminary. Therefore, his expectation for Uganda was that it would also be compulsory to possess a certificate from Namiryango Boarding School.

Second, Alexander raised the issue of finance by noting that each jurisdiction of the church was to be taxed for the general support of clergy and upkeep of individual parishes. Funds were also to be generated from certificates that verified that various sacramental rites had been performed. He maintained that :

> Every family [is] to pay 50 cts per month for the support of their [church], if unable to pay the amount per month then pay it per year together with the 2/59 cts for the church yearly Assessment, the clergy when they receive the amount as per specified. They will report the same to the synod when at assembles [sic] on the report forms provided.[29]

Third, Alexander was the prime mover in extending the circulation of *The African Orthodox Churchman*. He informed the Ugandan diocese that the newspaper was the best missionary asset of the AOC. He implored his followers to help share the burden of the cost of the paper, to seek subscribers and to provide Parish news.

Alexander's last concern for the Ugandan church was translating the liturgy into African languages because it was important for church members to have the liturgy in their native tongues and to move beyond a reliance on English. Even here, money was a pressing concern for Alexander :

> but as in everything we are short of money, and if we could get say (6) six men to advance us 100 shillings each, we would be able to get the Liturgies printed at Our press, and from the first 1000 copies that we sent to you here, you would be able to repay those that have loaned us the money....[30]

KENYA

As in the Uganda effort, Alexander was invited to Kenya by dissatisfied black religious leaders of budding separatist groups. He arrived in Mombasa on 8 November 1935. His visit to Kenya has to be set against a backdrop of mounting tensions between European Churches, notably the Church of Scotland Missions, which forbade clitoridectomy (female circumcision), and African religious groups over educational policy. During the late 1920's, two groups emerged that pressed for educational reforms: the Kikuyu Independent Schools Association (KISA) and the Kikuyu Karing'a Educational Association (KKEA). The battle centered on the Kikuyu group's determination to have an educational system that did not prohibit female circumcision.[31] As the crisis mounted, the Kikuyu left the Anglican and other European Churches. Appeals were made to the Department of Education and the Anglican Bishop of Mombasa to ease their plight by allowing female circumcision to be practiced. However, European leaders remained adamant in their opposition to the Kikuyu custom. The outcome of this altercation left the Kikuyu without any clergy to perform marriages and baptisms and led to contacts with the AOC.[32] Leaders of the Kikuyu movement, such as David Maima wa Kirogu, Johana Kunyiha Arthur Gatung'u wa Gathunna, and Philip Klande Gachera wa Magu, probably informed Alexander of their position on female circumcision before he left South Africa. Like polygamy, female circumcision was at the core of traditional Kikuyu values. Alexander may have opposed clitoridectomy personally; however, he was a most willing participant in providing pastoral and spiritual care for his new Kikuyu flock.

In the summer of 1936, Alexander informed Rev. Ernest of New York that he intended to reside in Kenya for at least 15 months and then go on to Uganda to visit Spartas.[33] In July of the same year, Johana Kuyiha, President of the Kikuyu Independent Schools Association, stated to Alexander :

> We have forwarded you the balance for L18 IOS. by telegram, and we are hoping that you will receive it before your getting this note. I shall be very pleased if you will send us telegram stating about your departure and arrival in Mombassa (sic).

> We also hope that your visit to Kenya will be an enjoyable time and that the work will be a nucleus in which Negro Race will set an example to the world indicating what the race can do itself without any external assistance of another race.[34]

Alexander's work schedule was quite busy:

> While in Kenya, Central Africa 1935-37, I baptized 8,000 (eight thousand) souls and on one particular Sunday I baptized 646 alone, confirmed 300, and married 150, one day so you can imagine how I must feel .... I do need a rest tremendously... [35]

B. F. Welbourne recounted "at a cost of L50 the Archbishop landed at Mombasa on 8th November 1935 and shortly afterwards started his ordination course at Gituamba.[36] Welbourne also provided other valuable insights concerning Alexander's tour:

> In addition to his ordination course, the archbishop also toured the Kikuyu Province with a car bought by the committee for him and he did a considerable amount of spiritual work . . .A less friendly observer says that he 'ordained, baptized and confirmed those whom he was paid to do' and left Kikuyu when it appeared to offer no further opportunity for financial gain . . . the KISA [KiKuyu Independent Study Association group bade him a grateful but firm farewell; he had done his work in providing them with orders . . .[37]

The fees Alexander charged for confirmation and baptism were in keeping with the regulations of the AOC and were not exorbitant. Some of the fees, of course, went into Alexander's church account. But he used some of it to purchase the certificates the church used to mark special events in the spiritual life of its members. Alexander noted on many occasions that because the printing company did not provide free handouts of certificates, he was obliged to charge a small fee to cover costs.[38]

Alexander also extended support to his Kenyan brothers and sisters to grant them spiritual autonomy, which meant respect for traditional values and ideas that European missionaries had degraded. The battle over clitoridectomy was settled. A priesthood and functioning laity were put in place to further the spiritual aims of the Kikuyu people. Alexander seemed to have provided a durable foundation from which to spread African Orthodoxy.

Although Alexander's East African mission began with promise in Uganda and to a lesser degree in Kenya, the missionary effort eventually ended in an abandonment of Alexander and the AOC. Welbourne provided a clue as to why the Ugandan group may have left the AOC :

> Before his departure the Archbishop was invited by a Greek employee of the Public Work Department, by name Vlachos, to baptize his children. Observing that the Archbishop did not use the Greek rite, Vlachos advised Spartas to write to the Greek Archimandrite Sarikas in Moshi, Tanganyika. Sarikas visited Uganda towards the end of 1932, (relations with Archbishop Alexander were immediately severed and the attempt begun to obtain recognition from the Orthodox Patriarch of Alexandria).[39]

From the above statement, it appeared that Alexander's brand of orthodoxy was not pure enough for Spartas. His drive therefore for true orthodoxy led him to the Greek Church. In the early 1920's, Spartas vowed to die or go to hell in order to achieve spiritual emancipation from Europeans. Nearly a decade later, Spartas sought entrance into a "menzuga" (European) church group. Psychologically, Spartas was never the militant black nationalist he projected.

At the same time, it should be noted that Welbourne was incorrect in stating that Spartas terminated his relationship with Alexander immediately. As late as June, 1935, Alexander was still in communication with Spartas about the prospect of going to Synod in America (and visiting Uganda). Alexander also stated that he would take several of the clergy with him to America for consecration. One would be from South Africa and the other from Central Africa, presumably Spartas' area. Spartas was, therefore, maintaining ties with the AOC ever as he pursued entrance into the Greek Orthodox Church from Meletios II, the Patriarch of Alexandria. Seemingly, he had his feet in both camps. Alexander provided a clue as to why Spartas left the AOC when he asserted that as soon as some individuals became priests they hungered to become bishops. In fact, Alexander recorded that Spartas departed abruptly from the AOC because he was not elevated to the rank of bishop. To be an African bishop in a European Church was indeed an achievement of great importance for many African Christians.

The issue of bishop, of course, was not the reason for the collapse of the AOC in Kenya. Alexander came to Kenya with the aim of implanting a truly independent mission church. The late Patriarch McGuire had given Alexander the same charge in the early 1920's that all churches in South Africa must be independent of the American parent body. Alexander most certainly informed his Kenyan group of the same guidelines. So the desire for the KISA to form its own churches (African Independent Pentecostal Church) was very much in keeping with the general missiology of the AOC. The other churches of the KKEA, under the leadership of Kiande an (at least 10) maintained a close relationship with the Archbishop, but by 1940, all Kenyan groups ceased contact with South Africa. Alexander held that financial distress, the increasing work load at pro-cathedral (Mother Church) and the inability to find a competent assistant created an atmosphere that killed his missionary efforts in other parts of Africa. The collapse of the AOC was a withering of Alexander's influence based on distance and his frustration at wrestling with European control and differing agendas.

We do not have much information about AOC developments in other regions of southern Africa. The church in Rhodesia was founded around 1929. One of the first names associated with the Bulawayo Church was James Poyah. Before this branch was sufficiently organized, Alexander informed Poyah that he expected all AOC parishes to help defray the cost of his American trip, and the infant church in Rhodesia was expected to do its part. Poyah informed Alexander in early February 1930 that :

> I have opened the work of the AOC the 1st of December 1929 and I am still working we are holding our service outside the Bulawayo Location about half mile from the location, for Bulawayo Municipality refused us to have a place in Location.... We have great trouble Bulawayo Town and location were all very confusing Natives against Natives Mashon [Mashona] boys and Matebele boys . . . through the help of Government the trouble is going over now.[40]

Poyah also asked Alexander to send him a church constitution, a hymnal, an English catechism and twelve AOC newspapers. Several days later, N.G. MaKoak, probably a Reader, reminded Alexander to contact the immigration office in Pretoria for passports for him and Poyah. MaKoak also stated that in regards to seminary that "I would like to come first and start my lessons which [sic] Mr. J. Poyah remains here carrying the work .... Mr. Poyah and I are busy ... among our people. One by one are coming to answer to the name of AOC."[41]

On the whole, Alexander was pleased with the growth of the AOC in Southern Rhodesia, but he stressed the church's financial status to Poyah :

> What I want you to understand is that the work here (Alexander means the church work in southern Africa) is still young. And I have to struggle to get the things I need, even in America, every congregation is busy trying to build the churches. . . We have no rich people in our churches and therefore each and everyone of us must do his bit towards the up building of the Church at large.[42]

Alexander also informed Poyah of the various fees which had to be paid for maintaining the Archbishop and the church in Rhodesia, performing religious cemmonies, and missionary efforts.

When Alexander visited Rhodesia in 1931, some problems developed between him and Poyah, but the church records do not reveal these issues. There is a gap of some years in the Rhodesian records, but late in 1945, they indicated that Poyah levelled a charge with the Rhodesian Native Affairs Commission (NAC) that Alexander had left the AOC to become a "witch-doctor."[43] In response, Alexander entertained the idea of bringing charges against Poyah to the NAC, but the tensions evaporated and Poyah may have remained within the AOC. It was not uncommon for Alexander to have terrible altercations with his clergy, and after several months, to smooth them over or completely forget them.

Another example of this is when an AOC priest, Mphamba, tried to assist Alexander in Rhodesia. Although the government authorities blocked Alexander's entry into Rhodesia, one may have expected that he supported Mphamba's efforts to secure his entry into Rhodesia. But Alexander rebuked Mphamba at the 1947 Synod with a harsh reprimand for "using Synod's money at the behest of his congregation." [44]

At this Synod, Alexander also extended his greetings to Rev. Joseph Mashasha from southern Rhodesia who had been baptized in the Anglican Church, but joined the AOC via the African Methodist Episcopal Church. But Alexander later rebuked Mashasha and placed him on a one year probation. The reasons for his stern action were not provided. He ordered Mashasha back to Rhodesia to prove himself worthy of his position. Mashasha provoked a schism in the black African Orthodox community when, 1963, he formed the Ruponiso African Church in Salisbury. The Ruponiso African Church contradicted AOC doctrine by viewing monogamy as the only correct form of marriage. Mashasha stated that "He feel [sic] the best thing is to keep away from those who want polygamy [polygamy] it is against our Christian feelings..[45] Alexander invited the entire church to discuss polygamy, but a compromise on the issue could not be reached."[46]

In Basutoland, missionary efforts produced a harvest of converts but not without controversies. In July, 1946, the Paramount Chief's Office in Matsieng informed Alexander that it rejected the AOC's application to establish a church under Rev. Hlong's sponsorship. Paramount Chief Mantsebo Seeiso stated : ". . . regret to inform you that this application cannot be approved in view of the fact that it may do more harm than good to the Church of England from which Hlong has been."[47] The Paramount Chief's response undoubtedly did not surprise Alexander since it reflected a larger conflict between the AOC and the Anglican Church over "flock raiding" and Anglican allegations that the AOC's claims to apostolic succession were invalid. Alexander was very successful in bringing Anglicans into the AOC fold in South Africa.

In November, 1946, Hlong borrowed five pounds from Alexander to repair his automobile.[48] The loan and Hlong's poor performance of duties brought his behavior increasingly under the scrutiny of Alexander, who inquired why Hlong had not kept him informed of his work in Basutoland. In early February 1947, Hlong told Alexander the church consisted of ninety individuals. Hlong also related a trip he took to Matelile for the first time since his resignation from the Anglican Church. The surprised people were told not to greet him. Hlong was an ex-priest of the Anglican church, and although Anglican officials in the area asked Hlong's former church members not to be friendly with him, some were.

Alexander attempted to visit Mafeteng the last Sunday in October 1947. Hlong informed him that a few chiefs would be in attendance as well as some officials from the District Commissioner's Office. Hlong expected Alexander to confer minor orders of Reader and Subdeacon on several individuals and provide confirmation for fifty more followers.

Several weeks later, Hlong reported back to Alexander on his visit's impact. He confessed that the Mafeteng area was a "most difficult place" for extending the orthodox message. Alexander was asked to avoid the "Hail Mary' and the sprinkling of holy water because many in the Mafeteng area were anti-Catholic. Hlong went on to say :

> The thing is this: I understand that when the Romans first came here, the priests crust [cursed?] other denominations and called them Satan's churches . . . gathering during the war to pray for soldiers etc., the Roman Catholics took no part in these services .... Now the Roman Catholic Church is badly noted in this part of the country . . . I do not even say that you are coming to confirm . . . but that you're coming to receive them in Church.[50]

> Hlong also encouraged Alexander to wear his golden cape (given to him by an admirer while he was in Brooklyn) on his trip to Basutoland so that all who saw him would be filled with pride at their African Archbishop and so that Anglicans would feel inferior.

At the 23rd Synod which met in October 1947, Hlong and Brother Mohomo were presented to the entire church as new members from Basutoland. Alexander called Basutoland the "Land of Ethiopia" on which his eyes had always been as well as Bechuanaland..... [57] Mohomo pleaded for an early episcopal visit to his country to eradicate some of the "difficulties' there.

The warm relations experienced at Synod quickly evaporated because of new in-fighting between Hlong and Alexander over the issues of money and trust.

Hlong seemed to have worked diligently to propagate the cause of the AOC and his attitude reflected his uncertainty over Alexander's changed perception of his character. Hlong stated "I do not know as to whether your Grace is referring to the

matter of admission of guilt by the police officer or to some other things which I do not remember...."[52] The Archbishop refreshed Hlong's memory and, in his typical didactic manner, admonished him about trustworthiness, faithfulness to AOC's teachings and paying debts. Because of Hlong's respect and admiration for

the Bishop, he must have been shaken by Alexander's comments. The Archbishop's comments, though harsh, were justified. After twenty years of laboring with difficult priests, Alexander was convinced that frankness was the best guide for interpersonal relationships with his priests. He wrote Hlong:

> you remember you put us in a predicament last time we met the D.C. [District Commissioner] by not telling us you had signed an admission of guilt form. You are now not carrying out the instructions we gave you when we left .... You are a new man in the church, and it is painful when a new man is found untrustworthy, no matter how well he speaks about himself, his doings must speak for him; and a man who makes a promise and does not keep it is not worthy to be put in responsible positions...[53]

Alexander also warned him that he should leave the church if he was not prepared to adhere to AOC doctrines. Alexander compared him unfavorably to Father Masiko, whom he called the Black Henry Newman and whom he deemed a wonderful man for giving his energies to build up the church. In actual fact, Masiko turned out to be a scoundrel who later caused a major crisis in the AOC.[54]

Alexander reminded Hlong that he had not dealt with some pressing issues; collecting the Archbishop's fees for confirmation, instructing the people in the ways of the AOC and refusing to ordain some unqualified people to the rank of subdeacon.[55] Alexander raised the theme of debts again: "You borrowed 101-from me to buy petrol, and promised to send it as soon as you got home, but now you are quiet. . ."[56] He mentioned that he did not like to rehash money debts, but an honest man would have paid something, however small. The on again, off again relationship between Hlong and the Archbishop continued into the 1950's.

In Pondoland East and West, the AOC made slow progress in establishing a new church. The AOC's emergence was closley linked with Ice Walker Mbina, an Anglican priest, who became restless under European mission domination in late 1946. It was unclear whether the infant AOC already existed in Pondoland or whether Mbina created the first branch. By 1950, the Pondoland AOC had experienced such slow growth under Mbina's leadership that during the mid-1950's, Alexander transferred him to Cape Town to utilize his talents better. Although not a man with much formal education, Mbina was an indefatigable worker and would later achieve the rank of bishop within the AOC. In early October 1946, Alexander asked him:

> We are taking this opportunity in writing you these few lines to inform you that we have [been] advised by the Campaign for Spiritual Freedom that you have joined the above church, if so we must congratulate you on the step you have taken, when we sing "God Bless Afrika". How can she be free when her sons are spiritual slaves.[57]

The church to which Alexander was referring was Holy Cross, located in Flagstaff, Pondoland. The Campaign for Spiritual Freedom was a newly organized movement for non-European clergymen and churches to gain greater spiritual autonomy and to arouse religious/race consciousness among lethargic black clergymen. Alexander also posted Mbina an application for the AOC plus a church constitution and canons.[58]

In November 1946, he expressed to Mbina the meaning of the separatist impulse of unity:

> We understand and appreciate your determination to come away from the white man's slavery; we sing Nkosi Sikelela i-Africa, but we keep the blessings away from Africa. We must come together and work for the upliftment of our Mother country.[59]

In May, 1948 Alexander informed Paramount Chief Botha Sigcau of Pondoland of Mbina's new status as director of Missions in Pondoland in the AOC and that Mbina had resigned from the CPSA :

> AOC is a denomination which has received full Government Recognition; governed by a Black Archbishop whose orders comes direct from St. Peter the Apostle, Fr. Mbina has been appointed Director of Missions for East and West Pondoland.[60]

The majority of the AOC's missionary efforts in Pondoland were tedious. At some point, Mbina was overwhelmed not only by the slow pace of recruiting members to black orthodoxy, but also by the constant guerilla war with the Anglicans. He was hampered in his early efforts by the few pennies he collected for traveling expenses.[61] He also noted that Anglican propaganda contended that he was spreading false doctrines and that the Anglicans attempted to use the Paramount Chief's influence to impede Mbina's ambitions. He complained that his mail was even tampered with and that he wrote the Flagstaff post-master, an Anglican, and threatened that if his mail were not delivered properly, he would file a charge against him. Mbina also related that :

> our people here are still ignorant, they believe on what has been said by white bosses; first time they were told that Mbina will be put in prison if preaches

> A.O.C. I went about people preaching going to town for my wine, and they began to follow. Now they are told there is no Bishop for A.O.C. You will never see it [a Black Bishop]......[62]

In 1948, Alexander visited Pondoland where he confirmed 112 individuals, 80 of whom were former Anglicans. He ordained three Readers and one subdeacon. Alexander was pleased that Mbina was providing instructions for fourteen catechists.[63] Of greater importance to Alexander was the fact that the young Pondo church paid all of his Travel expenses. The visit was a success, and he noted that all fees were paid without a "brawl".[64]

Despite this promising start, several minor problems plagued the AOC in Pondoland. A Reader by the name of Bidla was arrested, but Mbina did not state the reason for his incarceration. Tensions between Mbina and his new wife developed over the payment of lobola.[65] By far the greatest controversy was the affair surrounding Father Masiko, whose debt nearly caused ruin for the whole church, and who disliked Alexander noted :

> dropped down Alexander [to leave the AOC], because there is a bishop and two priests from Alexander, Egypt. They have come to organize churches and schools, and that school of mine is to be a lived [or alive (?)] now because we are to get help is not to be as Alexander's attitude who always claim money from us and chasing our congregations away by always claiming money and you don't see what is done by the money. This service is also Orthodox church it is under the Patriarch of Egypt it is called Coptic Orthodox Church, and Dr. Malan has accepted it, and gave it all privileges in the union ....[66]

Masiko probably intended to involve Mbina in a scheme to leave the AOC and join him in the Coptic Church. Mbina's loyalty to Alexander was secure, although in time, it would be severely tested. Alexander expressed his gratitude to Mbina for providing some financial assistance in regards to the Masiko matter:

> I want to take this opportunity of writing to thank you for the promptness in which you have sent me this remittance for the Masiko debt, because it means that if you do not send it I will have to worry and worry. .[67]

Masiko's debt aside, Mbina also experienced other economic difficulties. In (1947), he reported how his efforts to secure a modest level of comfort for his wife and children went wanting. He could not even afford to purchase a basic staple such as sugar. Nearly three years later, his economic situation had not improved and Mbina thanked Alexander for sending him two bags of mealies (maize). By 1951, his situation had become desperate. To Alexander he wrote :

> All these years I have been trying all means to do my rounds regularly, but now I have no more means and my congregations are not determined to pay traveling expense. [sic] shameful thing being the Priest and yet I have many debts....[68]

Mbina beseeched Alexander to consider his condition. He promised that in time, he would pay all church related fees, but he erred when he asked for the name and address of an AOC priest in America to "inform him of his work in South Africa...."[69] Alexander harshly responded:

> earn your money and stop crying . . . as to getting people in America to collect for our journey, that will never happen, because we must learn to rely upon ourselves . . . I do hope that you will see that we must have Race pride. I am personally going amongst those chiefs when I get there this year. When I was consecrated I promised the Patriarch that I would be the only medium through which we correspond to those in America, and I do hope to carry out that agreement.[70]

Mbina felt that Alexander's assessment of his predicament was narrow-minded, since Mbina had worked extremely hard to plant the AOC in Pondoland.[71] His defense led to a further confrontation between the two and the broadening of the dispute to include other issues. Alexander quoted pages and sections of canons and the seminary's syllabus to buttress his argument about Mbina's misconceptions:

> my reason for quoting the Constitution is to show you, that this matter of the Ministry is a personal matter between the candidate, the Priest, and his Bishop, no conference or synod can force the Primate to delegate his power to any individual . . . Father Mdatyulwa also wanted to hold a District conference, I had to show him that as a Priest, he has no authority to do so . . . what he was entitled to hold was quarterly conference...[72]

The tensions between the two apparently eased; nonetheless, Mbina later complained to Alexander about his home being in disarray, his children being unsupervised and his need for a new wife. Moreover, he complained that Alexander had refused to answer his letters concerning receipts for church monies posted to the Archbishop.[73]

In another powerful exchange, however, Alexander took Mbina to task :

> I have advised you to call your own District Conference and invite me to come and hear what all the trouble is about, but you say that you cannot, because you are going to Basutoland .... Why are you so determined that I should not come to St. Marks, are you afraid that I will hear all about the trouble . . . first it is Mpengesi, then your brother; now Ntinjana . . . I refuse to write any more letters to any Congregation in your Archdeaconry....[74]

Mbina's ten page response was impertinent but provided a blow by blow rebuttal to Alexander's views. Mbina informed Alexander that he did not attach as much importance to being an Archdeacon as Alexander assumed. In cynical fashion, Mbina stated that the task of Archdeacon required much work, no pay and absolutely no gratitude. He asked Alexander why only Pondoland had been written on his appointment, if he had been appointed Archdeacon of East and West Pondoland, Umzimkulu and Natal, Qumbu and Willowvale.[75]

The ultimate insult from Alexander must have been the attack that stated that since Mbina was experiencing difficulties with his deacons and subdeacons, he would not ordain any more individuals for him. Mbina went on to say :

> Oh! Do you really mean that? Do you think that when your people leave, the reason is in you? Is it why these under- mentioned men left you? Rev. A. Z Twala, Rev. Albert M. Hbobo, Rev. M. J. Mpongwana, Rev. S. P. Mandzini, Rev. A. W. Mhawu, Archdeacon Hlong, Archbishop's Chaplain and Examiner Masiko, and W. F. Dupreez . . . Your Grace had I known I would not have struggled so much asking people to pay for Masiko's debt. You say you won't write anymore letters to any congregation in my Archdeaconry, Thank you very much for that.[76]

Whatever may have been the differences between the Archbishop and his Archdeacon, they appeared to have resolved the conflict. Perhaps Alexander understood the power of Mbina's critique of the men who left the AOC. Masiko, Hlong and Dupreez, left or had to be driven from the church due to Alexander's faults. By 1953, their relationship was still firm, and in April of that year, Mbina was promoted and transferred to Cape Town to better utilize his talent. Concerning the transfer, Archdeacon Julies of Cape Town informed Alexander that he was always willing to work with and support African priests. Although it had not been addressed forthrightly, some Coloured priests did not want to associate with or have Africans in their churches. Such a transfer commenced a new chapter in AOC history and Alexander would come to depend more and more on Mbina's advice. For the next decade, Mbina labored in the service of the AOC but eventually figured prominently in an effort to oust Alexander as head of the AOC in Africa.

ECUMENICAL EFFORTS :

The AOC's ecumenical spirit within South Africa in many ways generated more success than its missionary ventures as many churches became a part of the AOC. The three churches to be explored here featured the best and worst elements in attracting churches into a new spiritual union with the AOC. For the most part, Alexander extended a cordial welcome to many separatist churches. Unfortunately, many who entered the AOC did so not for spiritual reasons, but for the limited benefits provided by the government. Due to new pressure on black religious groups, many became affiliated with any government approved church. This political move brought protection from the government, but produced conflict in many instances because of a lack of sincere adherence to the creeds of the host churches. However, some groups worked diligently to assure that the merger would be a lasting one.

One example was Rev. William Hinnings of the Independent Church of Zion in Benoni, who represented the best in the ecumenical tradition. In October 1943, Hinnings asked Alexander to visit him to discuss the merger of their religious groups. Hinnings noted that there still existed several points of disagreement between them over such issues as infant baptism, the use of the Common Book of Prayer and preaching from the calendar (i. e., sermons coinciding with feast days of the church). Hinnings expressed a simple fundamentalist faith, a characteristic which pervaded all of his years with the AOC, in regard to the calender and faith. He informed Alexander that :

> We only preach from the Bible and we pray from our heart and in the spirit of God and the spirit must lead us to pray so there has been no arrangement made for members to be confirmed....[77]

He assured Alexander that his congregation wanted union, but he noted "...we don't feel we can change what we have already believed.."[78] Hinnings also wanted union with AOC in order to achieve government recognition, but at the same time, he desired a smooth transition for his congregation into the AOC.

The last issue which held up the merger was infant baptism, but they finally reached a general consensus on 7 November 1943. Hinnings informed Alexander that Rev. Lulwane, another separatist minister, had received his congregation into the AOC on 5 November 1943 before a packed church.[79] Nearly a hundred people were present at the ceremony and Lulwane was hopeful that another one hundred members might soon join the AOC from Kliptown.[80] Hinnings publicly voiced his joy at being under a black religious leader.[81]

Another chronic problem of the AOC was providing quality training for incoming ministers. In Hinning's case, Alexander wanted him to leave his place of employment, the Van Ryn Deep Mine, and attend seminary for three months. Hinnings was not opposed to entering the seminary at Kimberley, but the financial burden for him was too great. He begged Alexander to work out another arrangement so that he could become fully ordained to do God's work.[82] And work he did. Alexander, who was not an easy man to impress in his later years, elevated Himings to the rank of Archpriest by 1953 and made him one of his senior assistants. Others were not quite so fortunate. Many were exposed to Alexander's harsh tongue lashings. In Alexander's defense, some of those who were capable of attending seminary, concocted excuses not to attend, while others were too busy pushing their petty interests to make such a sacrifice.

Hinnings, too, experienced some difficult moments with Alexander. In the early stages of the merger of their churches, Alexander blasted Hinnings in a letter to Lulwane, who was in charge of the merger, that ". . . we are not going to break up our church on account of a single congregation who believe that they have been sent by God to do as they like." Alexander's criticism of Hinnings did not obscure his appreciation of Hinnings' fine qualities as a church servant. Years later, he noted that after the death of Hinnings' wife, the Archpriest attended Synod even though his personal life was full of great sorrow.

Hinnings' death in 1958 left a void in Alexander's life and in that of the AOC. Once Hinnings and his group decided to enter the AOC, they remained faithful stewards. They had entered the AOC not for selfish economic reasons, but to attain spiritual growth under black leadership. Hinnings always attended

Synod meetings, and he faithfully responded to all of Alexander's demands. It was this type of ecumenical merger that gave Alexander hope that he could build bridges with other groups despite the opprobrium of some clergy.

In contrast, the van der Westhuizens, leaders of the African Lutheran Church (ALC), merged with the AOC in order to maintain the autonomy of their church. Negotiations with the ALC probably commenced in 1955; however, a document (1 January 1956) stated that the AOC did not own or have control over the ALC's property unless the various congregations granted such ownership. Moreover, the Rev. Robert R. van der Westhuizen, son of the founder of the ALC, promised Alexander the right to visit his congregations and bestow confirmation upon them. Nearly a year later, van der Westhuizen informed Alexander that :

> My headquarters being at 141 Esthows Street No. 2, location Kimberley. I desire to be appointed woolly [wholly] under the AOC, and also that two following clergymen be temporary appointed till Synod meets: - namely Paulus Van der Westhuizen and Mark Mokae . . . And that I will submit to all rules and regulations....[84]

The van der Westhuizens used obscurantist tactics setting in motion unification with the AOC but denying Alexander's authority as their bishop and thereby retaining control of their churches. In November 1957, Alexander argued that the two groups' lack of interaction was highly unusual. He noted that Robert van der Westhuizen had signed a document on 9 April 1956 stating that he and his two ministers should be under AOC supervision, but that since the last Synod, there had been no contact and he had not seen Mr. Mokae, their priest. Alexander had complied with the Westhuizens' request not to pressure them for continued contact until they had completed fighting a case that may have involved church property. To Alexander's way of thinking, too much time had elapsed, whether there were problems or not. He reacted :

> Since your case has been finished, I expected you to come and inform me what is the outcome . . . it seems that you have not even told your member in No. 2 that you have joined the African Orthodox Church, of what are you afraid ? I am not ashamed of my ministry nor of the African Orthodox Church, one thing I am proud, 'It is recognized'....[85]

Alexander gave the appearance that if the new members did not respond quickly to his satisfaction, he would sever church relations with the ALC. Of course, this did not occur, and in January 1951, Alexander and the church council of St. Augustine were still in a quandary over the nature of their relationship with the van der Westhuizens. Neither Alexander nor any AOC official had seen any of the ACL's officials or visited any of their churches. Brother M. Jafta made a motion, seconded by Brother Schoema, to form a delegation consisting of Alexander and three other members to visit the van der Westhuizens to resolve their difficulties.

The father and son team found the scheduled time for the visitation an inconvenience and rescheduled the meeting for 13 January 1957, but the meeting did not occur. In March, Robert van der Westhuizen asked Alexander not to give up on his group, but for God to grant him patience, and that very soon he would have victory over his enemy and provide Alexander with all of the details.[86]

Alexander explained to van der Westhuizen that he had been patient and that no other organization would have allowed a group to use its name for over a year and not have received pertinent information or any communication. He warned the ALC group that if communication had not improved by Easter, he would dissolve the merger. Van der Westhuizen's son responded by saying "I think your Eminence will remember that in the night I and my father were there together that you promised not to worry him as I took the matter over..."[87] The problem was that ALC's two leaders had not entered into the agreements with the AOC in good faith. In fact, van der Westhuizen, Jr. seemed perturbed with Alexander's mild inquiries. The younger van der Westhuizen stated:

> Really I must say that it grieves me to see and hear that after all this explanation in legthy discussions that the matter has not been fully comprehended by his Eminence...[88]

Robert van der Westhuizen advised that the most convenient way to resolve the issues between their groups was a conference; and that Alexander and ALC officials would have to travel about and gather opinions from the ALC's membership.

It is puzzling why Alexander continued with this charade for so long; nonetheless, he responded to the matter of a conference by saying he was very much in the dark as to the location, time, or date of the proposed conference. He reiterated the ALC's lack of compliance with the declaration they had made before the Commissioner of Oaths. He expounded on the AOC's relationship with other separatist churches seeking merger:

> I want you to understand that your churches are not the first to be admitted into the African Orthodox Church. Archpriest Solomon Manyali was also selfstanding, and when he had already held his meeting with his people he wrote to me; after the second letter he called me to come and receive them into the church; I went and when two congregations refused to come with him, he left them...[89]

Alexander highlighted the situation of Archpriest Mayali at St. Marks in Basutoland to demonstrate his patience with the ALC group and to emphasize the swiftness with which ministers could make important decisions, even if their congregations were hesitant in making such crucial moves. He extended the deadline beyond Easter in the hope that the situation would be resolved amicably.

In May, Robert van der Westhuizen informed Alexander that the 31 May would be the scheduled time of their meeting if the Archbishop were agreeable. Van der Westhuizen suggested that he be allowed to perform a marriage between Coloureds at the Cathedral, St. Augustine of Hippo.[90] There exists no evidence to suggest that the proposed meeting or wedding ever occurred; however, in early November, van der Westhuizen informed Alexander he would not attend Synod, but Paulus, his son, would take all of the reports to the conclave.[91]

Throughout 1958, the records indicate that no communication was maintained between the ALC group and the Archbishop. Then without warning, Alexander, with the usual pepper in his pen, ended the merger between the two groups. The Archbishop intimated that Richard Robert van der Westhuizen was a liar and a dishonest soul who forced his son to become ordained in the AOC. Alexander suggested that the purpose of such a tactic was aimed at allowing the senior van der Westhuizen to continue "under the name of the African Lutheran Church, as it is now three years since that day you have never had one of your members confirmed by me...." [92] According to Alexander, Paulus was a man who was exactly like his father, full of untruths. He said that he would write a letter to the proper authorities to provide notice of the termination of the relationship. The brief letter directed to the superintendent of the No. 2, Location in Kimberley, stated :

> This is to inform you that the Rev. Richard R. vd Westhuizen. . . is no more connected with the above church . . . he with many excuses failed to bring his people to receive any of the Samarnents which must be performed by a Bishop .... We have informend [sic] him by registered letter that we are going to inform your office and that of the manager of Native Affair of the City Council,Kimberly, known that he and his son have no right to use our name ...[93]

Apparently, the elder van der Westhuizen never intended to embrace the authority of the AOC, but entered into an arrangement with the Archbishop to further his ambitions and to protect his church from the new stringent measures being introduced by the government against unrecognized churches.

In contrast, the Ethiopian Catholic Church (ECC), under the leadership of Archbishop Surgeon L. Motsepe, embarked upon a spiritual union with the AOC out of a sincere need to become part of the AOC team. This boosted the AOC, not only because the ECC was a solvent organization but also because it had over fifty ministers and a substantial membership in ECC churches in 12 African locations. The merger of the two groups produced a firmer foundation from which to launch African Orthodoxy in the black community.

In September, 1958, Motsepe stated to Louis Van Branden of Lady Selborne, that the was no longer in the ECC but the AOC. He noted that it was an excellent church in good standing with the government and Motsepe encouraged Van Branden to 'take up orders" and join the AOC so Van Branden could provide pastoral care for the Coloured congregation in Benoni.[94]

However, in June 1959, Motsepe sought an audience with Alexander on the matter of incorporation with the AOC. If such were the case, Motsepe was not correct in stating that the merger between the two groups had been finalized. He informed Alexander that his organization was represented throughout South Africa and Bechuanaland.[95]

Alexander responded by saying that he and Motsepe knew each other intimately. He felt that he should be quite candid about the matter under consideration. He noted that the merger was possible as long as the welfare of their people and service to God were primary. He warned Motsepe that if the union were simply for self advancement, then it was doomed to failure. He asked Motsepe or one of his priests to come to Beaconsfield to discuss preliminaries. Many separatist churches, Alexander reported, were turning to the AOC for shelter since the government's Bill on Unrecognized Churches was issued.[96]

Mother Alexander's death in 1958 left the Archbishop pensive and worn. He informed Motsepe of her death and of their nearly 57 years of married bliss. He also made Mbina aware of Mother's passing. He thanked Mbina for his kindness during his moments of sorrow and provided him with information concerning the upcoming union with the ECC. There was a sadness that characterized the remaining portion of his life. Now alone and more cantankerous than ever, Alexander forged ahead with his work, travel and voluminous correspondence.

In late June 1959, Motsepe again made it clear that he deemed amalgamation with the AOC extremely important. He wanted to hurry to Beaconsfield to commence negotiations. However, it was not as soon as Alexander wished, as Motsepe was scheduled to preside over his Natal and Zululand Synod.[97]

Motsepe desired to be appointed Bishop of the Transvaal, and he presented Alexander with his educational credentials:

> I hold the Metropolitan Certificate (Church of the Province of South Africa) and have passed in these subjects . . . 3. Doctrine 4. Christian Worship 5. Teaching Method and Child Psychology.... I am taking studies with the Wolsey Hall Oxford in England.... I also have a certificate from Moodies Bible Institute of Chicago, USA ...[98]

Motsepe urged Alexander to confer the title of Doctorate of Theology upon him and, perhaps, after his consecration, to apply to America for the D. D. (Doctorate of Divinity) as Alexander had recommended on an earlier occasion.[99]

The smooth proceedings, as mentioned above, encountered a minor barrier when Motsepe asked Alexander "to reopen this discussion...."It may be assumed that the loose financial and organizational structure suggested by Motsepe was not completely to Alexander's liking. Motsepe had proposed in July that :

> We want to be strong ... create a Reserve Bank.... your party is freely working without interference and our party also is free to work . . . have Conference or Synod together once a year where each party denote and equal number or amount of money to be invested as a reserve fund to be owned and governed by an affiliated executive of both parties.[100]

In the past, Alexander had entertained similar ideas on mergers that were not firm. The record does not indicate whether or not the Archbishop accepted some of Motsepe's ideas or whether they were rejected outright. If difficulties existed, they were resolved quickly because Alexander instructed Motsepe to bring his church into the AOC fold. Since the church was located in the Transvaal, Alexander felt more comfortable in allowing Motsepe to handle the details of the merger.

Motsepe proceeded with formal authority from Alexander to contact Reverend Edwards Mhlangu, of Witbank, head of the Eastern Bantu Methodist Church to finalize their churches' merger. Mhlangu was informed by Alexander that on 22 July 1957, Motsepe and his 51 ministers were conditionally baptized and confirmed. Alexander made it clear to Mahlangu that such conditions were not applicable to his group, the reason being that they were Protestants and not Catholics. Motsepe submerged himself in work in the Transvaal and Alexander seemed pleased with his new bishop. The storm, however, that would split the AOC asunder in 1961 was not yet on the horizon. The marriage between the two Catholic groups was firm. The future looked bright.

In Chapter Five, several issues will be explored in detail: the rise of apartheid, the response of the AOC to racist legislation and the importance of race/identity questions for Alexander. In addition to this, the rebellion within the Anglican Church is highlighted. Still another important issue that will be explored is the attack by Anglican Church officials upon Alexander because some of their priests were "persuaded" to join the AOC.

Endnotes

1. The Primate's Charge 1928 (Box-3, Folder-37, DWA Papers), p. 1.

2. *Ibid.*,. p. 1.

3. *Ibid.*, p. 1.

4 Letter from DWA to Thos Godlo, 2 May 1929 (Box-9, Folder-103, DWA Papers).

5. Synod Minutes, 1925-1933 (Box-2, Folder-34, DWA Papers), p. 402.

6. *Ibid.*

7. The Primate's Charge, 1928 (Box-3, Folder-37, DWA Papers), pp. 2-3.

8. *Ibid.*

9. Letter from D. F. Brown to DWA, 30 April 1929 (Box-9, Folder-103, DWA Papers).

10. Letter from DWA to D. F. Brown, I May 1929 (Box-9, Folder-103, DWA (Papers).

11. *Ibid.*

12. Letter from DWA to J. R. Damane, 23 May 1928 (Box-9, Folder-103, DWA Papers).

13. Letter from DWA to J. P. Poyah, 23 January 1928 (Box-9, Folder-99, DWA Papers).

14. The government's stringent demand that it would recognize only marriages by state officials meant public saving of monies by limiting the right of inheritance general assistance for "unofficial" marriages.

15. The issue of priests being exemplary was a problem that Alexander struggled with for over forty years. At Synod and during district conferences, he put forth the same message about being honest, spiritual, and hard working.

16. Men such as Sikewbu, Masiko, Damane, Likning, Maitland, Dithebe and several more brought disgrace upon the AOC for their criminal activity, immoral behavior and insubordination to DWA.

17. Letter from Rev. T. Burns to DWA, 22 October 1928 (Box-9, Folder-103, DWA Papers).

18. Ruben S. S. Musaka Sparta, "The Patriarchal See In Africa (?)", *Negro Church Official Organ Of the African Orthodox Church*. 1927-1931, Volumes 5-9 (Millwood, New York: Kraus Reprint Co., 1977), Vol. Vl, No. 11, December, 1928, p. 3.

19. Letter from DWA to S. S. Sparta, 11 February 1929 (Box-9, Folder-101, DWA Papers).

20. *Ibid*.

21. Letter from Sparta to DWA, 10 January 1929 (Box-9, Folder 101, DWA Papers).

22. *Ibid.*

23. F. B. Welbourn, *East Africa Rebels: A Student of Some Independent Churches*, (London: London SCM Press, 1961), p. 81.

24. "The African Othodox Churchman", *The Negro Churchman*, Vol VII, No. 7, August, 1929, p. 5.

25. Although Sparta was only a reader (a lay person who reads the scriptures and lessons of the Mass), he was instrumental in bringing to the fold of the AOC a priest and sixty-seven members in less than a year.

26. The Primate's Charge, First Annual Synod of the Uganda Diocese, 1952 (Lox-4, Folder-136, DWA Papers), p. 2.

27. *Ibid.,* p. 2.

28. *Ibid.*, p. 3.

29. *Ibid*.p. 3.

30. *Ibid.*

31. Jomo Kenyatta, *Facing Mount Kenya: The Tribal Lift of the GikuYu* (New York: Vintage Books, 1965). See also Welborne's response to the Kikuyu educational movement, op, cit., pp. 144-152.

32. *Ibid.*

33. Letter from DWA to Rev. William Ernest, c. 10 June 1936 (Box-9, Folder109, DWA Papers). It should be noted that Sparta added an "s", the masculine form, to his surname (Spartas) when he made contact with Greek Orthodoxy in the 1930's.

34. Letter from Johana Kuyiha to DWA,1 July, 1935 (Box-10, Folder-127, DWA Papers)

35. Letter from DWA to the Rev. William Miller, 16 July (ca) 1939-1940 (Box 9, Folder-109, DWA Papers).

36. Welbourne, *op.cit.*,148.

37. *Ibid*, p.149

38. *Ibid*, p. 88.

39. Welbourne, *op, cit.*, pp. 88-89.

40. Letter from James Poyah to DWA, February 1930 (Box-9, Folder-99, DWA papers).

41. Correspondence Register, 1963, (Box-7, Folder-73, DWA Papers).

42. Letter from Poyah to DWA,1 January 1930 (Box-9, Folder-99, DWA Papers).

43. Synod Uinutes, 1933-1961 (Box-3, Folda-35, DWA Papers), p. 211.

44. *Ibid*, pp. 259-260.

45. Correspondence Registry, 1963 (Box-7, Folder-73, DWA Papets).

46. The question of polygamy was not an issue for many black Christians who were ex- Anglican and urban. Rural peasants, however, were still in tune with their traditional culture which held polygamy in high regard.

47. Letter from Paramount Chief's Office to DWA, 11 July 1946: Mafeteng, Basutoland (Box-8, Folder-85, DWA Papers).

48. Letter from Paramount Chief's Office to DWA, 11 November 1946 (Box-8, Folder-85, DWA Papers).

49. Letter from DWA to Hlong, 19 November 1946 (Box-8, Folder 85, DWA Papers).

50. Letter from Hlong to DWA, 21 October 1947 (Box-8, Folder-85, DWA Papers).

51. Synod Minutes, 1933-1961 (Box-3, Folder-35, DWA Papers), p. 247.

52. *Ibid*, p. 247.

53. Letter from DWA to Hlong, 2 December 1947 (Box-3, Folder-35, DWA Papers).

54. Newman was an Irish bishop who greatly extended Roman Catholicism in America during the late nineteenth century.

55. Letter from DWA to Hlong, 12 December 1947 (Box-8, Folder-85, DWA Papers).

56. *Ibid.*

57. DWA to Ice Walter Mbina, 18 October 1946 (Box-8, Folder-92, DWA Papers).

58. *Ibid.*, Mbina's earliest correspondence with DWA reflects an illiterate man; however, all later letters are in standard English. He must have acquired a good secretary.

59. Letter from DWA to Mbina, 19 November 1946 (Box-8, Folder-95, DWA Papers).

60. Letter from DWA to Paramount Chief Botha, June 1947 (Box-8, Folder-92, DWA Papers).

61. Letter from Mbina to DWA, 14 July 1947 (Box-8, Folder-92, DWA Papers).

62. Letter from Mbina to DWA, I September 1947 (Box-8, Folder-92, DWA Papers).

63. Letter from DWA to Hlong, 24 May 1948 (Box-8, Folder-85, DWA Papers)

64. *Ibid.*

65. Letter from Mbina to DWA, 3 July 1950 (Box-8, Folder-92,DWA Papers).

66. Letter from Masiko to Mbina 2 October 1950 (Box-8, Folder-92, DWA Papers).

67. Letter from Mbina to DWA, 22 January 1951 (Box-8, Folder-92, DWA Papers).

68. Letter from Mbina to DWA, 12 February 1951 (Box-92,DWA Papers).

69. Letter from Mbina to DWA, 6 March 1951 (Box-8, Folder-92, DWA Papers).

70. Letter from DWA to Mbina, 12 March 1951 (Box-8, Folder-92, DWA Papers).

71. Letter from Mbina to DWA, 10 April 1951 (Box-8, Folder-92, DWA Papers).

72. Letter from Mbina to DWA, 16 April 1951 (Box-8, Folder-92, DWA Papers).

73. Letters from Mbina to DWA, 13 August 1951 and 26 November 1951 (Box-8, Folder-92, DWA Papers).

74. Letter from DWA to Mbina, 8 January 1952 (Box-8, Folder-92, DWA Papers).

75. Letter from Mbina to DWA 22 January 1952 (Box-8, Folder-92, DWA Papers), p. 2.

76. *Ibid.*, P 9

77. Letter from William Hinnings to DWA, Independent Church of Zion, Brakpan, 5 October 1943 (Box-8, Folder-84, DWA Papers).

78. *Ibid.*

79. Letter from Hinnings to DWA, 7 December 1943 (Box-8, Folder-84, DWA Papers).

80. Letter from Hinnings to DWA, 6 December 1943 (Box-8, Folder-84, DWA Papers).

81. Synod Minutes, 1934-1961 (Box-3, Folder-35, DWA Papers), p. 153.

82. Letter from Hinnings to DWA, 4 January 1944 (Box-8, Folder-84, DWA Papers).

83. Letter from DWA to Jerimiah Lulwane, 14 November 1943 (Box-8, Folder-87, DWA Papers).

84. Letter from Van der Westhuizen to DWA, 4 September 1956 (Box-9, Folder-102, DWA Papers).

85. Letter from DWA to Van der Westhuizen, November 1956 (Box-9, Folder-102, DWA Papers).

86. Letter from Van der Westhuizen to DWA, 27 March 1957 (Box-9, Folder-102, DWA Papers).

87. Letter from Van der Westhuizen to DWA, 11 April 1957 (Box-9, Folder- 102, DWA Papers).

88. *Ibid.*

89. Letter from DWA to Van der Westhuizen, 15 April 1957 (Box-9, Folder-102, DWA Papers).

90. Letter from Van der Westhuizen to DWA, 20 May 1957 (Box-9, Folder-102, DWA Papers).

91. Letter from Van der Westhuizen to DWA, 3 October 1957 (Box-9, Folder-102, DWA Papers).

92. Letter from DWA to Van der Westhuizen, 11 September 1959 (Box-9, Folder-102, DWA Papers).

93. Letter from DWA to Superintendant No.2 Location, Kimberley, September 1959 (Box-9, Folder-102, DWA Papers).

94. Letter from Surgeon L. Motsepe to Louis van Branden, 9 September 1958 (Box-9, Folder-96, DWA Paper).

95. Letter from Motsepe to DWA, 6 June 1959 (Box-9, Folder-96, DWA Papers).

96. Letter from DWA to Motsepe, 10 June 1959 (Box-9, Folder-96, DWA Papers).

97. Letter from Motsepe to DWA, 20 June 1959 (Box-9, Folder-96, DWA Papers).

98. Letter from Motsepe to DWA, 23 June 1959 (Box-9, Folder-96, DWA Papers).

99. *Ibid.*

100. Letters from Motsepe to DWA, 7 July 1959 (Box-9, Folder-96, DWA Papers).

CHAPTER 5
THE EYE OF THE STORM: APARTHEID AND BLACK RESISTANCE

The emergence of apartheid in 1948 did not signal a radical departure from established racist laws and customs. However, it was an intensification of these restrictions with a rigidity and thoroughness. The concept of apartheid was first used by Dr. Malan in the early 1940's to define the total "separateness" of the races of South Africa. The idea, according to Afrikaner nationalists, was to ensure the mutual respect and the development of each race's culture, nationalism and economic wellbeing. It was decisive for unifying fragmented Afrikaners, ensuring Afrikaner political hegemony over all South Africa, and smashing any black political and economic challenge. Black groups received none of the alleged benefits of apartheid and by 1960, the standard of living for Africans had declined to the level of the 1920's.[2]

The election of 1948 was not won simply on the platform of race separation, although it was a central building block in the apartheid edifice. Dr. Malan and a small circle of Afrikaner intellectuals advocated the advancement of Afrikaner economic business interests, the need for an Afrikaner identity distinct from other Europeans, the sacredness of the Afrikaans language and the social evils of communism.[4] This wide range of concerns attracted middle class supporters, many of whom were active members of the Broederbond, who desired greater Afrikaner participation in the nation's political life, as well as farmers and workers who flocked to the purified camp because of promises of protection of white employment from black labor. Malan's Nationalist Party, in cooperation with Havenga's Afrikaner Party, presented an image of defending "whiteness" at all cost. Of course, the rhetoric of "whiteness first" and the demand for a permanent solution to the "native problem" made excellent political hay on election day. However, the Nationalist Party attack on the "liberalism" of the Smuts' administration had no foundation, since Smuts' United Party never advocated full equality and complete citizenship rights for Africans and Europeans.

In 1948, Dr. Malan firmly asserted that apartheid was not a policy of repression, although sometimes it might adversely affect Africans. He went on to state in regards to African political rights that:

> I have emphasized that the abolition of Native representation in the Assembly is a policy that we have indeed laid before this house and before the people for approval . . . and we have it from the mouth of General Hertzog himself that it is the best policy for our people . . . if we refuse to do so, . . . then we would be unfaithful to the people and the people's highest interest. Then we would be betraying South Africa and European civilization .... The question of the penetration of Natives, their further and further encroachment on the European so that more and more is equally coming about between Europeans and non-Europeans, affects South Africa deeply. Our survival as Europeans depends on the solution of this problem....[5]

While Dr. Malan may have been sincere in stating that apartheid was not a policy of repression, his successor, J. G. Strijdom, bluntly called for "baaskap' (or absolute domination) to ensure the racial survival of Europeans and their continual superiority in the political/economic arena. The legislation which came cascading forth after 1948 was designed to achieve this end. The most prominent of the new laws were the Mixed Marriages Act (1949), the Immorality Act (1950), the Population Registration Act (1950), The Reservation of Separate Amenities Act (1953), and Extension of University Education Act (1959). The spirit of these new regulations stemmed from the Afrikaner fear of miscegenation, which shaped their identity and their moral ethical values. The neo-Marxist analysis of the function of ideological illusion in capitalist societies has merit, but the Afrikaners' visceral reaction to miscegenation was not simply a mechanistic reflex to the capitalist mode of production.

A new viciousness marked the years after 1948. This new climate of racial intolerance triggered new levels of African resistance. Even the twenty-fourth

Synod of the AOC in 1948 exhibited an attitude of resistance. It started out with lively discussions of matters like temperance, but on its second day, Alexander blasted the Nationalist Government by calling apartheid a false doctrine. He noted that the government was quick to condemn any individual who stood up for his rights as a communist; but their real intent was taking away all rights of non-Europeans. Alexander proceeded to direct the Synod to draft a resolution against the government's mandate of Proclamation 1890. He felt the act was undemocratic, designed to smash African nationalist organizations and an unnecessary interference with the right of free association. He was:

> convinced that in the ordinary laws of the country there is adequate machinery for dealing with cases of robbery, fraud or any other form of swindling and accordingly urges the government to withdraw the Draft Proclamation....[7]

But Proclamation 1890 faded in importance as the full weight of apartheid measures made their impact felt upon South Africa. During the AOC Synod in October 1951, Alexander introduced two members of the Non-European Unity Movement (NEUM). The first speaker was W. Rhoda, secretary of the NEUM, who related that profound changes were taking place in South Africa. He provided the following data: the annual profits from the mines stood at 20 million pounds and of this sum, 14 million pounds were channeled to the government.

> The farmers get about 7 1/2 million and the people are underfed, as they are too poor to exist: He then referred to what happened in 1946, when the police were called out and a number of Africans were killed .... He also pointed out the way in which millions of Africans were represented in Parliment [sic]; namely 9 million of the Africans were represented by three members in Parliment [sic] and two million of the whites were represented by 25 members in Parliment [sic], whereas all the coloureds were to be represented by four members ....[8]

Rhoda's figures on parliamentary representation may have been recorded incorrectly; nevertheless, the essence of his message was that coloureds and, in particular, Africans, were receiving extremely meager portions of the wealth of their society. In the realm of politics, Africans had absolutely no voice in determining their destiny. The ugly constitutional fight to remove coloureds from the common roll was still five years away, but some within the coloured community must have approached the future with a sense of dread that the worst was yet to come.

The next speaker was J. J. Myers. He briefly touched upon Freedom of Speech, the Pass Laws, the Land Tenure Bill and the need to abolish the Poll tax. He declared that the entire system of civil and criminal laws had to be revamped. In his annual Synod address, Alexander lashed out at the Nationalist Government for putting into place laws that suppressed the economic, educational, and spiritual aspirations of Africans. These laws had been designed to deny full adulthood suffrage to non-Europeans and to make them slaves in the land of their birth. For instance, the Mixed Marriages Act was cruel because it placed the onus of determining the nationality of the marrying parties upon the marriage officer. Alexander added that "some of the older people who took no notice of the Proclamation, found themselves in Court and were later released." [9] In those cases in which one spouse was classified racially different from the other, forced separation was mandated. The suffering to family and friends was enormous.

Alexander rejected the Group Areas Act of 1950, which empowered the government to proclaim business and residential areas for a particular race group. He noted that this law demanded that "each race must develop on their own lines."[10] He argued instead that:

> since we all have accepted Christianity, which knows no race or creed, no greek [sic] nor Barbarian, slave nor free, yet here the Nationalists with their voortreker mentality, believe that Non Europeans are still in the embryo stage.[11]

The introduction of the Coloured Representation Bill (or Separate Representation Of Voters) in 1951 plunged South Africa into a constitutional crisis because Dr. Malan contended coloureds could be deprived of the vote without a two-thirds majority decision of a joint sitting of Parliament. A long and acrimonious struggle ensued over Malan's position.

First, he was able to get the measures passed separately in each house by a too much space narrow margin. This move by the Prime Minister was unanimously declared unconstitutional by an appellate decision. Malan was determined to destroy Coloured participation in the electoral process; he sought to create, via a new bill, a High Court of Parliament that would have the power to invalidate decisions of the Appeal Court. Again, Malan's scheme was defeated. In 1954, at 80 years old, he resigned as Prime Minister.

The drive to remove Coloureds from the Cape roll, however, was achieved by Malan's successor, J. G. Strijdom. In 1955, Strijdom was able to get a new bill passed, the Senate Act, which increased the Senate from forty-eight to eighty-nine members, thereby creating greater voting power in areas with slight Afrikaner majorities. Afrikaner nationalists, now augmented by the Senate Act, removed coloureds from the voting roll in 1956.

In the early 1950s, Alexander viewed the Coloured Bill as retrogressive legislation since once the vote was taken away, coloureds would be represented by four whites in Parliament. Addressing the AOC Synod, in 1951, he argued that English-speaking whites had only raised their voices in protest because they feared that their turn would eventually come. He also raised the issue of the plight of his African brethren:

> But what about the African People? Those who were given the franchise in the Cape Province, and were robbed of their birthright; is there no redress for their wrongs? Are they forever to be the battle-core and shuttlecock of different Political Parties, when they come into power? Are they then, because of their colour to be despised? .... Or is it that the Non-European is feared, because of his aptness to pick up any trade...[12]

Lastly, Alexander addressed the Native Representative Council (NRC) which he viewed as a tool of the Nationalist government that made it difficult for anyone with pride or a sense of responsibility to serve in such an institution. This Council had come into existence after Cape African voters were removed from the common roll by the Representation of Natives Act (1936). The Act reduced black parliamentary representation to three elected white members for the Cape and four white members in the Senate for all of South Africa. The NRC was purely an advisory body with no power to implement its recommendations. Alexander felt that a significant outcome of this legislation was the coming together of black groups to defend their rights:

> the legislation, which has been passed at this session of Parliament, by its harshness, had made it possible for Non-Europeans to unite and go into one camp; the coloured man with his pride and prejudice against the African; the Indian with his race consciousness at India's freedom, realizes that unless he pools his resources with them by their leaders in India, to make friends and assist the inhabitants of the countries in which they live; they will find themselves isolated.... [13]

Alexander cited a strike by 96 coloured union workers (he provided no date or place), as proof of the black race's ability to strive for political goals. The strike inconvenienced many, but Alexander believed if limited solidarity could be maintained for a week, the authorities would grant concessions. But concessions from the apartheid system were meager indeed. Even after tens of thousands had participated in the Defiance Campaign in 1952, the South African state made no concessions.

Apartheid laws also impinged directly upon the independent black Christian community. Prior to 1948, the state set numerous guidelines for black separatist churches to follow. While some separatist churches existed in hostile relationships with the government, most separatist churches hungered for official government recognition of their churches. Although Alexander struggled for many years to obtain state recognition for the AOC, this new status brought a host of benefits. For example, Alexander boasted as early as 1941 that the AOC "stood above 600 other churches with no approval from the government" and that recognition was a great moment in the history of the church. Even the Mayor of Kimberley sent a letter of good wishes to Alexander and his church on their "elevation" by the state.[15]

Elevation by the government meant each new incoming church had to comply with various regulations concerning marriage officers. The Marriage Officer's job was perhaps the most important one that came with government recognition. By analyzing the Marriage Officer's role within the separatist church, a more lucid picture can emerge in terms of regulations and benefits.

The individual seeking the position of Marriage Officer had first to apply to the Native Affairs Department (later the Office of Bantu Affairs). Since separatist priests and ministers needed to move about freely to attend to the needs of their fellows, they was exempted from the pass system. Here again, exemption from carrying a pass was obtained through another application. A recognized Marriage Officer also received a railway identification card which entitled him to a reduction in fares. For the struggling AOC during the 1930's and 1940's, a railway card for its priests was a welcomed economic benefit. There was also the matter of wine used in church services. Africans needed a permit to purchase wine, and the state allowed only priests to purchase wine.

An excellent example of expanded state control over religion was the Tomlinson Commission (1955), which is best known for laying the foundation for the Bantustan system. According to Davenport, the purpose of the commission was:

> to conduct an exhaustive inquiry into and to report on a comprehensive scheme for the rehabilitation of the Native Areas with a view to developing within them a social structure in keeping with the culture of the Native and based on effective socio-economic planning . . . that there is little hope for evolutionary development towards a common society....[16]

But the commission also addressed the role of religion in the African separatist churches. Certain reformist expressions of Christianity would be encouraged for them; however, certain "Bantu customs" such as "witchcraft" would be deemed undesirable. Indeed, the state preferred a black theology that was reformist and malleable to the needs of the state. By the mid 1950's, Alexander adjusted to the apartheid state by abetting separate development in order to protect the interest of his church. He informed the Rev. Henry Basson, in 1956, that the Tomlinson Report demanded:

> that all men to be ordained, at least in the Non-European Churches should be std [standard] 7. Can you see how I am struggling to make it your business to learn to write more carefully, but you don't seem to take any notice of it . . .[17]

The demand for a standard seven education for black clergy placed an almost insurmountable burden on them. Moreover, all transactions with the government were done in English and Afrikaans. Alexander insisted that a literate clergy would better serve the needs of the AOC.

While registration offered certain benefits, the AOC clergy were nonetheless still subjected to a wide range of controls. For example, after Father Mbina moved to Cape Town in 1956, he could not purchase books from abroad. He asked Alexander to obtain them:

> I am just from the Post Office to post the money order for the AO Church History book but they refused that I do so-they say the law refuses that we order books from overseas. So now I send the sum of 1-10 pounds to you to kindly order it for me....[18]

The Archbishop fared no better with the Department of Commerce and Industries in a vain attempt to obtain a communion chalice for the church. Because it was a great inconvenience to his congregations, Alexander wrote the Exports and Imports section of the Department, after six months, to ask why the order had not been filled.[19]

The Director's response was that "your case has been given careful consideration and whilst the inconvenience which will be caused by the non-receipt of these goods is appreciated, it has not been found possible to accede to your request."[20]

Despite the fact that AOC priests were exempted from carrying passes, this benefit did not extend to their families. Mbina's experience highlighted the plight for urban African families. He asked Alexander to remember to write the Department of Interior for a permit for his family. Mbina was concerned because of a report that "some women were caught by the police who came to Cape Town without a permit ...."[21] During the 1950's, African women were increasingly being subjected to influx controls, and men, who were unable to obtain the necessary documentation for their wives and children, could not prevent there return of their families to Bantustans. Mbina understandably was not about to risk bringing his family to Cape Town without the authorities' consent.

NATIONALISM OF AFRIKANER RELIGION:

The issue of influx control faced by Mbina's family was due to the hegemony of Afrikaner power which combined religion and nationalism into an ideology of political dominance. The religious struggles within the Afrikaner community, however, highlighted the limitations of Alexander's religious ideas and mission training. Afrikaner religious views must be explored to contrast the theology of submission with the racist/nationalist theology of "self determination". Developing within the Afrikaner community were social, political and economic forces that produced tragic consequences, in general, for South Africa and in particular for the black races of that society. The AOC and other separatist churches were ill-prepared to cope with the politico-religious domination of the Afrikaner.

The drive for Afrikaner political domination commenced in the 1920's and 1930's with debates and ideas concerning a civil religion, the poor white "problem", and the co-equal status of Afrikaner nationalists emerged with English in education and government. By the 1930's, a group of purified Afrikaans nationalists emerged who desired to implement a program of Afrikaner political advancement as well as a social/economic system of rigid racial segregation.

They channeled their energies into the Nationalist Party led by Dr. D. F. Malan, who preached a program that was the harbinger of the apartheid policies that aimed to maximize the economic exploitation of black labor and to reduce physical or social contacts between Europeans and "lesser" developed groups.

Central to Afrikaner nationalist philosophy was the notion of a civil religion which held that God had imbued all history with ultimate meaning. According to its advocates, nowhere in the universe was God more intimately involved in the affairs of men than in the Afrikaner nation. The Calvinist tradition of God's sovereignty over human affairs marked the Afrikaner's sacred history. They believed historical events were rooted in time and space and occurred because God preordained them. For instance, the Great Trek was proof of their "selection" as chosen people. The Afrikaner victory at Blood River on 16 December 1838, also signified that God had affirmed a covenant with His children. A solemn oath to celebrate the occasion marked the victory over thousands of black "savages."

Conversely, many Afrikaners viewed the Anglo-Boer War (1899-1902) as an omen of God's displeasure with the Afrikaner people. This terrible conflict wrought massive destruction on Afrikaners and their land; some 26,000 Afrikaner men, women and children died in British concentration camps from starvation and disease. Historical events revealed the handiwork of God's retribution or magnanimity to His chosen people. For Afrikaners, their selection was defined in terms of their whiteness. By definition, the blackness of Africans meant their "non-selection"; Africans were considered things, not human beings. Afrikaner sacred history defined Afrikaners as the "oppressed" and black Africans as the "oppressor." This religious attitude was tinged with a powerful economic motive - the African literally was a "beast of burden" to be worked and used as the Afrikaner deemed proper.[22]

Afrikaner ideologues used many examples of their mistreatment historically to forge a program of ethnic upliftment and to build a new group identity In contrast, during the 1920's and 1930's. The views and issues of the AOC were very narrow and hampered by a theology of submission which blocked Alexander from exhibiting an independent ideology in order to produce a secular and spiritual liberation for Blacks. Instead, he was content with being accepted by Europeans as a leader of a recognized separatist church.

Afrikanerdom, however, reworked the "universal' themes of Christianity to produce a "new" chosen history full of earthly power. But within the social experience of Africans in South Africa, many events could have served the useful purpose of building a civil religion for the AOC. For example, the Land Act of 1913 and the conquest of Africans and "coloureds" during the nineteenth century may have served as key ingredients in developing a formula for a "civil" religion of "liberation" Alexander's refusal to be a "slave" in the spiritual dwelling of Europeans could have been extended to the spheres of economic and group identity. His "God-talk" could have made plain that oppressed Blacks were the select of God and that it was only through militant struggle against the oppressor that God would raise them up and renew the covenant with his chosen African people.

Religious Afrikaner ideologies, on the other hand, hammered out a "sacred" history to enhance their liberation. Sacred history became the "civil religion" when the ideas of God's involvement in Afrikaner history merged with public displays of devotion, commemoration, and political speeches. Indeed the idea of a civil religion functioned as the linchpin of organizing society and the state around crucial historical events. Within Afrikanerdom, historical events assumed extraordinary dimensions. The public celebrations of events and holidays such as Kruger Day or Republic Day were filled with thanksgiving and pride in Afrikaner ethnicity and community. Howevr, no public celebration was as meaningful as the *Geloftedag,* the Day of the Covenant, held 16 December. On that day, God's people publicly reaffirmed their obedience to divine law.

Producing even greater levels of emotional intensity were the massive holy pilgrimages to shrines such as Vroue Monument (1913) and the Voortrekker Monument (1938). The defenders of Afrikanerdom felt that these shrines were worthy of veneration and they rested upon hallowed ground. Civil ritual, therefore, complemented sacred history by the joining of heaven and earth. Such a merger, at best, was diabolical; civil religion was the "mother" that would later give birth to apartheid.[23]

During these same years, Alexander concentrated on his missionary and ecumenical efforts. His theological and religious beliefs did not keep pace with developments in the Afrikaner community. By 1948, his views had actually retrogressed from his fire and militancy in the late 1920's (see Chapter three). In part, his theological/religious views atrophied due to his focus on his infant Church's day to day operations. Of greater importance was Alexander's adherence to a theology of submission which stressed resolving societal problems or conflicts through appeals to morality that stressed "loving one's enemy", "turning the other cheek" and never using violence to achieve political or social aims. This theology of submission made the arena of change the Christian conscience. Once the oppressors experienced a "change" of heart, justice and economic fair-play would be extended to include the long abused African have-nots.[24]

As appealing as the humane notions of the theology of submission may have been, far too many Africans attempted to make these views a reality. Afrikaner religious/ theological thought rejected loving one's enemy or turning the other cheek. Its advocates sought to energize every aspect of the Afrikaner existence to ensure their dominance in society. And after 1948, Afrikaner religious/theological thought justified massive violence against Africans in their struggle for liberation. But what Alexander and almost all mission educated Africans failed to comprehend in their struggle for economic and political power was that appeals to Christian conscience and morality were not based upon power. Indeed the appeals were powerless in attempting to achieve goals which could only be induced from a position of power. In other words, if Europeans refused to grant economic and political fair play, Alexander and others like him, possessed no means of force to obtain their desired ends, since violence was absolutely rejected in all situations. The Afrikaner, however, did not reject violence and would eventually use state power to ensure the economic survival of their kind.

AOC, THE ANGLICAN CHURCH, AND THE NON-EUROPEAN UNITY MOVEMENT:

As Africans struggled for group survival, they could not, however, rely upon the state to insure their economic survival or to redress their grievances. Even within European churches, Africans fought to emancipate themselves from religious subjugation. James Z. Mdatyulwa was confronted with this problem within the Anglican Church. Mdatyulwa's budding nationalism brought him into direct conflict with European authorities which later forced his departure from the church. Mdatyulwa entered the AOC in 1946 and rejected the authority of the Anglican Church. Beyond any doubt, he was the most gifted and the most critical thinker of all the priests under Alexander. He introduced Alexander to the Campaign for African Spiritual Freedom, and he hoped that his new spiritual leader would encourage other clergy to join the campaign.

Mdatyulwa's departure from the Anglican Church was set in motion by R. F. Yates, a Johannesburg church official, who informed Mdatyulwa that he had been "talking service" at Robinson Deep in violation of express orders of the Archdeacon that no one could participate in services without a Sub-Catechist's Certificate.[25] Mdatyulwa's response was revealing:

> As far as I am concerned, I took Fr. Masiko's invitation as official. He was a priest in the parish and he was looking after the particular area in which he asked me to assist . . . I shall, however, refrain from taking services in your parish . . . I am informed that the Archdeacon made a public announcement at Robinson Deep . . . He is alleged to have given as a reason that I preach poisonous propaganda....[26]

The poisonous propaganda referred to Mdatyulwa's demand for greater black autonomy in spiritual matter. In the 1940's, the Anglican Church was still unprepared to bestow the rank of bishop on Africans, regardless of their personal qualities.

In November 1946, Mdatyulwa wrote to the Anglican Bishop of Johannesburg, G. H. Clayton, in a powerful exchange that severed his ties with the Anglicans:

> For some time now, you have no doubt been noticing the trend of my motions introduced for discussion . . . You know the view I have expressed not only in the Diocesan conference and Synods but also in Province conference of the Anglican Church. You no doubt must have realized that I was one of the ever increasing thousands who are not happy about things as they were and as they still are . . . My criticism of the position has always been expressed in unminced words though with a reasonable amount of moderation, while many who felt as I did, unfortunately did not have the courage to make open declaration of their conditions....[27]

Mdatyulwa noted that some of Clayton's white assistants, who were experts on African affairs, were overtly antagonistic to articulate Blacks who had different opinions concerning the position of Blacks in the Anglican Church. "The very idea of making an attempt," Mdatyalwa noted, "to reform an organization which did not belong to Africans was folly."[28] On several occasions, he suggested that indirect actions by the Europeans made it plain that Blacks were not wanted even though some Africans had been slow to comprehend the matter.[29]

Mdatyulwa was brutally frank when he told Clayton that no equality existed between white and black in church or state:

> The action of your chief bishop in Capetown (sic) in associating himself with a cable which refuted allegations made by Sir Maharaj Singh against South Africa's treatment of my people . . . has put the clock of confidence back in your church, many years back. His action, and the failure of the other bishops to condemn him, has disappointed those who have laboured under the impression that the church of the Province of South Africa . . .

was the champion of the causes of the under privileged . . . the liberation of the African will not come from the House of Parliament in Capetown (sic) or from the Administrative Building in Pretoria, his salvation will not come through the white man's church in which he has no future....[30]

Mdatyulwa presented four major conclusions as to why it did not pay to belong to the Anglican Church:

1) The white bishops were very un-Christian in not giving consideration to having African bishops;

2) The discriminatory treatment of ministers based upon color as embodied in the Constitution and Diocesan Regulations of the Anglican Church;

3) The Diocesan Synods and Conferences had played with the feelings of African people; and

4) Much of their discussion was a deliberate attempt to confuse the issues in order to cripple the national struggle of African people for their rights.

Mdatyulwa recognized that good white Christians existed within the Anglican ranks. He admired them and believed they were a blessing to South Africa. Nonetheless, he confessed that the existence of such Christians could not alter the fact that Africans refused to borrow Archbishop Clayton's phrase, to be "tolerated guests, in white churches". Mdatyulwa, therefore, cut his religious umbilical cord with the Anglican Church and entered the new life of black separatist Christianity.[31]

In April 1946, he attended his first AOC Synod. He expressed pleasure at not being associated with a European Church since he had spent so much of his life in one. The great need, he believed, was for the church work to do be done by the laity, and for the ministry to take the Gospel to those who had nothing. Alexander asked Mdatyulwa to address the issue of separatist churches. He responded by saying that the members of the AOC were Catholics and that other denominations such as the E. G. African Catholic in Zion had no idea what was meant by Catholic, although it was part of its church title. Mdatyulwa then posed an important question: "Why do the Africans break up into bits....."[32] Africans and Coloureds, according to Mdatyulwa, knew and felt they had no home in European churches.[33] He also stressed that these groups must not be despised but befriended and that these "sects" be drawn "little by little to Catholicism."[34]

As a Catholic church, the AOC found itself under attack during the 1940's. The origin of the conflict was rooted in Alexander's ability to build the AOC membership at the expense of the Anglican Church. Anglicans from the pulpit and in the press waged a guerrilla war against the AOC to retain their membership. Alexander openly stated that the attacks were proof of the growing strength and importance of the AOC in South Africa's religious community.[35]

In 1941, the Anglicans circulated a pamphlet attacking the AOC. Alexander informed Mbina shortly after his break with the Anglican Church that "we know they [i.e. the Anglicans] will strive to persuade you to withdraw your resignations, being afraid your people will follow....." [36]

In 1947, Hlong informed Alexander of the role of Bishop Gibson , the head of the Church of Province of South Africa (CPSA) in his "crusade" against the AOC :

> What is the matter with Gibson! [?] It shows how narrow-mineded [sic] he is. Can he really dare condem [sic] the AOC[?] What a splendid idea of the C.O.P. [Church of the Province]. We shall be prepared to welcome those priests if at all they come to us....[37]

Hlong later provided greater insight into the ongoing controversy:

> Those of the C.O.P.S.A. who attacked the AOC should feel ashamed for using false statements .... What was at the back of the minds of the writer was nothing but prejudice. Secondly they thought much of their white skin that no one would dare to answer them... you [Alexander] have them by the throat.[38]

Episcopi Vagantes, written in the late 1940's by an Anglican scholar, explored the murky area of wandering bishops (men who are highly mobile but not attached to any specific church or See). The scholar was forced to conclude that the AOC's credentials were valid but 'irregular'; i.e., not obtained through established procedures whereby every new bishop-elect must have three bishops place their hands upon the consecrated for his orders to be valid. However, the orders of Joseph Rene Vilatte, which consecrated McGuire, were not "established", and many within and outside of the Anglican Church, knew this. If the proselytizing efforts of the AOC had been unsuccessful, this question of legitimacy would not have surfaced at all.

Alexander was not a timid man; he did not flee from an altercation with the Anglican Church. His counter-attack was thorough and characteristically biting. Nevertheless, he informed Hlong in 1947 of some of the other activities of Bishop Gibson:

> Canon Manyali writes from Matatiela [that] Bishop Gibson gave his clergy an outline and condemnation of the AOC, at Synod, and at a conference of catechist, he drew their attention to this black Archbishop when a catechist stood up and asked his bishop, why all the worry about this black archbishop, and the AO Church; there are many churches governed by black clergy and we never hear anything about them at Synod now we are warned.... We wanted to elect Calata to be our bishop you said he had Phthisis, then we elected Mhletywa you didn't agree, it is a long time that we want a black bishop.[39]

The number of members the AOC gained from the Anglican Church cannot be exactly ascertained. Much more certain is the fact that Alexander, Hinnings, Hlong, Mbina and Mdatyulwa were all former members of the

Anglican Church. The real threat which concerned the Anglican leaders was not so much with membership, but with the AOC's potential. Of course, the growth did not occur; the apartheid storm, commencing in 1948, rained violence, economic hardship and death on Black groups in South Africa. The AOC, then, like other black churches, struggled not only against European churches for membership, but also against more repressive government legislation. Indeed, if other black separatist churches were also raiding the Anglican fold, then retaining black membership was a problem of the first magnitude.

An important factor which may have exacerbated the conflicts between the Anglican Church and the AOC was the Non- European Unity Movement (NEUM) which attracted coloured clergymen seeking spiritual autonomy from European-controlled denominations. On the political front, the radical ideas of the movement called for "a direct onslaught against oppression...."[40] The militant rhetoric of the NEUM dismayed moderates who formed separate organizations. The NEUM also attracted many colored intellectuals and activists in the Western Cape. Unfortunately, the NEUM's position of non-collacoration was tantamount to no action at all, and its net impact upon the masses, African and colored, was nil.[42]

During the early life of the NEUM in the 1940's, Alexander served as Vice President of the Kimberley branch. Historically, Coloureds had received better social and economic treatment than Africans, but Alexander insisted that Coloureds needed emancipation more than their African brothers. Pressures from the NEUM must have strained relations between coloureds and European-controlled groups if the dominant churches perceived themselves to be losing membership.

Linked to NEUM was the Campaign for African Spiritual Freedom, which also espoused a progressive separatist religious message. James Z. Mdatyulwa, a leading AOC advocate of the new Black organization, informed Alexander of his desire to attend the Unity meeting in September 1946.[43] Mdatyulwa disclosed that he wished AOC clergy to join the campaign and that he hoped "to have an opportunity to explain its workings and aims ...."[44] to Alexander. The rise of the

Campaign signalled a more intense drive by black people to end their spiritual and political bondage. Such activity by Africans and coloureds must have unnerved the European religious community. The Anglicans, in particular, were hostile to their endeavors. The European religious establishment, regardless of denomination, correctly understood that black religious rebellion had the potential to undermine all white authority in South Africa.

The Campaign for African Spiritual Freedom served as an ancillary factor in rekindling black Christian separatist sentiments. The center of the new religious rebellion was Johannesburg. This city possessed a long history of militant/black Christian activity because of the increased numbers of Blacks in the labor force and the urbanization of the area which ensured the survival of black Christian separatist ideas. The campaign, therefore, was a continuation of the rich heritage which rejected European religious instructions as infallible. In the words of Alexander, the campaign come into existence "to ameliorate the lethargy and helplessness of the clergy."[45] Mdatyulwa stated that the campaign was the "talk of the town" in Johannesburg:

> The white men are beginning to feel that there is something going on they are busy making investigations behind our backs....[46]

In order to ensure the survival of the campaign, Mdatyulwa asked Alexander in early 1947 for a loan to help sustain his work:

> because we in Johannesburg are a new group and have no congregation to appeal to. Moreover, the main battle ground for the spiritual freedom of the Non-white races of this continent is undoubtedly going to be Johannesburg. The rest of the AOC in South Africa and beyond is going to be supported by this area once it is built up and given a chance to be on its feet....[47]

Mdatyulwa's remarks concerning Johannesburg's role as "savior" of the AOC were premature. The campaign collapsed because between 1948 and 1958, the Nationalist Party mounted a racist campaign which sapped most of the energy of the AOC and other African organizations. The intense oppression of these years moved the black struggle from the nonviolence of the Defense Campaign to the revolutionary actions of "Spear of the Nation" (Umkhonto we Sizwe) of the early 1960's.[48] The powerful black issues exploded into the Black Consciousness Movement.[49] By 1971 the Black Power rhetoric caused much anguish within the white power structure. More than ever, some Asians and Coloureds were identifying as Black/African. The issue of race and identity for Alexander, therefore, must be revisited. The growing radicalism of the 1960's, must not obscure the very intense battle over race reclassification that raged in the Cape. Many Asians and coloureds absolutely refused to be categorized as black. Seemingly, Alexander made peace with being black; however, his relationship to his Africanness must be examined.

Alexander came to Kimberley to organize the AOC among the Coloureds of that area and not Africans. As he solicited support for his charitable endeavors, it was always for some coloured cause. Alexander, in fact, established an orphanage for coloured children during the late 1930's or early 1940's. On the success of the organization or how many children were provided services, the record was silent. At the same time, Alexander was involved in other organizations in the coloured community. He was president of the Northern Cape Coloured Ministers' Fraternal, an active member of the Kimberley Schoolboard, and maintained close ties with the Ex-Coloured Servicemen's Association. Alexander's identity was shaped by his great participation in the coloured "world." The rigid enforcement of the Population Registration Act during the 1960's forced Alexander to confront the issue of race as never before.

The Population Registration Act, passed in 1950, declared that all racial groups, such as Europeans, Asians, Indians and Coloureds, must possess registration cards with photograph and identification number. By 1963, the government was implementing its policy of registration and race classification, causing widespread panic and anger. Within the Cape Province, these feelings were strong since that area contained a disproportionate number of coloureds and "almost" whites. The Sunday Times of Diamond Field Advertiser featured a headline entitled "BORDERLINE WHITES WORRIED' The article (1963) stated in part:

> Although the Gevernment's identity card system is due to be in full working order by February 1, it became clear this week that many of South Africa's "borderline" Whites - especially in the Cape Province have failed to apply for their identity cards because they fear they will be classified as Coloured. . . with only 11 days left, some of them are said to be in a state of panic and are appealing to City Counsellors and Members of Parliament for advice.[50]

The article provided some family history on Alexander, and it stated that as a child he was sent to America. This, of course, was absolutely not the case; the mystery was why Alexander provided this untruth. The article stated that Alexander was classified as a "native." Alexander responded by declaring he was Coloured and the classification process was unjust because the government's official, Mr. Morgan, did not allow him to present details of his background, not simply for himself, but for all Coloureds. In an editorial, Alexander highlighted details of his encounter with Mr. Morgan:

> I lived in Pretoria and Johannesburg, nor was I ever stopped by policemen at nights for a special pass, but here just in three minutes I am made to accept classification which is absurb [sic]. When I refused to take the document, he told me that I would be arrested. I am, sir, ready to go to jail for a principle....[51]

Alexander resisted his classification as an African on the grounds of his family background and history. He openly stated that there was absolutely nothing wrong with being an African; nevertheless, he insisted he was coloured. This idea of being Coloured was simply a creation of the European mind which over the centuries, was used to divide Africans on the basis of skin color Since wealth, power, status and worth were almost the exclusive properties of those with white skins, individuals with dark skins were assumed to be worthless "Colouredness" in terms of identity, and race was intertwined with "Europeanness" and was hostile to any form of "Africanness". So all over the African diaspora, Alexander shared with many of his new world cousins, the unconscious belief that things rooted in European/Western experience were superior to most things rooted in that which was African/Black The profound process of cultural distortion and negation of self was the inevitable consequence of European mission/secular education which contaminated the thinking of Africans on both sides of the Atlantic. [52]

In the next chapter, we must resume the theme that the post World War II years brought a host of church related problems for Alexander.

Endnotes

1. Phyllis MacRae, "Race and Class in Southern Africa." *African Review*, IV, 2 (1974): 237-57. See also Shula Marks' "Liberalism, Social Realistics, and South African History." *Journal Of Commonwealth Political Studies*, X (1972): 24349, and "African and Afrikaner History." *Journal Of African History*, XI, 3 (1970): 435-47.

2. Francis Wilson, *Labour in South African Gold Mines, 1910-1969* (Cambridge: Cambridge University Press, 1972), p. 12.

3. Leonard Thompson, 'Afrikaner Nationalist Historiography and the Policy of Apartheid." Journal Of African History, III, 1 (1962): 125-41, and Dan O'Meara's "The Afrikaner Broederbond, 1927-1948: Class Vanguard of Afrikaner Nationalism." *Journal Of Southern African Studies*, III,2 (1976): I56-86, V. 3 and "Analyzing Afrikaner Nationalism : The Christian-National Assault on White Trade Unionism in South Africa, 1934-48." African Affairs, 77, 306 (1978) : 45-72, V. 77.

4. T. Dunbar Moodie, *The Rise of Afrikanerdom: Power. Apartheid. and the Afrikaner Civil Religion* (Berkeley: University of California Press, 1971). See, in particular, chapter 12.

5. C. M. Tatz, *Shadow and Substance in South Africa: Study in Land and Franchise Policies Affecting Africans. 1910-1960* (Pietermaritzburg: University of Natal Press, 1962), p. 131.

6. Greater insight into Afrikaner history is given in the following articles : Martin Legassick's "Legislation, Ideology and Economy in Post-1948 South Africa." *Joumal of Southern African Studies,* I, 1 (1974): 5-34; "The

Frontier in S.A. Historiography. *SUAS Seminar Paper. II,* (1978): 1-34; and "Review of Five Hundred Years: A History of South Africa." *African Historical Studies,* III, 2 (1965): 491-6.

7. Synod Minutes, 1933-1961 (Box-3, Folder-35, DWA Papers), pp. 278-279.

8. Synopsis of Proceedings of 27th Synod, October 1951 (Published by AOC, private collection of Patriarch Sweeting), p. 4.

9. *Ibid.*, p. 14.

10. *Ibid.*, p. 13.

11. *Ibid.*, p. 14.

12. *Ibid.*, p. 13.

13. *Ibid.*, p. 14. For a harsh analysis of African nationalism, see Fadma Meer's "African Nationalism—Some Inhibiting Factors." In H. Adam (ed.) *South Africa: Sociological Perspectives* (1974): 121-57.

14. Synod Minutes, op, cit. (DWA Papers), p. 125.

15.*Ibid.*, pp. 123-125.

16. T. R. H. Davenport, *A Modern History,* 3rd edition (Toronto and Buffalo: University of Toronto Press, 1987), p. 375.

17. Letter from DWA to Henry Basson, 20 August 1956 (Box-8, Folder-82, DWA Papers).

18. Letter from Mbina to DWA, 23 April 1957 (Box-8, Folder-92, DWA Papers).

19. Letter from DWA to Director of Exports and Imports, 23 June 1950 (Box-10, Folder-118, DWA Papers).

20. Letter from Director of Exports and Imports to DWA, 20 luly 1950 (Box-10, Folder-118, DWA Papers).

21. Letter from Mbina to DWA, 5 February 1954 (Box-8, Folder-92, DWA Papers).

22. The idea that the African was a beast or beastlike is linked to the alleged sexual prowess of the black savage. For discussion of such attitudes, read Winthrop D. Jordan, *White Over Black: American Atttitudes Toward the Negro. 1550-1812* (Baltimore, Maryland: Penguin Books Inc., 1969), pp. 28-40.

23. Religion as an independent agent has produced as much social change and social dislocation as the economic factor in history. I am convinced that the Afrikaner Revolution in 1948 would not have been victorious had the religious ethos of their struggle not been present.

24. Malcolm X's position of religious oppression was that the "have nots" -the exploited - should use any means necessary to liberate themselves.

25. Letter from James Mdatyulwa to R. F. Yates, 7 November 1946 (Box-8, Folder 94, DWA Papers).

26. *Ibid.*

27. Letter from Mdatyulwa to G. H. Clayton, Bishop of Johannesburg, 19 November 1946 (Box-8, Folder-94, DWA Papers).

28. *Ibid.*

29. *Ibid.*

30. *Ibid.*

31. Mdatyulwa noted that after can ful consideradon, he was cuthng all des with the Anglican Church; he sent Bishop Clayton his resignadon only as an act of cartesy.

32. Synod Minutes, mL cj~ (DWA Papers), p. 227.

33. *Ibid.*,

34. *Ibid.*,

35. "The African Orthodox Churchman" was written by DWA. It was the official newsletter of the AOC; however, I have located only one of these pamphlets, which consisted of four pages. 1947 (Box-2, Folder-19 DWA Papers).

36. Letter from DWA to Mbina, ca 1944 (Box-8, Folder-85, DWA Papers).

37. Letter from Hlong to DWA, 24 February 1947 (Box-8, Folder-85, DWA Papers).

38. Letter from Hlong to DWA, 17 February 1947 (Box-8, Folder-85, DWA Papers).

39. Letter from DWA to Hlong, 22 February 1947 (Box-8, Folder-85, DWA Papers).

40. Ian Goldin, *Making Race: The Politics and Economics of Coloured Identity in South Africa* (London and New York: Longman, 1987), p. 58.

41. *Ibid.*, p. 58.

42. Gavin Lewis, *Between the Wire and the Wall: A History of South African "Coloured" Politics* (New York: St. Martin's Press, 1987), p. 242.

43. Letter from Mdatyulwa to DWA, 30 September 1946 (Box-8, Folder-94, DWA Papers).

44. *Ibid.*

45. Letter from DWA to Mbina, 18 October 1946 (Box-8, Folda-92, DWA Papers).

46. Letter from Mdatyulwa to DWA, 21 November 1946 (Box-8, Folder-94, DWA Papers).

47. Letter from Mdatyulwa to DWA, 14 January 1947 (Box-8, Folder-94, DWA Papers).

48. Tom Lodge, *Black Politics in South Africa Since 1945* (London and New York: Longman, 1983). See, in particular, chapters 10, 11, 12. David Merrnelstein (ed.), *The Anti-Apartheid Reader : The Struggle Against White Racist Rule in South Africa* (New York: Grove Press, 1987). See, in particular, chapter 7.

49. Gail Gerhart, *Black Power in South Africa* (Berkeley: University of California Press, 1978). For how the black power concept impacted upon religion, see Basil Moore's *Black Theology; The Southern Voice* (London: C. Hurst and Co., 1973). Much that is contained in the black power position was part of the broader philosophy of Pan-Africanism. An excellent introductory volume to Pan Africanism is P. Olisanwuche Esedebe's *Pan-Africanism; the Ideas and Movement. 1776-1963* (Washington, D. C.: Howard University Press, 1982).

50. "Borderline Whites Worried," Diamond Field Advertiser, 20 January, 1963 (Box-2, Fokler-26, DWA Papers).

51. Diamond Field Advertiser, 1 March 1963 (Box-2, Folder-26, DWA Papers).

52. The following volumes have provided a painful encounter with education, identity and exploitation : Carter G. Woodson, *The Mis-Education of the Negro*, (New York Ams Press, 1977), Sulayman S. Nyang, *Islam. Chrianity, and African identity,* (Brattleboro, Vermont Amana Books, 1984), Albert Memmi, *The Colonizer ,and the Colonized*,

(Boston: Beacon Press, 1965), Paulo Freire, *Pedayogy Of the Oppressed*, (New York Continuum, 1985) and Frantz Fanon, *The Wretched Of the Earth*, (New York : Grove Press, Inc., 1968).

CHAPTER 6
AOC IN THE POST WAR YEARS: CONFLICT AND EXPANSION

The years following the Second World War were very difficult ones for Alexander as he searched for answers to continuing church leadership problems. One of the most pressing issues was that of finance which nearly brought ruin to the AOC because some of the clergy used the church funds for personal reasons, some refused to repay church loans; and some even stole from their churches.

Fortunately, Alexander had some priests of good character. One outstanding priest was James Z Mdatyulwa who brought intellectual prowess and intense dedication to the uplifting of his people. His bonding to Alexander over the next decade developed into a father/son relationship. From their first meeting, Mdatyulwa offered advice and opened his innermost feelings to Alexander. For example, he sent Alexander a copy of his resignation letter to Archbishop Clayton (which Mdatyulwa neglecteded to post) and he instructed Alexander that it should be released to the press for "propaganda purposes."[1] There is no evidence to suggest that Alexander released the resignation letter to the press, perhaps because that same letter contained a discussion about a priest that Alexander found troublesome. In the letter, Mdatyulwa plotted :

> Now, Your Grace, if I must give you my candid opinion, I believe that it is not in the interests of our work to keep Archdeacon Bamvana at Vrybrug ... he be transferred next January .... from correspondence to you and me, he keeps on talking about Colesburg .... As it will cost nothing to us to send him there, I suggest that be be allowed to go .... Let him go to this place and commit suicide. It may be he is right and we are not. If he succeeds there, all honour to him if he fails and is ruined; he will have nobody but himself to blame....[2]

The outcome of events for Bomvana was not revealed in future correspondence.

Nonetheless, in early January, 1947, Mdatyulwa petitioned Alexander for a loan from the Cathedral Building Fund. Alexander refused to approve the loan. Mdatyulwa expressed disappointment, but he understood why he was rejected. Some priests would have soured if Alexander had not provided the funds Mdatyulwa's spiritual high from being involved with the AOC was reflected in a very warm exchange with Alexander in December 1947. Filled with the Christmas "spirit" and good humor, Mdatyulwa told Alexander he had not forgotten his birthday; he would give one gift for Christmas and his birthday. Alexander's new spiritual son noted:

> Mark Anthony, making an oration over the body of Caesar said: the evil that men do lives after them; the good is often interred with their bones. As you pass over these many Christmas Days, greater is the work and fuller becomes the record of such work done .... We pray, therefore, that in your case, the good that you have done should never [be] interred with your bones when the 'sun' sets, but should remain towering above your Grace as an undying monument to be sung by generations to come as an unchallenged and unchallengeable indication that has also produced prophets, Bishops and priests, saints and leaders and champions of the nation's cause.[3]

Mdatyulwa's salutations concerning Alexander's spiritual well-being gave way to more mondane issues--monetary matters. He candidly revealed the stealing of church funds to Alexander. Mdatyulwa noted "things" must be left confidential. He stated that Rev. Mhawn brought no "dollar Money" or the Archbishop's support to Synod and:

> a) The Good Shepherd people paid their dollar money and your support. In addition they elected Mhlakotshane and Nombamba as delegates, but at the station Nombamba was told to go back the money is not enough. It appear that Mhawn and Mtshaisa divided the money between themselves, Nombamba's train fare given by the people as well as the dollar money and Episcopal support. They do not know that these moneys were not reported at Synod . . .[4]

Mdatyulwa's source wanted to know what happened when Mhawn, Mtshaisa and Mhlakotshane attended Synod. Mdatyulwa also noted that Mhawn had taken monies from the Children of Mary's fund[5] and was extremely disrespectful to some members of the congregation when questioned about the monies. Mdatyulwa demanded that action be taken and provided Alexander with two ideas for obtaining the truth: 1) Alexander should write directly to the church warden and request a report of all monies sent to Synod and of the funds in the church's bank account; 2) Alexander should write directly to Mhawn asking for a similar financial report, and if the requested information were not forthcoming, he would be bound to set up a commission of inquiry.[6]

Mdatyulwa's advice bore fruit He gleefully reported to Alexander:

> Nombamba told me how Mhawn got a shock of his life .... I am also keen that Mtshaisa should come to Beaconsfield because I think he is poisonous there .... One of the greatest acts, ... was the typing of the article on church wardens which, unfortunately, is not in our own Canons Book .... Your letter came together with a letter from Nombamba [.] In it he states that they had a Church Council meeting .... Rev. Mhawn opened and proceeded to tell them that the Archbishop gave him authority to keep in his hands all monies. He also informed them that he bad written to the Primate inquiring as to who wrote the letter that exposed all these things . . . further, he took away church warden rights from Nombamba. This moved the whole congregation to anger. . .[7]

Mdatyulwa wanted retribution. He demanded that Mhawn return all church funds and resign; if not, Mhawn should be charged with theft by "conversion." Mdatyulwa agreed with Alexander that what Mhawn got from the Anglicans was priest "wood" and it was only fit for making fire--not priesthood.[8]

But, in mid-March 1948, Mudatyulwa sent a conciliatory note to Mhawn. He asked him not resign but a write a letter of apology and seek a transfer. The change of heart on Mdatyulwa's part may have resulted from serious reflection on the matter and his understanding of Christian forgiveness. Both Alexander and Mdatyulwa could project toughness in making decisions; at the same time, both had the ability to demonstrate genuine compassion for their fellow human beings.[9]

Mdatyalwa waged a constant struggle for the upliftment of his people regardless of denomination Mdatyulwa, like Alexander, embraced as his motto taking the mission of the AOC to the byways and outcasts of South Africa.[10] He concretized this sentiment by fighting for Blacks in the Queenstown location[11] in the early 1950's:

> Our church has been launched at a time when Queenstown is faced with civic disturbances. The council of the town has decided to introduce Pass regulations and to remove a portion of the location and demolish the houses. As these matters have a direct effect on the life of the people, the church cannot be silent and look in the face of injustice and oppression. Your servant here has tried to lift up the voice of the church against these destructive decisions and will continue to do so.[12]

Because of Mdatyulwa's firmness and superior articulation of ideas, Alexander appointed him Organizing and Propaganda Secretary of the AOC in the early 1950s. It was in this capacity that Mdatyulwa came into conflict with Alexander. But it was the conflict around the Masiko affair that consumed so much of Alexander's time and energy. Father Masiko was a former Anglican who became a part of the AOC at the same time as Mdatyulwa. Alexander was full of praise and was content with Masiko's initial work in Kliptown (although Masiko did not submit his reports for two Synods), so Alexander was unprepared for the bombshell which exploded in 1950.

Alexander wrote Herman H. Julia, Chancellor of the AOC, of the dastardly deed that Masiko perpetrated against their group:

> I was sitting in the office last Thursday the Sheriff walked in, and said that he had an order from the Magistrates Court in Johannesburg, to attach anything belonging to the AOC .... as I know the Sheriff, Mr. Harhoff, he told me to go to the solicitor who had got the order and their agents here in Kimberley. Messrs Duncan and Rothman . . . I have written to all members of the Primate's Executive, and have sent them this copy of the New Canons that we must pass at the next Synods.... [13]

Alexander shed further light on Masiko's misdeeds to Samuels Manyali, a priest of Qacha's Nek:

> Masiko started a school in Kliptown, and although money was given by the people to pay the rent, which he never did, the owners of the building tried to get him out, but he refused, so they took him to court, he lost the case, and as he had nothing he gave the address of the Church here in Beaconsfidd, so they got an order, and have come to wire up all our property .... and now we have to pay 325 pounds ... I have written him warning him about the matter, but as he is crooked...[14]

Nothing in the history of the AOC so vexed and disturbed Alexander as the Masiko affair. In his initial discussion with Mdatyulwa on the matter, there was no hint of the conflict to come between them. Alexander stated:

> On page 3 of your letter, we come to the matter of Masiko's debt. You may say that we have gone over it, but you must agree that you are partly to blame for the predicament we found ourselves, because when Archdeacons Hinnings and Mbina, with myself met in your house in Queenstown, before your ordination to the Priesthood we left the documents of the case in your hands, with the promise from you to take care of the matter...[15]

Alexander lamented that he and Mother Alexander had "put all our money, our health and all we had to build up the church...."[16] Now others had simply entered the AOC and reaped the benefits. Alexander complained that he was treated this way because he was viewed as "a black old man...."[17]

Throughout 1950 and 1951, Alexander kept the pressure on concerning the Masiko debt and asked Mdatyulwa to draw up laws to safeguard the church in the future.[18] Mdatyulwa admitted that the Masiko situation was partly his fault but that it was due to his poor health, and he pledged to do more to bring about resolution of the burdensome debt Then on August 14 1951, Mdatyulwa asked Alexander to remain aloof from the petty quarrels of his subordinates and "Pray for us! Don't take offance [!] Pray! As a priest I must implore you to go down on your knees...."[19] On August 22, Mdatyulwa held that in the matter of Masiko's debt, he made repeated appeals and even threats to produce funds to pay the debt. But his pleas had produced no results.

Alexander's furious rebuttal stated that Mdatyulwa's letter of August 14 was most insulting and undeserved. He noted that an attack from an uneducated soul was understandable; however, coming as it did "from one who always shouts about his loyalty...." was a bitter pill. He took Mdatyulwa to task:

> As to the Masiko case, you have the cheek to tell me, that I must not strain myself, mentally or spiritually; it may be nothing to you, because you never sacrificed a penny in the building up of the AOC Church . . . You also say that I am continually quarrelling with my subordinates Yes! to those who are liars . . . honest and conscientious men, . . . find me easy to work with and at Synod you will have to substantiate your accusation....[20]

He told Mdatyulwa that he did not "ordain" him; Alexander felt he was not one "of those fellows who knocks about the street, playing at ministry . . ."[21] Mdatyulwa must have been shaken by Alexander's criticisms. But a few months later, their relationship was back; to normal.[22] Mdatyulwa was busy with his duties at St Cyprian while Alexander was on one of his proselytizing missions. Alexander reported the following incident to Mdatyulwa to show him how the Anglican Church was still maltreating Africans:

> I went to Rev. Mbuto, who is now at Benoni, but he was out and I found his wife she told me they are tired of the Anglicans, and hope to be out; then of the 25th we went again, and found him . . . as he was tired of the church, they are 100 years old, and not one African has made an Archdeacon, or an Assistant Bishop....[23]

By 1954, however, a cloud again gathered over the relationship betw Mdatyulwa and Alexander. Mdatyulwa was brought on moral charges before the AC

Senate which nearly stripped him of his priesthood. Mdatyulwa's remarks vagu detailed the problem:

> I am sorry about it all . . . yet it is not in my make up to be partisan or racialistic .... I am an enemy of such attitudes ... My own concern . . . was to confess my own guilt and plead for merciful handling ....[24]

Mdatyulwa noted that Mbina was very vindictive and tried to destroy him. Mbina's role, however, is not made clear in the church records. Mdatyulwa was aware of the fact that he could have ruined Mbina's career on professional and moral grounds due to Mbina's second marriage which was not performed in the AOC.[25] Much of the vindictiveness of the clergy was from their jealousy of the father/son relationship between Mdatyulwa and Alexander. Mdatyulwa remarked, though not without bitterness, that "This is why this whole affair cut deeper . . . those clergyman who had been envying my position of sonship, who could not understand . . would shout 'There you are! His special darling'!"[26]

Alexander intervened to save Mdatyulwa from expulsion from the AOC. His account of the incident, on the other hand, did not provide much clarity on the charges against Mdatyulwa, but he asked his spiritual son to alter his behavior:

> As you say Mbina could have warned you, but he did not do so, nor warn you that you are treading on dangerous ground, well it is over, but I am extremely sorry . . . my advice to you again is get married, and settle down, you cannot keep going on as formerly, you are breaking your old mother's heart.[27]

The AOC Senate proceedings strengthened the bond between Mdatyulwa and Alexander. Mdatyulwa wanted Alexander to clarify the "Masiko's friends" remark during his tribulations. Alexander suggested that the remark was made to serve notice to those in the AOC who still supported and wanted Masiko to return to the fold. He went on to say that the AOC was not anyone's playbox. Masiko reapplied for admission, but Alexander vowed to bar him forever from his former duties at Orlando, Kliptown and Pimville. The religious activities in these churches sank to a very low level due to Masiko's poor leadership. Alexander noted with some malice that the same condition existed under Mbina's leadership in the Transkei. Alexander was correct in his position that the AOC should have been flourishing in the above areas. Sometimes, due to the smallness of mind or the lust for power of the priest involved, the important work of the AOC was subverted.[28]

Mdatyulwa's death in 1958 caused much grief in Alexander's household. His last brief note to Alexander asked for a Xhosa Hymn and Prayer Book because Mdatyulwa's was so ragged. Alexander paid for the casket and Mbina conducted the service. Mdatyulwa was a likely candidate to succeed Alexander as the next Archbishop; no one else was mentally hardy enough to fill Alexander's demanding shoes. Mdatyulwa was deserving of this responsibility, not only because of his education, but because of the quality of his religious vision. For him, the church was in the vanguard of the struggle to defend the interests of the oppressed. Central to his theology and his understanding of mission was the need to battle the forces of evil, i.e., racism, exploitation and religious chauvinism. He understood that such a battle could not be waged within the cultural and racial confines of the Anglican Church; the alternative was religious separation and spiritual emancipation. The joy and pain Mdatyulwa found within the AOC was part of an ongoing spiritual search for black authenticity and liberation.[29]

Although Mdatyulwa silently endured the verbal abuse Alexander heaped upon him, he no doubt understood it was merited. On the other hand, others within the AOC were not as obedient or as insightful as Mdatyulwa. They thought Alexander was mean and uncaring. But he was harsh only in circumstances which provoked these acid responses. For example, Father Herman H. Julies decided to acquire some property to build a new church in 1955. From the inception of the plan, Alexander informed Julies that the owner of the property was not making a gift to the AOC and that the owner stipulated "that she has two tenants on the premises, and do not want them removed...."[30] Alexander made it clear that the stipulation must be removed if the property were to be purchased.

From 1948 to 1950, Julies begged Alexander for financial or moral support. Alexander informed Julies that his purse was empty. "You must be aware that I have sacrificed my inheritance to build up the AOC church at its infancy. I have nothing at present to give, as I am naked . . ."[31] Several months later, Alexander reinforced his position of not having spare funds by declaring that any extra funds would be used for Mother Alexander--she had lost sight in one of her eyes--because of "all her sacrifices in assisting me in establishing the AO Church.."[32] Morally Alexander supported Julies, but in November 1950, Julies expressed his disappointment with Alexander's lack of support to build a school. Julies now argued that a church would be too expensive and that the Depanment of Education would make some funds available in erecting a school.[33]

Alexander then not only provided moral support, but also provided Julies with authority to borrow money. This turned out to be a foolish move by Alexander, "I want you to realize," Alexander wrote Julies, "that the letter of Authority which I gave . . . is with the understanding that you are responsible for the payment of the loan...."[34] Alexander confessed to Julies that he was aware that many felt he was harsh. Alexander candidly explained that he asked for cash for all transactions and did not extend credit so that amicable relationships would be ensured.[35] Nevertheless, in 1955, Julies and Alexander were at odds. It may be assumed that with Alexander's constant prodding, Julies and his church members were attempting to repay their bank loan. But Julies reneged on the L50.000.00 borrowed from the AOC's treasury, with the promise to pay six percent interest on the loan. Alexander responded with characteristic bluntness. He wanted the church's money back.

Julies' cry was that pressure of work: prevented him from communicating with Alexander sooner, and he was making every effort to repay the L50.000.00. Alexander revealed two years later that Julies had defaulted on the loan in Cape Town; the bank loan and money from the church fund remained unpaid. He stated that in a letter from Messieurs Hogan-Fleming and Company that they obtained a written letter from the Court to take AOC property. Alexander admitted that

Hogan and Company were correct in their assessment of Julies: "That a man in your position in the church whose words cannot be trusted, is not worthy to hold any responsible position such trustee or archdeacon or otherwise."[36] Harsh comments, but comments which were provoked by Julies dishonesty and, therefore, deserved.

For nearly ten years and after many headaches for Alexander, the struggle to make his clergy responsible continued; however, his new Bishop-Elect, Motsepe, was a responsible and skillful man. His entrance into the church in 1959 was marked by his energy and desire to make the AOC a greater institution, so Alexander stressed to him the importance of education for the clergy:

> My dear Bishop when you are holding your Synod at Orlando . . . impress upon your clergy . . . to be ordained . . . the offices . . . some will have to be relinquished and others to be examined . . . some of them will not agree . . . the Government: is very determined to see that all clergy is capable and educated, and so is the church....[37]

Motsepe also was of the opinion that an educated clergy was needed to move the work of the AOC forward. He suggested that the quality of membership was more important than quantity. This reference was made in regards to the Ethiopian Catholic Church in Zion, which Motsepe was amalgamating into the AOC. Motsepe admitted to Alexander that some of his clergy were not qualified and they must work to "make a thorough overhall [sic] of the staff...."[38]

A few days later, however, Alexander suggested to Motsepe that all illiterate priests with only a standard 2 education were of better service to the church than many of the educated.[39]

The relationship between Alexander and Motsepe was very cordial. Any small task that Alexander needed accomplished Motsepe performed For example, Alexander asked Motsepe for a list of recognized churches in the Transvaal. Motsepe worked diligently until he produced it. Concerning that list, Alexander noted that no Ethiopian Church was named and he thought that strange since it was purported that they were strong in that area.[40]

Motsepe's stature in the AOC received an enormous boost when he became the Marriage Officer for the entire Transvaal.[41] Alexander felt that Motsepe was more than qualified to oversee the expansion of the AOC there. Motsepe was also quite pleased to receive his railway concession card which gave him reduced travel rates. If there were any problems between him and Alexander, it was far too late for Motsepe to have qualms of conscience. On October 29, 1959, Motsepe's church and property were transferred to the AOC:

> We therefore make it known that the church formerly known as the Ethiopian Catholic Church; has handed all their rights, assets and property movable and immovable to the care of the Provincial trustees of the A.O.C., ... that I Surgeon Lennon Simeon Motsepe formerly the Archbishop of said Church has entered the said AOC, with all my clergy....[42]

In the AOC's negotiations with other separatist churches, Motsepe was also in the final stages of bringing the Eastern Bantu Methodist Church (EBMC) into the AOC. In a special meeting between the AOC and EBMC officials, Motsepe conveyed to the group the events that had transpired between them during the last two years. Motsepe noted that EBMC group urgently wanted official recognition and was willing to pay fifty pounds for the service. AOC guidelines prevented such dealings and Alexander would not give his blessings to the transaction. Of course, Motsepe informed the group that the transaction must be done correctly so that misunderstandings would not generate ill feelings. The EBMC was allowed to woship as they wished, and after three years of probation, the AOC would recommend them for recognition. On the other hand, Motsepe outlined what the AOC expected for their support: the AOC annually taxed each minister 3.0.6 pounds and expected the same of the EBMC. The AOC would also provide other amenities such as sacramental wine, confession certificates and marriage certificates.[43]

The Rev. Khoza provided a brief history of the EBMC, which was founded in 1944 and he highlighted the financial assets of his church.[44] Rev. Khoza was pleased with all that was stated, but was unable to finalize the arrangements until he obtained approval from their church authorities after their conference.[45] Consequently, in November 1959, the Witbank group was willing to enter the AOC. Motsepe reported the following to Alexander:

> I am writing from Witbank where I arrived yesterday . . . to meet the President of the E.B.M.C.... The meeting was a good one ... an agreement that they all become members of the AOC and hold credentials there of . . . we were careful . . . we don't commit ourselves nor the church . . . agreed to all our suggestion . confirmed their offer again to pay the Archbishop's sopport . . . 50.0.0 pounds per year . . . father let us give this matter a trial of 3 years. Send to me their credentials and they are ours . . . This very building in Witbank will be ours and I told them a reception should be given for the Archbishop....[46]

Thus, the EBMC was absorbed into the AOC.

Meanwhile, in Cape Town, Mbina was adjusting to the new environment since his tansfer from Pondoland. He met his congregation in 1953 and was quite pleased with the Easter service. Alexander informed Mbina that "the African Orthodox Church was organized in Cape Town some time in 1932 by Mr. Arthur Maits, then a member of the St. Augustine Pro-Cathedral . . . he had gone to Cape Town, and started a Sunday School amongst the coloured children...."[47] In similar respect, Mbina, like Maits, was also a pioneer in building a second church under the leadership of an African priest.

Mbina's work progressed with its share of minor problems. He had to apply to the authorities for a housing permit, then to another agency to bring his family to Cape Town and acquire proper documentation to build the new church. All the transactions were completed, but not without applications being lost and new ones submitted. These problems Mbina expected, but on the other hand, he raised his concern that a "colour bar" existed within the AOC. He stated in 1955:

> Re: The Good Shepherd Mission when I first went to East London for the funeral of the late Ven. Arch. W. Alexander, I noticed that the two Parishes were so close together not even a mile apart; personally I do not like it; it seemed as though to some people it would give an impression that the

> AOC has colour bar one would say in East London, African and coloured people are not united; why should there be two porishes in one location . . each of these has not even got 50 communicants . . . today I thank God that this has come to our Primate that the Parish should be one under one Priest in East London .....[48]

Mbina may have stated to Alexander at the funeral of Alexander's son that two parishes in close proximity disturbed him. Mbina mailed this letter as a follow up ploy to reinforce his displeasure and, in addition, to provide some pressure to ensure that Alexander dealt with the problem. Although Alexander proclaimed he was black and that race prejudice was anathema to him, it was notable that he did not respond in writing concerning the issue of the color bar. Of course, coloureds were not considered African, and many sought to maintain their status by claming European ancestry. Mbina had raised an ugly part of South Africa's life within the AOC. Alexander, identified as coloured by the system, should have dealt with the issue in a forthright way to maintain his integrity and Christian brotherhood. If Alexander did not face the challenge openly, then he failed spiritually and for the second time in his long life, he refused to deal with racism in the AOC.

Alexander's lapse on the color bar matter was not as great as Mbina's lack of moral certitude. Nonetheless, he complained loudly to Alexander regarding the disgraceful behavior of some young women within the AOC:

> Your Grace, I do not want to tell the awful things I discovered in East London, . . . because you are busy with church concerns . . . St. Barnabas is full of [uneducated] women, I mean women with no respect, I have no words to describe them . . . Moreover, there are even girls in this case, young girls prepared to speak rude), against a priest about fornication.....[49]

Poor moral actions! This was the great weakness of Mbina. Alexander complained to Motsepe that he was weary of sending Mbina money to fix his decrepit car and ". . . then they continually overload it with unnecessary women . . ..."[50] On another occasion, Alexander remarked that Mbina desired every well-dressed woman he saw. Mbina married a second wife knowing that she had not received legal separation from her husband. Besides all of this, Mbina even attempted to destroy the career of Mdatyulwa. Flawed as he was, Mbina was still loyal to Alexander and was still committed to spring the mission of the AOC.

Alexander needed Mbina's loyalty to accomplish several small but meaningful tasks. For example, when Archpriest Manyali was in the hospital in Qacha's Nek, Alexander asked Mbina to write a strong letter to Father Makhoabane to visit his Archpriest. Then, too, Alexander wanted Mbina to inform the Ethiopian Order the reason Somerset, a priest, left the AOC and to inform them of the 'type' of man they were to receive into their congregation; one who refused to pay his debts.[52]

In 1960, Mbina, along with Alexander and Motsepe, made plans for the visit of the Patriarch to South Africa. Alexander informed Mbina of the a good news of the merger between the AOC and the Eastern Bantu Methodist Church Alexander stated that although the group was on a three-year probationary period, he expected to absorb all their ministers and property. Such good tidings of 1960 had, by late 1961 turned sour for Alexander. As American and South African officials demanded that he abdicate the chair as Archbishop and Primate of the African Province.

Alexander refused to leave the AOC, and a bitter struggle commenced over the control of the organization. It is this conflict and schism that is explored in the next chapter.

Endnotes

1. Letter from Mdatyulwa to DWA, 21 November 1946 (Box-8, Folder-94, DWA Papers).

2. *Ibid.*

3. Letter from Mdatyulwa to DWA, 22 December 1947 (Box-8, Folder-94, DWA Papers).

4. Letter from Mdatyulwa to DWA, 19 January 1949 (Box-8, Folder-94, DWA Papers).

5. *Ibid.*

6. *Ibid.*

7. Letter from Mdatyulwa to DWA, 9 February 1949 (Box-8, Folder-94, DWA Papers)

8. Letter from Mdatyulwa to DWA, 23 February 1949 (Box-8, Folder-94, DWA Papers).

9. Later from Mdatyulwa to DWA, 19 Demmber 1949 (Box-8, Folder-94, DWA Papers).

10. Letter from Mdalyulwa to DWA, ca 1949 (Box-8, Folder-94, DWA Papers).

11. The 1950's was a period of increased urbanization for Africans which produced intra-African conflicts, as well as a housing shortage. This shortage meant that many Black families lived in squalid conditions.

12. Letter from DWA to Herman H. Julies, 19 June l950 (Box-8, Folder-86, DWA Papers).

13. Letter from DWA to Samuels Manyali, 19 June 1950 (Box-8, Folder-90, DWA Papers).

14. Letter from DWA to Mdatyulwa, ca 1949 or 1950 (Box-8, Folder 94, DWA Papers)

15. *Ibid.*

16. *Ibid.*

17. Letter from DWA to Mdatyulwa, 17 June 1950 (Box-8, Folder-94, DWA Papers).

18. Letter from Mdatyulwa to DWA, 14 August 195I (Box-8, Folder-94, DWA Papers).

19. Letter from DWA to Mdatyulwa, 18 September 195I (Box-8, Folder-94, DWA Papers).

20. *Ibid.*

21. *Ibid.*

22. Alexander sometime invited many of the conflicts within the church by his inconsistent enforcement of rules and regulations. Some priests were allowed to return to the AOC who clearly should have been barred. However, Mdatyulwa was one of his loyal supporters and therefore deserving of gaining reentrance into the church.

23. Letter from DWA to Mdatyulwa, 1 March 1952 (Box-8, Folder-94, DWA Papers).

24. Letter from Mdatyulwa to DWA, 2 November 1954 (Box-8, Folder-94, DWA Papers).

25. *Ibid.*

26. *Ibid.*

27. Lettter from DWA to Mdatyulwa, 5 November 1954 (Box-8, Folder-94, DWA Papers)

28. *Ibid.*

29. It should be noted that Mdatyulwa was working on a major manuscript of the history of the AOC.

30. Letter from DWA to Julies, 14 March 1948 (Box-8, Folder-86, DWA Papers).

31. *Ibid.*

32. Letter from DWA to Julies, 22 November 1950 (Box-8, Folder-86, DWA Papers).

33. Letter from Julies to DWA, 18 November 1950 (Box-8, Folder-86, DWA Papers).

34. Letter from DWA to Julies, 30 November 1950 (Box-8, Folder-86, DWA Papers).

35. Ibid.

36. Letter from DWA to Julies, 22 June 1957 (Box-8, Folder-86, DWA Papers).

37. Letter from DWA to Motscpc, ll September 1959 (Box-9, Fo der-96, DWA Papers).

38. Letter from Motsepe to DWA, 22 September 1959 (Box-9 Folder-96, DWA Papers).

39. Letter from DWA to Mosepe, 24 September 1959 (Box-9, Folder-96, DWA Papers).

40. Letter from DWA to Motsepe, 2 September 1959 (Box-9, Folder-96, DWA Papers).

41. Letter from DWA to Motsepe, October 1959 (Box-9, Folder-96, DWA Papers).

42. Letter of transfer of Church property, 20 October 1959 (Box-9, Folder-96, DWA Papers).

43. Special Committee Meeting (Eastern Bantu Methodist Church), 24 October 1959 (Box-9, Folder-96, DWA Papers).

44. *Ibid.*

45. *Ibid.*

46. Letter from Motsepe to DWA, 15 November 1959 (Box-9, Folder-96, DWA Papers).

47. Letter from DWA to Mbina, 4 September 1953 (Box-8, Folder-92, DWA Papers).

48. Letter from Mbina to DWA, 2 April 1955 (Box-8, Folder-92, DWA Papers).

49. Letter from Mbina to DWA, 2 April 1955 (Box-8, Folder-92, DWA Papers).

50. Letter from DWA to Motsepe, 23 October 1959 (Box-9, Folder-96 DWA Papers).

51. Letter from DWA to Mbina, 26 November 1959 (Box-8, Folder-92, DWA Papers).

52. *Ibid.*

53. Special Committee Meeting, *op, cit.* (Box-9, Folder 96, DWA. Papers). The Eastern Bantu Methodist Church was financially more secure than the AOC. Both Motsepe and Alexander shared an eagerness to acquire the EBMC properties. The AOC added at least four churches, a farm, a school and 13 ministers as a result of the merger.

CHAPTER 7
SCHISM AND INDEPENDENCE WITHIN THE AOC

Since Alexander's visit to the U. S. in 1927, his ties with the AOC in America had been maintained through correspondence. In 1960, two American AOC leaders visited South Africa, but instead of solidifying bonds between the two branches of the church, their visit set off a major internal dispute within the South African AOC and eventually led Alexander to form his own church separate from the American AOC.

This conflict, however, was not on the horizon when Alexander convened the 1959 Synod. He raised the issue of bringing the American Patriarch James I to visit South Africa to consecrate new bishops. The Patriarch was ready to make the trip, but according to South African law, he needed a written invitation. This formality and the lack of a carefully planned itinerary delayed his visit until June 1960.

During this period, Motsepe became an integral part of Alexander's team. Alexander nominated Motsepe to be Bishop of the Diocoese of Transvaal and Mbina as auxiliary bishop. As had happened all during Alexander's experience with the AOC, the South African church did not have funds to entertain the Patriarch and his Primate as they would have wished. The guests paid almost all of their expenses themselves. The small amount Mbina borrowed became another of the financial problems for the church, as they were unable to repay the money on demand.

Whatever the financial burden, Alexander was enthusiastic about James I's visit. He addressed his people:

> I am sure that everyone of you here would like to kiss his Beatitude's ring. I personally would like to do so since it is a long time [since] I did it in America, and I again I [sic] nominated him to the Patriarchal throne when I was in Kenya. Negroes in America speak of Africa with sincerity more than the South Africans.[1]

Motsepe and Alexander devoted their attention to the Patriarch's visit. Alexander was disappointed that certain arrangements had not been made for the Patriarch and Archbishop Robinson.[2] Motsepe replied that plans had not materialized because the parochial councils had not agreed on the dates to entertain the Patriarch. Alexander wearily responded, "my plea was all in vain . . . give into them so that we can blame them tomorrow....."[3] In early January 1960, Alexander was still unable to provide Motsepe with a definite date for the arrival of Patriarch James I.[4]

The AOC's pride in seeing Patriarch James I and Archbishop Grant Robinson, Primate of the American Province, on South African soil was evident when they finally arrived in Kimberley on June 25, 1960, to see firsthand AOC operations in South Africa and to aid in the consecration of Mbina and Motsepe as bishops.[5] When Motsepe entered the AOC fold in June 1959, Alexander nominated him to be bishop of the Diocese of Transvaal and Mbina as auxiliary bishop. Alexander later noted that be informed the Patriarch of his desire for the two to be nominated since he believed they were truly qualified.

Alexander also remarked that there were others who were not worthy of elevation. He had promised the late Patriarch McGuire never to consecrate any bishop without McGuire's consent. But Alexander confessed that temptations had been placed before him by ministers, some of whom were European, who had offered him money to consecrate them as bishops. Alexander had stood firm against these temptations, and now James I was on African soil to elevate rightfully those whom Alexander deemed worthy of such an honor.[6]

Although Mbina was embarrassed by the lack of funds to entertain the church dignitaries from America, he and the American fathers travelled to Cape Town, Pretoria and Springs, using funds from the Patriarch McGuire's pocket. Alexander instructed Mbina to borrow money whenever possible, assuring him that the Synod would assume financial responsibility. But the Patriarch and Primate Grant covered all but L19.5 of their costs. Despite reassurances to creditors that they would be repaid, creditors threatened legal action to recover the remainder. No documents exist to show how this matter was resolved.

Several other controveries erupted that demanded the intervention of James I and Primate Grant during their brief South African sojourn. For instance, infighting between Mbina and one of his coloured priests, Rulash, led to threats by them to sue each other. This infighting spread to an attack on Alexander. Motsepe accused him of wrongdoings; therefore, the Archbishop threatened to seek a legal course of action.[7] This prompted Archbishop Grant to state that the church did not permit its members to sue each other. He reasoned that, according to Canon Law, no patriarch, primate or bishop could encroach upon another's jurisdiction.

Patriarch James I also expressed the need for the word "Kaffir" to be defined during Synod (1960). This was because a coloured priest had used "Kaffir" to refer to Blacks within the AOC. Alexander commented that it was an Arabic word meaning one who does not "believe" The Patriarch had not been aware of its pejorative connotation, but he argued that such language should never have been uttered by a Christian and that apartheid should not be exercised in the Church of Christ.[8] The Patriarch also regretted that there were those who did not want to mix socially with their black brothers.[9]

On 19 October 1960, the Synod questioned the cost of the Patriarch's visit. Alexander had not found it necessary to keep a detailed account of expenditures, although Mbina had collected nearly L100 to defray the costs.

This controversy disintegrated into Alexander demanding Bishop Motsepe to pay L5 for the consecration certificate and L30 for "entertainment" for the Patriarch. In addition, Mbina said Rev. Palmer sent Alexander L10, but the records showed L5. All of this led to an expanded debate concerning the accountability of church funds.

At Synod, Patriarch James I was incensed to discover that money had been contributed towards his trip. He used L10 of his own money to pay a portion of his medical expenses; nevertheless a balance remained. Shortly thereafter, the Patriarch's entourage went to Cape Town and paid most of their own expenses Motsepe and the Patriarch paid for the Patriarch's trip to Rhodesia. In regards to money matters, the Patriarch highlighted America's role for such an expensive visit:

> General Synod in the USA did not raise $4,000 for a social visit. From 1927, since the consecration of the Primate of S. Africa, the General Synod wanted to know what is going on with the church in Africa. We are to give a full report when we return to America. The Conclave of Bishops will receive our report. The full report will be made on the 9th of May, 1961.[10]

On 16 May the Patriarch stated that he only provided money to Archbishop Alexander because the archbishop told him that his church body contributed very little to his economic well-being.[11]

Alexander did not help matters; indeed, he provided additional ammunition to be used against him by purchasing an automobile in the late 1950's, which he claimed was for general church use. [12] The question of Alexander's authority, thus, became entangled in this "crisis." The car's purpose became an issue because several new outstations opened, and the car facilitated Alexander's contacts with his congregations.

On 21 October, the matter of the Primate's car surfaced because Mr. Eden, the ear dealer, wanted "to square up all debts...."[13] In response to Bishop Motsepe's inquiry, Bishop Mbina emphatically stated that the church owned the property and that the car was not Alexander's personal vehicle.

The issue of funds refused to disappear. Points and counterpoints were raised concerning accountability, the Patriarch's funds, and how monies should be reported and disbursed. No other Synod in the history of the AOC devoted so much time and energy to the issue of funds.

At the Patriarch's request, a special committee was formed to explore the purchase of the car. Were the newly elected Bishops, Motsepe and Mbina, deliberately undermining Alexander's authority? Alexander produced a receipt; however, it "did not exactly mean that the ear belongs to the church."[14] Mbuna also produced a letter from Alexander, which asked each clergyman to donate L20 towards purchasing the car.

Archbishop Grant, on the other hand, suggested that a delegation go to Mr. Eden and inform him that the car belonged to the church. Grant raised a very pertinent question: "Did the Provincial synod buy the car for the use of the Primate but belonging to the African Orthodox Church?"[15]

The Patriarch was also concerned with what was in the chunch records on the issue. The secretary then read from the church minute book that the car was not the private possession of Archbishop Alexander:

> Although this car is registered in Archbishop Alexander's name, it is for the church and then we feel proud about it. It is our car, not Archbishop's.[16]

With the ownership of the car settled, the Synod promised to make payments for the months of October and November.

The car incident caused church members and officials to focus on other aspects of Alexander's financial dealings. Mother Mbina, head of the special committee during the 1960 Synod, was delegated to "investigate" matters of Alexander's entire administration of the church. Of particular interest to church officials, including the Americans, was how Alexander spent money on a day-to-day basis. However, she reported that Alexander stated there were no old bank books because when Alexander traveled to Kenya during the 1930's, he left all of the church's property in his office. Upon his return, he discovered that the office had been broken into and all documents, with the exception of a few books, had been destroyed. Alexander, of course, may have kept some of the "destroyed" documents.[50] It seemed farfetched that from 1949-1959, Alexander did not have in his possession any financial documents.

Several months after the American Prelates left South Africa in late 1960, the AOC exploded in conflict and turmoil. Alexander proceeded to let Motsepe know his feelings concerning the mischief he believed the African American Prelates had caused:

> I am . . . writing . . . to let you know that since you and the American Prelates have left Kimberley, I have received two letters, one from Archbishop Richard Grant, Primate of the American Province, and a supposed to be Bull from the Patriarch James the First, suspending me from all my work as Archbishop and Primate of the African Province....[18]

At the 1961 Synod, however, it was apparent that Alexander and the new bishops of the church were on a collision path. The collision occurred at the 1961 AOC Synod when Alexander contended that some of the questions raised about church finances were part of an effort to oust him as Archbishop. Alexander charged that after the consecration of Mbina and Motsepe, the Patriarch and Archbishop Grant gathered news about him that was untrue and "unbecoming [of] men in their position."[19] To make matters worse, the Patriarch reduced the size of Alexander's Province and left him with "only you [church members attending Synod] present here today."[51] Rhodesia, Basutoland and parts of South Africa had been parceled out to Mbina and Motsepe.

Because the American group favored Mbina and Motsepe, Alexander questioned their loyalty. He judged that there were "some" who took the "Oath of Canonical Obodience", but at "the first opportunity they skipped away" and refused to be responsible for the debts which they had assisted in making and agreed to help pay.[21]

Alexander stated that Mbina and Motsepe "was [were] made to ask a lot of unnecessary questions."[22] Alexander remarked that Mbina was also with the "mob" against him. From Alexander's perspective, the questions and demands for information were a frame-up to undermine his authority. What astonished him most was that James I demanded all annual church reports from 1927 to 1960. Alexander stated fifty copies of the annual report were posted to America in 1958; yet, the American officials maintained they never received the report. Alexander refused to provide replacement documents to the Patriarch. After Alexander left

Synod, Mbina, as vice-chairman of church Affairs, allowed the "mob" to do whatever they desired because he was the chief instigator against Alexander.[23]

Alexander stated to Mbina that since the American Prelates used a lawyer to suspend him, he, in turn, had acquired a lawyer and was determined to fight the matter in court. He told Mbina that the Americans possessed no authority to enter his province and take control since all of his documents were in order as legitimized by the late Patriarch McGuire. Alexander wanted to know why Motsepe asked Mbina not to provide him with money and church documents. Another priest of the church, Sikwebu, also apprised Alexander that Motsepe had asked him not to provide information to Alexander.[24]

It must be noted that from the early stages of the conflict, Motsepe had cast his fortune with the Americans and had advised them on Alexander's shortcomings. Mbina, however, had remained firmly loyal to Alexander and had urged him to take bold action:

> We there came to a conclusion that we of this Diocese should leave the AOC and form the Holy Orthodox Church and we have a membership of more than 2,000 . . . we can strive for recognition. If we fail we shall join any recognized African Church that has Catholicism. I . . . have asked you often to call together the Bishop and Clergy . . . but you failed . . . that we make ourselves a Church and free ourselves from the Americans....'[25]

This bitter altercation placed Alexander and the American prelates on an irreconcilable collision path which opened the door for a separate and independent church free from American control. This was indeed a dangerous road because it meant schism. Alexander was bound by his vows of obedience to accept without question the directives of the Patriarch, but he did not The contumaciousness of Alexander, in part, stemmed from the prelates using an attorney to oust him. This removed the conflict from the religious realm and placed it before civil authorities.

By the end of November 1961, Mbina urged Alexander to convene a special Provincial Synod in early 1962 to resolve the problems they faced. To Mbina, the only solution was "to break away from the Negroes and be governed in Africa ...."[26] He reaffirmed his support for Alexander:

> In your letter you mentioned that let's be close together. This Diocese and myself never thought of separating from you . . . We still really regard you as our Archbishop and Primate so your Eminence never worry about this side....[27]

Alexander took Mbina's advice because he convened a special Synod in December 1961. At that special convocation, Alexander was elected head of the AOC of South Africa. He informed Mbina in late 1961 or early 1962 that:

> We must fight this matter to the end, my lawyer has told me that I get in touch with one of the Nationalist members of Parliament, and explain the whole matter to him.... I personally will fight to get free of those Americans, I want to have nothing to do with them any more . . . I wonder what all those ministers will be doing now that Motsepe has passed away, especially Libham, Matthee, Sikwebu.[28]

Motsepe's death in late 1961 radically altered the nature of the struggle because no bishop was now pitted against Alexander. The plot to dethrone Alexander ground to a halt. In early 1962, Patriarch James I also died, and he was succeeded by Patriarch Peter IV who was open to reconciliation with Alexander.[29]

However, in April 1963, Mbina reported to Alexander that he was irked because Patriarch Peter IV had written several letters to priests in his bishopric. Mbina did not give a reason for the interference, although he had warned Peter IV on several occasions to write only to bishops. He laid out a general plan for restoring Alexander and outmanuevering Peter IV by convening a special provincial meeting after the consecration of three new bishops.[30] Moreover, in October 1963, twenty one clergymen were chosen to address the Patriarch and inform him to:

> leave us in the continent with an independent church that was given by the late Patriarch Dr. McGuire to Archbishop Alexander for Africa. The church in Africa must have her own Patriarch like the Russian Orthodox Church where there are many Patriarchs . . . The church in Africa has a Primate in Ghana what then of South Africa and Rhodesia ? [31]

The above letter does not indicate how the twenty-one ministers were chosen.

Mbina revealed to Alexander that the clergy was ready to force the Patriarch to meet its demands. Although Peter IV was willing to offer the rank of Patriarchal Vicar to Mbina, Mbina was adamant that the only rank which would meet his approval was for Alexander to become Patriarch of Africa. Mbina noted again that Alexander must do his part in the struggle:

> How will all these come through if you are standing outside the church allowing the trick of these young Rev. Tsotsi [gangsters] to hinder you from being restored? Do you think that your enemies who pretended to be your best friends while you were in good standing in the church, wish that you be restored? Julies, Ackrman, Motsepe, Matthee and many others are now the people who will write to the Patriarch fighting that you should not get your restoration.... I have been given the rank of being Patriarchal Legate. I know that in other words I am his errand boy.... [32]

Part of Mbina's strategy was to silence the bishops during the special gathering; only the clergy would present demands because Mbina knew that if the bishops led the charge for the radical demands, they would risk being excommunicated. Mbina urged Alexander, therefore, to submit all reports, provide a complete financial accounting (even if he spent some monies for his personal use) and forward McGuire's documents which affirmed the independence of the African church.

Alexander was prepared to put Mbina's plan into action. He informed Mbina that he would humble himself and imitate Christ to ensure the AOC's survival. He laid out his plan to Mbina:

> On Easter Monday I will sit and write out my reports for 1961-2. The 1960's report was taken by the date Patriarch and his Chancellor; then I will have to have the documents that were compiled by my attorney duplicated, so that I can send you two or three copies. I do fully realize that one cannot fight from the outside... All those whom you have named are my enemies. The deeper I read into your letter the more ashamed you make me.... From what the Patriarch writes, I am glad that he realizes that I brought the African Orthodox Church to Mother Africa. One of the biggest mistakes I made was when I took Motsepe into the Church, without consulting you others of the Senate ... Although I am advanced in age, God has kept me until this day. I am glad to see that the patriarch Peter IV has a more Christian [attitude] than James I...[33]

The generosity of the new Patriarch, nonetheless, required that Alexander provide "an accounting of the church finances and properties entrusted to him ...." and that he "must serve his probationary period of time before . . ."[34] Alexander could be elevated again to a high position within the church.

Peter IV acknowledged that Alexander was responsible for bringing the Episcopate to Africa and that he was due compassion because of his advanced age. However, the American Patriarch raised the need for the possibility of two Primates for the Motherland. Peter IV stated:

> your apartheid laws are now strictly enforcing the ethnical division of races. Since he [Alexander] is coloured, then he can only administer to coloured members of our churches in South Africa. This will leave us free to appointing another to lead the Bantus....[35]

Mbina shared Peter IV's letter with Alexander. It may be assumed that Alexander did not treat the idea lightly of confining his leadership within the church to coloureds only. But he was still eager to complete all the necessary documents for healing the deep divisions within the AOC.

However, over the next several months, the relationship between Mbina, the AOC in America and Alexander fell apart altogether. In November 1963, Alexander's reacted hostilely to Mbina's letter of the month before, pleading for general information and urging Alexander to forward all reports to the AOC authorities in America.[36] Alexander, however, absolutely refused to take the olive branch from Mbina. The heated response to Mbina was signed by Jacobus Alexander, Alexander's grandson; however, the letter was written in Alexander's distinctive handwriting. Alexander queried Mbina

> we want nothing to do with the Americans, as to the church, we are busy with its building up (1) you ask me about . . . Rev. Mphomane . . . don't you think it would be wise for you to write to him . . . (2) why should we send you all particular of what we are doing, are you acting the part of a patriarch? (3) . . . our constitution, why must we send you a draft thereof, are you the government? . . . According to competent legal opinion, we are still within our rights for refusing to give these reports, from 1927 to 1959, and it is only that competent advice that we have formed our church . . . The Primate asks when are you going to repay his L 7....[37]

Nearly forty years earlier, Alexander's consecration in Boston had conveyed a powerful message: there existed only one Holy Catholic Apostolic Church and schism was anathema to all true believers. Alexander understood the path on which he had now embarked. He had long preached that the AOC was not a "tribal" church and that the survival of the AOC should not hinge upon any one individual. He felt he had no other choice but to defy the American bishops and establish an independent church in South Africa.

Before Alexander took those final steps for independence, a bewildering set of claims and counter claims emerged over who was the AOC's legitimate leader. Mbina informed Alexander in early 1963 that Maqanda, a priest, had stated to the local government authorities in Port Elizabeth that S. S. Mphomane was the AOC's head. Mbina went on to say that he terminated Mphomane's office as Administrator pro tem on 5 February 1963 and officially stopped all of Mphomane's activities within the AOC. The confusion mounted when Mphomane ousted Lennox D. Duma Sibham as Rector in charge of the church in New Brighton (Port Elizabeth). Alexander was dismayed when he was informed about this action by Mbina.

Ironically, in early 1964, Mphomane who claimed a separate source of independence, again sought shelter under Alexander's control. Alexander informed him "I am also glad that you have found out the unreliability of those Americans."[38] Alexander observed that he forwarded copies of Mphomane's letter to members of the Church's Executive Committee to consider Mphomane's appeal. By 1967, however, he and Alexander were locked in a court battle.[39] Mphomane contesting that Alexander had no authority over him and that the excommunication by the Port Elizabeth Conference, is inconsistent with the constitution of this church and is invalid, void ... of no effect...."[40] It may be reasonable to conclude that Mphomane re entered the AOC under Alexander's control; however, when events turned sour for Mphomane, he initiated a law suit to block Alexander's ex-communication order.[41]

This ex-communication only magnified the authentic leadership question within the church. In early 1964 there were several leaders claiming AOC authority: Alexander, Mphomane, and Sibham. Moreover, Mbina moved to oust Maganda, a priest, as part of the ongoing struggle to determine who was the legitimate head of the church. Alexander then dropped the bombshell that Mbina had been ex-communicated by the American Prelates;[42] at least four centers of AOC autonomy existed. The reason for Mbina being ousted by the Americans was not provided; however, by late 1963, Alexander rejected the olive branch from the Americans via Mbina. What conditions or events that precipitated Alexander's refusal may never be known; all the partcipating actors provided no clues.

In retrospect, the history of the AOC would have been quite different if Alexander had made a second journey to America. He had great plans to take Mbina and Motsepe to America for their consecration, but the sharp 75% rise in the cost of steamship tickets from Cape Town to Southampton derailed their plans. Another obstacle to his plans was that some of his congregations which premised to support the venture "had not contributed a penny up to now .... "[43] The result of his failed plan (1963-1964) was the conflict that forced Alexander to establish a new division of the AOC completely under his control.

The new division was launched after a visit to the Minister of the Interior:

> We got in contact with Dr. D. L. Venter, M. P., for Kimberley South, who got in contact with Dr. De Klerk, Minister for the Interior, who through his Secretary advised us that he could do nothing for us; the law stood at present; but if we changed the name by adding or deleting, something could be done....[44]

Based on that advice, Alexander added "province Republic of South Africa" to the name of his division.

John Kemm of the Council for Coloured Affairs helped to facilitate government recognition for Alexander's new church. Kemm related the Archbishop's plight to Bosman, the Secretary for Coloured Affairs, who provided Alexander with legal advice via the Coloured Affairs barrister and advised him to have an appointment with De Jager of the Coloured Affairs Office.

In July 1964, Alexander met De Jager who examined him concerning the history of the AOC. Alexander revealed that there were fourteen churches under his authority and that he was elected Primate of the new group in 1961 at Synod.[52] Alexander noted that De Jager wished him well at the end of their meeting and forwarded all necessary documents to Pretoria. Alexander was appointed the Marriage Officer for South Africa with the power to solemnize marriage between all non- Europeans.[46]

Despite his new appointment as a Marriage Officer and the province of South African division being firmly in place, Alexander still resented his ouster from the American AOC. He noted when James I and Archbishop Grant applied to extend their visas a second time (1960), they were refused and "asked to leave the country. . ."[47] In addition, Alexander charged that the bishops in America were "yes-men" of the Patriarch; however, when the bishops voted and found him not guilty of insubordination, it could be that they were independent of the thinking of James I.

Alexander's leadership problems did not sap his capacity to work the last five years before his death. His life contained hope and pathos. His most heart wrenching experience was the forced removal of Alexander and his church from Beaconsfield. The Group Areas Act, which he deemed a monster, made his most terrifying nightmare a reality. In 1968, he provided this tragic assessment:

> Yes! It will be a wrench from the usual as I have lived here [for] 45 years, but the laws of the land demands that separate development should be implemented, and I am willing to move for all the people of the church are living there in the floors, Homestead, Homevale. And the time has come when I must follow them ...[48]

Alexander eventually made his new home in Colville, a coloured township.[53] He commenced building a new Cathedral of St. Augustine of Hippo. A very generous donation of 500 Rand from De Beers greatly assisted him in erecting the new structure [50] His capacity for work then was only slightly reduced by the move to Colville although he was in his early 80's. He related to Rev. Sikwebu that I am not of [100] % 00, as I have been too busy during this festival session...[51]

The great leap forward by Alexander in building construction was aided by his clergy, consequently, he urged them to be responsible and to honor all promises. Particularly disturbing to him was the lackluster performance of his new Bishops. He noted that Maqanda and Sikwebu were elevated to help ease the burden of the church duties, not to make the burden heavier. He warned that they would not be consecrated until they built their cathedrals. He reasoned that when his wife was sick, he had acquired two churches, and he expected no less from his Bishops Elect. He refused to allow the "bishops to carry out their Episcopal duties in homes..."[54] He also admonished them not to recommend uneducated men for the ministry. He declared that he and the chaplain determined who entered the ministry. It must be noted that Alexander was invariably taking back straying ministers into the church. This character trait hampered the proper administration of the church.

The problems Alexander was now experiencing were more serious because he was in the final years of his life and a successor was not on the horizon to provide for continued church growth. Far too many of Alexander's priests were flawed. For example, Jacobus Alexander informed his grandfather that rude and high-minded ministers should be kicked out of the AOC.[53] Jacobus Alexander found the behavior of the Rev. Nombamba especially obnoxious. There were others such as Arendse, Post and Sikwebu who were thorns in Alexander's side.

Sikwebu's actions were particularly revealing. Alexander had elevated Sikwebu to the rank of Bishop-Elect. Such a position required faithfulness to the Archbishop and to the constitution of the AOC. Sikwebu told Alexander "that a half-a-loaf is better than no bread...."[54] Sikwebu opined that Alexander should be content with the few dollars he received from the clergy rather than face penury. But Bishop-Elect Sikwebu's sense of responsibility as a leader of the AOC should have dictated a greater concern for Alexander's welfare; and he should have been diligent in encouraging others to provide the necessary monies for the archbishop's stipend.

Jacobus Alexander was not saddened by the departure of the caliber of such men as Maganda and Sikwebu. Jacobus felt that unruly clergy who returned to the fold of the AOC might create more mischief or come only for financial gain. He noted that another priest, Somerset, had returned to the church in hopes of gaining a pension promised by the Americans. Jacobus argued forcefully that the clergy who left the AOC should stay out or submit themselves to strict values in all future dealings with the church.[55]

Alexander did not always heed his grandson's advice. Nonetheless, he used Jacobus as his confidant. He was so grateful that Jacobus responded to all of his concerns and kept secret all information Alexander shared with him. He urged Alexander to take vacations and not worry so much about the affairs of the AOC. Jacobus affctionately called Alexander the Chief and urged him to "Fight the good Fight." Jacobus knew better than anyone that his grandfather was a warrior and most deserving of respect from his clergy.

The clergy's behavior was uppermost in Alexander's mind shortly before his death in 1970. In a circular issued to all Bishops-Elect and clergy, Alexander stated it was necessary to write a second circular because so few clergy responded to the first. Alexander refreshed their memories by stating that they were the ones who deprived him of his congregation and now they provide no support to his stipend fund. Alexander placed the burden of complacency upon the Bishops-Elect:

> I wonder if those Clergy whom I nominated realize that paying this stipend fund is part of their test. . . if they cannot carry out a promise R2.0.0 how can they expect me to believe them. . . In selecting the men whom I thought would be of assistance to me in organizing the Parishes, and in setting an example to the clergy under them, we are still in the same rut in fact worse....[59]

There was no reason to assume that the Bishop-Elect Sikwebu and the clergy radically altered their actions of non-support for the Archbishop; they continued in their traditional pattern of financial sloth.

This painful process of schism ended all connections with the mother church in America and by the end of 1969, Alexander was now completely in charge of a new division of the AOC created in South Africa.

Endnotes

1. Letter from DW.A to Motsepe, 13 January 1960 (Box-9, Folder-96, DWA Papers).

2. Letter from DWA to Motsepe, 17 December 1959 (Box-9, Folder-96, DWA Papers).

3. *Ibid*

4. *Ibid.*

5. Synod Minutes, 1934-1961 (Box-3, Folder-35, DWA Papers), p. 607.

6. Correspodence Register, 1959 (Box-6, Folder-70, DWA Papers).

7. Synod Minutes, *op.cit* (Box-3, Folder-35, DWA Papers), p. 679.

8. *Ibid.*

9. *Ibid.*, p. 660.

10. *Ibid.*

11. *Ibid.*, p. 661.

12. *Ibid,.* p. 682.

13. *Ibid.*, p. 683.

14. *Ibid.*, p. 701.

15. *Ibid.*

16. *Ibid.*

17. *Ibid.*

18. Letter from DWA to Motsepe, 10 May 1961 (Box-9, Folder-96, DWA Papers).

19. *Ibid.*, P. 709.

20. *Ibid.*

21. *Ibid,.* p. 710.

22. *Ibid.*

23.*Ibid.*

24.*Ibid.*

25. Letter from Mbina to DWA, 26 June 1961 (Box-8, Folder-92, DWA Papers).

26. Letter from Mbina to DWA, 25 November 1961 (Box-8, Folder-92,DWA Papers).

27. *Ibid.*

28. Letter from DWA to Mbina c. 1961 (Box-8, Folder-92, DWA Papers). In the typical "Alexandrian" mode of financial dealings, he reminded Mbina that Motsepe died owing him L13.0.0.

29. Archbishop Grant, Primate of America, was elevated to Patriarch. Perhaps he felt that the maltreatment of Alexander was too harsh, and the schism within the church was not necessary. The record indicates that Peter IV, Grant, made a sincere effort to bridge the gap between the Mother church and the AOC in South Africa. What dashed the hope of reunification, of course, was the problem that arose between Alexander and Mbina.

30. Letter from Mbina to DWA, 5 April 1963 (Box-8, Folder-92, DWA Papers).

31. *Ibid.*

32. *Ibid.*

33. Letter from DWA to Motsepe, 17 April 1963 (Box-9, Folder-96, DWA Papers).

34. Letter from Patriarch Peter IV to Mbina, 6 March 1963 (Box-8, Folder-96, DWA Papers).

35. *Ibid.*

36. Letter from Mbina to DWA, 24 May 1963 (Box-8, Folder-96, DWA Papers).

37. Letter from DWA to Mbina, November 1963 (Box-8, Folder-96, DWA Papers).

38. Letter from DWA to S. S. Mphomane, 21 January 1964 (Box 9, Folder 97, DWA Papers).

39. Letter from Mphomane to Bantu Affairs Office, 15 December 1967 (Box-9, Folder-97, DWA Papers).

40. *Ibid.*

41. *Ibid.*

42. Synod Minutes, *op.cit.*, p. 712.

43. Primate's 33rd charge, October 1967 (Box-4, Folder-55, DWA Papers).

44. Report of His Eminence, 1963-64 (Box-4, Folder-55, DWA Papers).

45. Correspondence register, 1965 (Box-7, Folder-75, DWA Papers).

46. *Ibid.*

47. "Th Voice of the Primate", Vol. 1, No. 1, 1966, Published by the AOC (Box-2, Folder-l9, DWA Papers), p. 2 .

48. Letter from DWA to Jacobus Alexander, 1 March 1968 (Box-8, Folder-79, DWA Papers).

49. Letter from Mbina Iris Mbina to Sister Maria Rulash, c. April 1968 (Box 8, Folder-79, DWA Papers).

50. Letter from DWA to Harry Oppenheimer, 2 December 1968 (Box-10, Folder-123, DWA Papers).

5l. Letter from Patterson S. Sikwebu to DWA, 19 April 1969 (Box-9, Folder 100, DWA Papers).

51. Alexander's demands upon his Bishops-Elect were reasonable. He had made many sacrifices to build the AOC. For example, he left Mother Alexander in Johannesburg for two and one-half years to commence his ministry in Kimberley.

53. Letter from Jacobus to DWA, 21 March 1969 (Box-8, Folder-79, DWA Papers).

54. Letter from Jacobus to DWA, 24 July 1968 or 1969 (Box-8, Folder-79, DWA Papers)

55. Letter from Jacobus to DWA, 28 July 1969 (Box-8, Folder-79, DWA Papers).

56. Circular No. 3, from DWA to all Bishops Elect and clergy, 13 March 1970 (Box-9, Folder-107, DWA Papers).

CHAPTER 8

CONCLUSION: AOC AND AFRICAN AMERICAN HISTORY

This concluding chapter highlights key issues raised in this study: the influence of the African American experience on the separatist movement in South Africa, the reasons for the schism within the AOC, the color identity question, and some final remarks on Pan-Africanism and Black theology.

The American experience was influential in the development of the independent Church movement in South Africa. Three factors generated concern for Africa: sociopolitical conditions of the late 19th century, Bishop Turner's Christian nationalism and Marcus Garvey's program of Africa for Africans.

First, the pervasive racism and wide-spread segregation between 1880 and 1920 created a perception among poor Blacks that America was not their home. As their economic and personal security deteriorated, they sought relief through emigration schemes to Africa This outward thrust opened channels of communication which were mostly religious in nature. Christianity, therefore, became a vehicle for reformist demands by middle class Blacks in America and Africa.

In the South African context, missionaries, educators, students and ideas moved between the African and the African American communities. The interplay of these factors influenced Blacks in South Africa to build churches, schools and lines to achieve western education. They emulated their American cousins. In conjunction with this, a small but dynamic group of Blacks in America desired a reconnection with Africa to redeem Africans throughout the diaspora. Black Christian nationalism called for building a new civilization in Africa free from European exploitation. No one more forcefully believed in African redemption than Bishop Turner. Since Blacks were maltreated in America and denied citizenship rights, he argued that Africa must be redeemed for Blacks who rejected America as home, and for Blacks on the African continent who wished to rebuild Africa and recapture the splendor of a glorious past. Armed with a deep love for Africa and a deep distrust for whites, Turner had a positive impact upon the Black educated elite of South Africa. Tuner's baptism of thousands spurred on the independent church movement. His fiery anti-white rhetoric instilled pride in his South African counterparts.

Marcus Garvey's newspaper, *The Negro World* sustained black political and religious nationalism throughout the 1920's. Garvey challenged the status quo by asking: Where are the black heads of state? Where are the black armies to protect the African people? He influenced generations with his message of race pride, black self-determination and land autonomy. These ideas and values were expressed in the pages of *The Negro World* and struck a responsive chord with Daniel William Alexander.

Alexander learned about the AOC from reading *The Negro World*, his subsequent trip to America in 1927 brought him into direct contact with the Black American experience. The American experience was very dear to him and he thought that Patriarch McGuire was a man among men. Some years later, he desired to raise money for various church projects and to renew contacts between the Mother Church and branches of the AOC in southern Africa. The schism which occurred within the AOC in 1961 severed Alexander from future monetary and emotional support from the mother church.

What attracted African churchmen to African American based theology, and why did the AOC encounter with religious Pan Africanism fail? First, African churchmen were attracted to the racial autonomy of some of their religious ideas. Under McGuire's leadership, the AOC also stressed black economic and political development free from white control. African Christians in South Africa took pride in these racial ideas which reinforced a belief they could achieve the same religious independence as their American cousins. Such a linkage elevated their religious rank and prestige. There was no difficulty in transplanting AOC's religious views into South Africa because, as in America, mounting segregation and maltreatment of Blacks fostered programs of upliftment and spiritual emancipation.

Although the AOC's religious beliefs made headway in South Africa, their Pan Africanist ideals did not. Pan Africanism meant that Africans and those of African descent were "chained" together in struggle/solidarity against racial and economic exploitation. The pariah status of those in the African diaspora sparked a discussion concerning a philosophy of how to enhance their liberation.[1] It was out of this spirit of race consciousness and the desire to provide spiritual emancipation for Blacks that Patriarch McGuire extended his hand of fellowship to Alexander.

The schism which tore the AOC of South Africa asunder was rooted in economics and a struggle for power rather than in ethnic or cultural differences. The AOC in America was a poor church, but the AOC in South Africa was even poorer. Alexander was always taking funds from his right hand to pay debts on the left. Lack of money prevented him from making trips to America to keep the bonds of support and respect strong and firm. Sufficient funds may have provided him with greater opportunities to travel abroad, thereby keeping the channels of communication open .

The reasons why the American bishops came to South Africa in 1960 were to reopen channels of communication and to consecrate Motsepe and Mbina as bishops. There is nothing in the AOC archives to suggest that James I or Primate Grant were displeased with Alexander's performance as Archbishop. The events, therefore, that led to schism emanated solely from South African actors. Once the American fathers were on African soil, events escalated into demands for Alexander's ouster. Motsepe was the central figure who turned the American prelates against Alexander.

What is less clear were Motsepe's motives for demanding Alexander's ouster. The only account of this emerging altercation was presented by Alexander, who noted that Motsepe told the American prelates many lies and half truths concerning his character. The American leaders sided with Motsepe in the feud, but their reasons for doing so were never clearly expressed. Perhaps they believed that after thirty-five years of Alexander's leadership, it was simply time for a change at the helm. Or they may have found Alexander's system of record keeping seriously flawed and deemed him incompetent.

The toughness which Alexander displayed during the schism characterized his entire life. Had he projected a "softness" toward meeting adversity, the AOC would not have lasted under his leadership for nearly a half century. His greatest achievement, of course, was the AOC becoming a government-recognized church in 1941. He had to overcome the problem of many restrictions placed upon "native" churches by The South African government. He had to fill out mounds of paperwork, took many insults from the government and expended considerable energy monitoring the government to ensure that the AOC's documents were received by the authorities.

Alexander also had to take on the multi-faceted problems related to the institutionalization of the AOC inside and outside of South Africa. To him, leadership and finance were the most vexing issues. He constantly searched for qualified men to become a part of the AOC leadership. Most of the time Alexander was unable to attract superior clergymen. His stern hand kept most of them in line, but they only performed at a modest level. His efforts to recruit qualified clergy in Basotoland and Rhodesia also produced a limited harvest. Problems of leadership were closely related to the matter of providing a strict accounting of funds. Some of his clergy kept some church monies for their own use, after they had received their salaries. This type of dishonesty plagued the AOC throughout its existence.

He also struggled with the profound dilemma of race and identity on two fronts. On the church front, Alexander remarked that coloureds needed to terminate their spiritual bondage; his grandson, Jacobus, agreed that coloureds could not be ". . . the eternal hewers of wood and drawers of water ...."[2]

Alexander expected greater Coloured membership within the AOC. The AOC in America had a large black Caribbean membership. However, in South Africa, the majority of its members were black Africans. Clearly the race/identity question was at the genesis of the AOC which came into existence to be free from European control. But many Coloureds expressed an uneasiness with very close and personal relationships with Africans. Even within the AOC, some Colourds called Africans "Kaffirs." Some Coloureds did not want Blacks in their churches, and a request to Alexander to combine two churches in close proximity, one for Coloureds and the other for Africans, fell on deaf ears. The two churches gave the appearance that apartheid was supported within the AOC. Alexander, to be sure, tried to resolve such matters with tact and reticence.

Alexander could not avoid attempts by the government to reclassify him as "native" or African. The government deemed him an African, but he fought the classification. Physically, he did not have the appearance of a mulatto or European. Nonetheless, he could not embrace his blood, his people, his heritage driven by his rejection of Africanness, he took refuge in the sham notion of "colouredness."

My thesis is, therefore, that mission education reproduced in the black South African elite a reformed "mind-sets" which rejected activism for solving social problems. Alexander's demand for inclusion in South African society, whether racial, religious or political was not revolutionary or militant. The South African government resisted reformist demands by him and other mission-educated black clergy. Even more problematic was that he could not make a complete break from his missionary training. The danger of mission education, then, was that it constantly presented religion as supporting the status quo and working against political agitation and change.

This proclivity towards reform was expressed in a theology of submission which defined the South African problem as bad people experiencing a change of heart. This theological perspective impaired Alexander's vision of religious emancipation. He did not give enough attention to those separatist churches which interpreted scripture as God's liberating message to free his chosen people, the exploited black masses.

Shortly before his death in 1970, a new theological perspective, Black Theology, was introduced into South Africa. A few black theologians declared war on Eurocentric theological views. The essence of Janes Cone's position was that Christian salvation was not only emancipation from individual sin but also from the corporate sin of poverty and white exploitation. In his seminal study, *Black Theology and Black Power*, Cone argued that God was on the side of the black oppressed masses, and the struggle of black people to empower themselves in white racist America was morally, biblically and theologically sound. Black theology had already been articulated by many African religious leaders such as Kimbangu, Chilembwe, Matswa, Nehanda and Mgijima.

Alexander did not tap this rich heritage of resistance. Of course, we cannot state with any certainty that he would have embraced black theology. Allen Boesak, too, did not use this rich history in exploring the rich of black theology in South Africa However, in his eloquent *Farewell to Innocence : A Socio-Ethical Study on Black Theology and Power*, he made the valid point that the biblical message was one of liberation. Any notion of liberation of the African in South Africa (or the United States) must take into account the long history of the exploitative relationship between European groups with power and African groups struggling to obtain power for themselves.[3]

The idea of winning acceptance must be explored in the wider framework of Alexander's popularity. Newman suggested that the Archbishop's claim to a valid apostolic succession may account for his general appeal. Since so few separatist church leaders could state such a claim, it "sets Alexander apart from the charismatic leadership of other independent churches and places him and the African Orthodox Church in a unique position vis-a-vis the traditional churches."[4] This, of course, may be so for a few who understood the importance of the heritage of apostolic succession for Catholicism, in Eastern and Western churches. On the other hand, greater weight should be given to the feet that the AOC was a recognized church by the government. Alexander recalled with great pride that over six hundred churches were knocking at the government's door for recognition. This status provided the AOC with a unique and elite position among separatist churches. Coupled with this elite status was Alexander's "magnetic' personality. His ability to lead and to "charm" even his adversaries was well established throughout separatist circles.

Alexander's well established leadership as a key player in fostering religious emancipation or self determination is his lasting achievement in the Ethiopian movement His reformist concerns for leadership separate from European controlled churches was part of the training ground for Africans, in general, to assume greater responsibility for their destinies after the "abolition" of colonialism. His individual efforts in Kenya, Uganda, Basutoland, Rhodesia and South Africa was part of a limited Pan African thrust for the redemption of Africa. At the same time, his extensive efforts were proof that Africans were capable of self rule. He, therefore, was a living symbol of the potential of Pan Africanism.

Although the AOC waged some resistance against apartheid, it did not engage in a scorched earth policy of liberation by any means necessary, due to the ethic of turning the other check, of course, within the Afrikaner community, the theology that emerged was one of power to ensure the survival/dominance of Dutch descendants. Alexander interpreted scripture, on the other hand, not in terms of earthly power but as being humble or bearing the cross. So many Africans, oppressed throughout the diaspora, held to the notion that suffering must be endured to achieve a brighter heavenly crown.

This history of the AOC is, therefore, a part of the extensive ties that existed between Africans in South Africa and "New World" Africans in the United States of America. The history of the AOC is also American history. Garvey came to greatness in America; McGuire established the AOC in Harlem, and Alexander became a bishop in Boston. Africa, North America and the Caribbean merge produced the history of the AOC. Daniel William Alexander's death on 14 May 1970 marked the end of a formative chapter in the AOC's history. He was the last living link to Patriarch McGuire and Marcus Garvey. Of his 67 years of religious service, 45 years were spent in the service of the African Orthodox Church. Early in the 1950's, James Mdatyulwa expressed his hope that all the good which Alexaneder had done would not be interred with his bones. In turn, I hope this thesis, in some small way, publicizes some of his good works.

1. E. U. Essien-Udom *Black Nationalism : A Search for Identity in America* (New York Dell Publishing Co., Inc., 1964). Essien-Udom describes the efforts of Blacks in the Nation of Islam as being middle class. This is correct; however, the broader picture suggests that the Nation of Islam has put into action a program of liberation, i.e., to eradicate the pariah condition of Blacks. See also Banard M. Magubane, *The Ties that Bind: African American Consciousness of Africa* (Trenton, New Jersey: Africa World Press, Inc., 1987). Magubane argues that due to the worldwide pariah status of Blacks, Pan-Africanism is a major tool used to combat psychological and economic "helplessness".

2. Letter from Jacobus to DWA, 6 July 1969 (Box-8, Folder-78, DWA Papers).

3. Alexander was certainly an important figure who helped institutionalize the independent church movement in southern Africa. In East Africa, however, the picture is more difficult to evaluate because Sparta left the AOC to enter the Coptic and other Greek Churches. Due to Sparta's chameleon religious character, he broke the historical continuity of Alexander's work in that region. It would not be an exaggeration to say that Alexander was the "Patron Saint" of Orthodox African Christians in Uganda. In other words, if Alexander had not spent those several months in Uganda establishing a strong separatist church foundation, the African Greek community would have had a much slower pace of development and a much more difficult fight to gain acceptance in the Greek-controlled churches.

4. Sec Newman,*op.cit.,p.* 17.

THE AOC ARCHIEVES

The African Orthodox Church records are housed at Pitts Theological Library, Emory University. The archives hold extensive correspondences between Archbishop Daniel William Alexander and AOC priests: Mdatyulwa, Poyah, Motsepe, Mbina, Julius, Hinnings, Masiko, and Hlong. Their letter covered such issues as finance, educational standards, problems with European controlled churches, government regulations for separatist church, and intimate personal problems. The letters reveal the colorful personalities of many of the AOC priests.

Other correspondence is preserved in the archives. One section in the archives is called "Members in Africa", which includes general correspondence with church people all over the continent of Africa. The "Miscellaneous" section also includes materials on topics which confronted Alexander. Two of the most important issues were the constitutional crises of the early 1950's which deprived coloureds of the right to vote and the color question which vexed South Africa. Alexander saved numerous news clippings concerning race reclassification and the problems he encountered with the apartheid system.

There are files that highlight the Pan-African nature of the AOC. Patriarch McGuire and Alexander entered into a religious association of separatist Christianity. The archives also highlight the requirements Alexander had to meet in order to become affiliated with the AOC. In addition, several travel diaries provided important information on Alexander's travels in Uganda, Kenya, Rhodesia, and America. In addition, the archives contain correspondence with church people and laity in England, Cuba, Sweden and the Bahamas.

Alexander's yearly addresses to the AOC are found in the voluminous "Synod" records. Alexander expressed his opinions on issues dealing with apartheid laws, the conduct of clergy, the schism with the mother church, attacks from the Anglican church, monies to defray the cost of the American trip and the need to support the Campaign for Spiritual Freedom.

There are two great limitations to this large collections of documents. First, there is a paucity of the information about Alexander's childhood and early adult life, his children and his wives. Second, there is a lack of information about Mother Alexander, who supported her husband for nearly fifty years in nurturing the AOC.

GOVERNMENT PUBLICATIONS

Cape of Good Hope. House of Assembly. *Report of the Select Committee on the Afrikaner Bond.* Cape Town: Government Printer, 1902.

DeWet Nel, M. D. C. *Industrial Development in Peripheral Areas.* Pretoria: Information Service of the Department of Bantu Administration and Development, 1960.

Fouche, Leo (comp.) *Report on the Outbreak of the Rebellion, and the Policy of the Government with regard to Its Suppression.* Pretoria: Government Printer, 1915.

India Information Services. *World Opinion on Apartheid.* New Delhi, 1952.

Jansen, Ernest George. *Native Policy of the Union of South Africa: Statements Made on 20 April 1950 and 19 May 1950.* Pretoria: State Information Office, 1950.

Jooste, C. P. *South Africa: Planned Policy of Chaos.* New York: Union of South Africa State Information Office, 1952.

Malan, Daniel F. *Apartheid: South Africa's Answer to a Major Problem: Letter from Dr. D. F. Malan . . . to The Reverend John Piersma . . . Grand Rapids, Michigan.* Pretoria: State Information Office, 1954.

Foreign Policy of the Union of South Africa. Pretoria: State Information Office, 1950.

Nicholls, G. Heaton. *Native Policy of the Union of South Africa.* New York: Union of South Africa State Information Office, 1945.

Report of Native Churches Commission Cape Town: Cape Times Limited, Government Printers, 1925.

Roberts, H. R., and K. G. Coleman. *Betterment for the Bantu.* Pretoria: Department of Native Affairs, n.d.

Strydom, J.G. *Separate Representation of Coloureds and Sovereignty of Parliament.* Address . . . at Joint Sitting, Houses of Parliament, February 15, 1956.

Union of South Africa. Department of Native Affairs. Bantu Education: *Policy for the Immediate Future:* Statement by Hon. Dr. H. F. Verwoerd, Minister of Native Affairs in the Senate of the Parliament . . . 7 June 1954. Pretoria: Government Printer, 1954.

House of Parliament. *The Cape Coloured Vote: A Common Roll or Political Apartheid.* Cape Town: Government Printer, 1953.

The Question of Race Conflict in South Africa Resulting from the Policies of Apartheid of the Government of the Union of South Africa. Proceedings of the United Nations. Pretoria: Government Printer, annual since 1952.

State Information Office. *Apartheid: South Africa's Answer to a Major Problem: Prime Minister D. F. Malan's Letter to an American Clergyman dated 12 February, 1954.* Pretoria: Government Printer, 1954.

PERIODICALS

Africa X-Ray Report: A Special Monthly Intelligence Service on Africa below the Sahara. Investors Intelligence, Johannesburg, 1954-59.

African Studies. Quarterly, Department of Bantu Studies of the University of Witwatersrand, Johannesburg, since 1921.

The Black Sash (Die Swart Serp). Monthly, Cape Town, since 1957. (English and Afrikaans.)

The Diamond Fields Advertiser. Daily, Argus group, Kimberley, since 1877. (English.)

Ilanga Lase Natal. Weekly, Bantu Press, Argus group, Durban. Founded by John L. Dube, first president of the ANC. (English and Zulu.)

Journal of Racial Affairs. Quarterly, South African Bureau of Racial Affairs, Stellenbosch, since 1949.

The Negro of Native Churches: The Official Organ of the African Orthodox Church, Vols. I 4, 1923-1926 and Vols. 6-9, 1927-1931. Millwood, New York: Kraus Report Co., 1977.

Race Relations News. Monthly, South African Institute of Race Relations, Johannesburg.

Thought: A Journal of Afrikans Thinking for English-Speaking. Quarterly, South African Institute of Race Relations, Johannesburg, since 1956. Mimeographed.
The World. Daily, Johannesburg, since 1932. Originally published as The Bantu World. Highest circulation of any Bantu newspaper. (English vernacular; sometimes Afrikans.)

Zonk. Monthly, Johannesburg, since 1949. A monthly for Africans, patterned after Drum. (Engglish.)

Books

Adams, Heribert and Herman Giliomee, *Ethnic Power Mobilized: Can South Africa Change?*, New Haven: Yale University Press, 1979.

Adas, Michael. *Prophets of Rebellion: Millenarian Protest Movements against the European Colonial Order*, Chapel Hill: University of North Carolina Press, 1979.

Adhikari, Mohammed. *"Let Us Live for Our Children": The Teacher's League of South Africa*, Cape Town: UCT Press (buchu books), 1993.

Alexander, Neville. *Education and the Struggle for National Liberation in South Africa*, Skotaville: Braamfontien, 1990.

Ani, Marimba. *Yurugu: An African-Centered Critique of European Thought and Behavior*, Trenton, NJ: Africa World Press, 1994.

Asante, Molefi K. *The Afrocentric Idea*, Trenton, NJ: Africa World Press, Inc., 1988.

_____ *Afrocentricity*, Trenton, NJ: Africa World Press, Inc., 1988.

Baeta, G.C. *Christianity In Tropical Africa*, London: Oxford University Press, 1968.

Ballinger, Margaret. *From Union to Apartheid: A Trek to Isolation*, New York, Praeger and London, Bailey Bros., 1969.

Berry, Mary F. and John W. Ballasingame. *Long Memory: The Black Experience in America*, New York and Oxford: Oxford University Press, 1982.

Bhana, Surendra & Bridglal Pachai. *A Documentary History of Indian South Africans*, David Philip, Publisher, Cape Town & Johannesburg, 1984.

Biko, Steve. *I Write What I Like: A Section of His Writings*, San Francisco: Harper & Raw, orig. edn, 1978.

Blackburn, Robin. *Ideology in Social Science*, Glasgow, Fontana/Collins, 1972.

Boesak, Allan A. *Farewell to Innocence: A Socio-Ethnical Study on Black Theology and Black Power*, Maryknoll, NY: Orbis Books, 1977.

_____ *Black and Reformed: Apartheid, Liberation, and the Calvinist Tradition*, Maryknoll, NY: Orbis Books, 1984.

Bonino, Jose M. *Doing Theology in a Revolutionary Situation*, Philadelphia: Fortress Press, 1975.

_____ *Christians and Marxists: The Mutual Challenge to Revolution*, Grand Rapids, Michigan: Eerdmans, 1976.

_____ *Toward a Christian Political Ethics*, Philadelphia: Fotress Press, 1983.

Bottomore, T. B. *Classes in Modern Society*, New York: Vintage Books, 1966.

BredeKamp, Henry & Robert Ross (eds.). *Missions and Christianity in South African History*, Johannesburg: Witwatersrand University Press, 1995.

Brotz, Howard M. *The Black Jews of Harlem: Negro Nationalism and the Dilemmas of Negro Leadership*, New York: Schocken Books, 1964.

Bryce, James. *Impressions of South Africa*, New York: The Century Company, 1898.

Bunting, Brian. *The Rise of the South African Reich*, Harmondsworth: Penguin Books, 1964.

Burkett, Randall K. and Richard Newman. *Black Apostles: Afro-American Clergy Confront the Twentieth Century*, Boston: G. K. Hall & Co., 1978.

Burridge, Kenelm. *New Heaven, New Earth: A Study of Millenarian Activities*, New York: Schocken Books, 1969.

Cabral, Amilcar. *Revolution In Guinea*, London: Stage 1, 1969; New York: Monthly Review Press, 1972.

Carter, Gwendolyn M. & Patrick O'Meara, (eds.). *Southern Africa in Crisis*, Bloomington: Indiana University Press, 1977.

Cell, John W. The Highest Stage of White Supremacy: The Origins of Segregation In South Africa and the *American South*, Cambridge and New York: Cambridge University Press, 1982.

Chidester, David. *Religions of South Africa*, London & New York: John Hinnells & Ninlan Smant, Routledge, 1992.

Chirenje, Mutero J. *Ethiopianism and Afro-Americans in Southern Africa, 1883-1916*, Baton Rouge: Louisiana State University Press, 1887.

Cilliers, S.P. *The Coloreds of South Africa: A Factual Survey*, Cape Town: Banier, 1963.

Clarke, Peter B. *Black Paradise: The Rastafarian Movement,* Wellingborough, Northamptonshire: Aquarian Press, 1986.

Cobley, Alan G. *Class and Consciousness: The Black Petty Bourgeoisie in South Africa, 1924-1950*, New York and London: Greenwood Press, 1991.

Cohen, Robin and Jean Copans, (eds.). *African Labor History*, Beverly Hills: Sage Publications, 1978.

Come, James H. *Black Theology and Black Power*, New York: Seabury Press, 1969.

_____ *Black Theology of Liberation*, Philadelphia: Lippincott, 1970.

_____ *God of the Oppressed*, New York: Seabury Press, 1975.

_____ *My Soul Looks Back*, Nashville: Abingdon, 1982.

_____ Speaking The Truth: Ecumenism, Liberation and Black Theology, Grand Rapids, Michigan: William B. Eerdmans Publishing Company, 1986.

Cooper, Frederick. Struggle For The City: Migrant Labor, Capital, and the State in Urban Africa, Beverly Hills: Sage Publications, 1983.

Crockett, Norman. *The Black Towns*, Lawrence: Regents Press of Kansas, 1979.

Clarke, John H. *Who Betrayed the African World Revolution? And Other Speeches*, Chicago: Third World Press, 1994.

Davenport, T.H.R. *The Afrikaner Bond: The History of a South African Political Party, 1880-1911*, Cape Town: Oxford University Press, 1966.

DeKiewiet, C. W. *A History of South Africa: Social and Economic*, London: Oxford University Press, 1957.

Delaney, Martin R. *The Condition, Elevation, Emigration and Destiny of the Colored People of the United States,* New York; Avno Press and The New York Times, 1968.

Denoon, Donald. *Southern Africa Since 1800*, New York: Praeger Publishers, 1973.

Desai, Ram. *Christianity in Africa as Seen by Africans*, Denver: Alan Swallow, 1957.

Doughty, Oswald. *Early Diamond Days: The Opening of the Diamond Fields of South Africa*, Longman, 1963.

Edgar, Robert. *Because They Chose the Plan of God: The Story of Billhook Massacre*, Johannesburg: Racan Press, 1988.

Enklaar, Ido H. *Life and Work of Dr. J. Th. Vander Kemp, 1747-1811: Missionary Pioneer and Protagonist of Racial Equality in South Africa*, Cape Town: A.A. Balkema, 1988.

Elkiins, W. F. *Street Preachers, Faith Healers, and Herb Doctors In Jamaica*, 1890-1925, New York: Revisionist Press, 1977.

Elphick, Richard and Herman, Gilliomee. *The Shaping of South African Society*, 1652-1820, Cape Town: Longman, 1979.

Esedebe, Olisanwuche P. *Pan-Africanism: The Idea & Movement*, 1776-1963, Washington, D. C.: Howard University Press, 1982.

Etherington, Norman. *Preachers, Peasants, and Politics in Southeast Africa, 1835-1880: African Christian Communities in Natal, Pondoland, and Zululand, London,* Royal Historical Society, 1978.

Evans, Maurice S. *Black and White in SouthEast Africa*, New York: Negro Universities Press, 1969.

Fanon, Frantz. *The Wretched of the Earth*, New York: Grove Press, Inc., 1963.

Fatton, Robert, Jr. *Black Consciousness in South Africa: The Dialectics of Ideological Resistance and White Supremacy*, New York: State University of New York Press, 1986.

Fauset, Arthur H. *Black Gods of the Metropolis: Negro Religious Cults of the Urban North*, Philadelphia; University of Pennsylvania Press, 1971.

Flint, John. *Cecil Rhodes*, London: Hutchinson, 1976.

Franklin, John H. *Reconstruction: After the Civil War*, Chicago and London: The University of Chicago Press, 1961.

Franklin, V. P. *Black Self-Determination: A Cultural History of the Faith of the Fathers*, Westport, Connecticut: Lawrence Hill Company, 1984.

Frazier, Franklin E. *The Negro Church in America*, New York: Schocken Books, 1966.

Fredrickson, George M. *White Supremacy: A Comparative Study in America and South African History*, New York: Oxford University Press, 1981.

Freire, Paulo. *Pedagogy of the Oppressed*, New York: Continuum Publishing, 1985.

Fremantle, Anne. *Mao Tse-tung: An Anthology of His Writings*, New York: A Mentor Book, The New American Library Inc., 1962.

Garrow, David J. *Bearing the Cross: Martin Luther King and the Southern Leadership Conference*, New York: Vintage Books (Random House), 1986.

Garvey, J. Amy. *Garvey and Garveyism*, New York: Collier Books, 1970.

Gerhart, Gail. *Black Power in South Africa*, Berkeley: University of California Press, 1978.

Gifford, Paul G. *The Religious Right in Southern Africa*, Harare: University of Zimbabwe, 1988.

Goldberg, David T. *Racist Culture: Philosophy and the Politics of Meaning*, Blackwell: Oxford, 1993.

Goldin, Ian. *Making Race: The Politics and Economics of Coloured Identity in South Africa*, London and New York: Longman, 1987.

Gool, Selim. *Mining Capitalism and Black Labour in the Early Industrial Period in South Africa in Critique of the New Historiography*, Stockholm. Lund, 1983.

Gossett, Thomas F. *Race: The History of an Idea in America*, New York: Schocken Books, 1985.

Graybill, Lynn. *Religion and Resistance: Politics in South Africa*, Prager Press, 1995.

Gutkind, Peter C., Robin Cohen, and Jean Copans, (eds.). *African Labor History*, Beverly Hills: Sage Publications, 1978.

_____ Peter Waterman (eds.). *African Social Studies: A Radical Reader*, New York: Monthly Review Press, 1978.

Guy, Jeff. *The Heretic: A Study of the Life of John Colenso, 1814-1883*, Johannesburg: Raven Press, 1983.

Hammond-Tooke, W.D. *The Bantu-speaking Peoples of Southern Africa*, London: Rutledge and Kegan Paul, 1974.

Hannaford, Ivan. *Race: The History of an Idea in the West*, Washington, D.C., Baltimore/London: The Woodrow Wilson Center Press The John Hopkins University Press, 1996.

Harlan, Louis R. *Booker T. Washington: The Making of a Black Leader, 1856-1901*, New York: Oxford University Press, 1972.

Harsh, Ernest. *South Africa: White Rule, Black Revolt*, New York: Monad Press, 1980.

Heard, Kenneth A. *General Elections in South Africa 1943-1970*, London: Oxford University Press, 1974.

Hepple, Alex. *South Africa: A Political and Economic History*, New York: Praeger Publishers, 1966.

Higgs, Robert. *Competition and Coercion: Blacks in the American Economy*, 1865-1914, Cambridge, Cambridge University Press, 1977.

Hinchliff, Peter. *The Anglican Church in South Africa*, London, Darton, Longman, and Todd, 1963.

Hirson, Baruch. *Year of fire, Year of Ash. The Soweto Revolt: Roots of a Revolution*, London: Zed Press, 1979.

Hodgson, Janet. *The God of the Xhosa*, Cape Town: Oxford University Press, 1982.

Houghton, Hobart D. *The South African Economy*, Cape Town: Oxford University Press, 1967.

Innes, Duncan. *Anglo America and the Rise of Modern South Africa*, New York; Monthly Review Press, 1984.

Jaarsfeld, F.A. Van. *The Awakening of Afrikaner Nationalism 1868-1881*, Cape Town, 1961.

Jabavu, D. D. T. *The Black Problem*, New York: Reprinted by Negro Universities Press, 1969.

_____ *The Segregation Fallacy, and Other Papers*, Lovedale: Lovedale Press, 1928.

Jackson, John G. *Christianity Before Christ*, Austin: American Atheis & Press, 1985.

Jacobs, Sylvia M. *The African Nexus: Black American Perspectives on the European Partitioning of Africa, 1880-1920*, Westport, Conn.: Greenwood Press, 1981.

_____ *Black Americans and the Missionary Movement in Africa*, Westport, Connecticut: Greenwood Press, 1982.

Jansen, E.G. *Native Policy of the Union of South Africa*, Pretoria: State Information Office of the Union of South Africa, 1950.

Jenkins, Paul. *The Recovery of the West African Past: African Pastors and African History in the Nineteenth Century*, c.c. Reindorf and Samuel Johnson (ed.), Basel: Basiert Afrika Bibliographien, 1998.

Johnston, Frederick A. *Class, Race and Gold: A Study of Class Relations and Racial Discrimination in South Africa*, London: Routledge & Kegan Paul, 1976.

Jones, Major J. *Black Awareness: A Theology of Hope*, Nashville: Abingdon, 1971.

Jones, William R. *Is God a White Racist? A Preamble to Black Theology*, Garden City, New York: Anchor Press/Doubleday, 1973.

Kallaway, Peter. *Apartheid and Education: The Education of Black South Africans*, Johannesburg: Fifth Impression, Raven Press, 1991.

Karis, Thomas and Gwendolyn M. Carter. *From Protest to Challenge: A Documentary History of African Politics in South Africa*, Vol. 1, 1882-1934, Stanford: Hoover Institution Press, 1971.

Katzenellenbogen, E. Simon. *South Africa and Southern Mozambique: Labour, Railways and Trade in the Making of a Relationship*, Manchester: Manchester University Press, 1982.

Kenyatta, Jomo. *Facing Mount Kenya. The Tribal Life of the Gikuyu*, New York: Vintage Books, 1965.

King, Kenneth J. Pan-Africianism and Education: A Study of Race Philosophy and Education in the *Southern States of America and East Africa*, Oxfor: Oxford University Press/Clarendon Press, 1971.

Kubicek, Robert V. *Economic Imperialism in Theory and Practice: The Case of South African Gold Mining Finance*, 1886-1914, Durham, NC: Duke University Press, 1979.

Kupe, Leo. *Passive Resistance in South Africa*, London: Cape, 1956, New Haven: Yale University Press, 1957.

Kwaa, Kwesi. Beyond the Colour Line; Pan-Africanist Disputatious: Selected Sketches, Letters, Papers and *Reviews*, Prah: Vivlia, 1997.

Laffey, John F. *Civilization and Its Discontented*, Montreal/New York/London: Black Rose Books, 1993.

Lamar, Howard and Leonard Thompson (eds.). *The Frontier in History: North America and Southern Africa Compared*, New Haven and London: Yale University Press, 1981.

Lantenari, Vittorio. *Religions of the Oppressed*, New York: Alfred Knopf, 1963.

Lewis, Gavin. *Between the Wire and the Wall: A History of South African Coloured Politics*, New York: St. Martin's Press, 1987.

Lewis, Rupert. *Marcus Garvey, Anti-Colonial Champion*, Londo: Karia Press, 1987.

Litwack, Leon F. *Been in the Storm So Long: The Aftermath of Slavery*, New York: Vintage Books, 1980.

Locke, Alain and Bernhard J. Stern. *When Peoples Meet A Study in Race and Culture Contacts*, New York: Progressive Education Association, 1942.

Lodge, Tom. *Black Politics in South Africa since 1945*, London and New York: Longman, 1983.

Logan, Rayford W. *The Betrayal of the Negro: From Rutherford B. Hayes to Woodrow Wilson*, New York: Collier Books, 1965.

Loubser, J.A. *The Apartheid Bible: A Critical Review of Racial Theology in South Africa*, Cape Town: Maskew Miller Longman, 1987.

Luthuli, Albert. *Let My People Go: An Autobiography*, London: Collins, 1962.

MacCrone, I.D. *Race Attitudes in South Africa: Historical, Experimental and Psychological Studies*, London: Oxford University Press, 1937.

MacMillan, W. M. *Bantu, Boer and Briton: The Making of the South African Native Problem*, London: Oxford University, 1963.

Magubane, Bernard M. *The Political Economy of Race and Class in South Africa*, New York: Monthly Review Press, 1979.

_____ *The Ties That Bind: African-American Consciousness of Africa*, Trenton, New Jersey: Africa World Press, Inc., 1987.

Mahan, Brian and Dale L. Richesin (eds.). *The Challenge of Liberation Theology: A First World Response*, Maryknoll, N.Y.: Orbis, 1981.

Majeke, Nosipho. *The Role of the Missionaries in Conquest*, Johannesburg: Society of Young Africa, 1952.

Mandela, Nelson. *Long Walk to Freedom*, London: Abacus, 1995.

Mandle, Jay R. The Roots of Black Poverty: The Southern Plantation Economy After the Civil War, Durham: Duke University Press, 1978.

Marais, J. S. *The Cape Coloured People*, 1652-1927, Johannesburg: Witwatersrand University Press, 1968.

Marks, Shula and Stanley Trapido (eds.). *The Politics of Race, Class, and Nationalism in Twentieth Century South Africa*, London and New York: Longman Inc., 1987.

Marks, Shula. *Reluctant Rebellion: The 1906-1908 Disturbances in Natal*, Oxford: Clarendon Press, 1970.

Marquard, Leo. *The Peoples & Policies of South Africa*, London: Oxford Paperbacks, 1962.

Martin, Tony. *The Pan-African Connection: From Slavery to Garvey and Beyond*, Dover, Massachusetts: Majority Press, 1983.

Maylam, Paul. *A History of the African People of South Africa: From the Early Iron Age To*, Cape Town and Johannesburg: Croom Helm, London, David Philip, , 1986.

Mays, Benjamin.*The Negro's God as Reflected in His Literature*, New York: Russell & Russell, 1968.

Mayson, Cedric. *A Certain Sound: The Struggle for Liberation in South Africa*, Maryknoll, NY: Orbis, 1985.

Mboya, Tom. *Freedom and Africa*, London: Andre Deutch, 1963.

Meier, August. *Negro Thought In America, 1880-1915: Racial Ideologies in the Age of Booker T. Washington*, Ann Arbor: University of Michigan Press, 1966.

Memmi, Albert. *The Colonizer and the Colonized*, Boston: Beacon Press, 1965.

Mermelstein, David, (ed.). *The Anti-Apartheid Reader: South Africa and the Struggle Against White Racist Rule,* New York: Grove Press, 1987.

Miranda, P. Jose. *Marx and the Bible: A Critique of the Philosophy of Oppression* (trans. John Eagleson), Maryknoll, N.Y.: Orbis, 1974.

Mobley, Harris W. *The Ghanaian's Image of The Missionary: An Analysis of the Published Critiques of Christian Missionaries by Ghanaians, 1897-1965*, Leiden, E. J. Brill, 1970.

Moodie, T. Dunbar. *The Rise of Afrikanerdom: Power, Apartheid, and the Afrikaner Civil Religion*, Berkeley: University of California Press, 1980.

Moore, Basil. *Black Theology: The Southern Voice*, London: C. Hurst and Co., 1973.

Morris, Donald R. *The Washing of the Spears: A History of the Zulu Nation under Shaka and its fall in the Zulu War of 1879*, London: Cape, 1966.

Naidoo, Jay. *Tracking Down Historical Myths: Eight South African Cases*, Johannesburg: A.D. Donker/Publisher, 1989.

Neill, Stephen. *Colonialism and Christian Missions*, New York: McGraw-Hill, 1974.

Nobles, Wade W. *Africanity and the Black Family: The Development of a Theoretical Model*, Oakland: A Black Family Institute Publication, 1985.

Nyang, Sulayman S. *Islam, Christianity, and African Identity*, Brattleboro, VT: Amana Books, 1984.

Oliver, Roland. *The Missionary Factor In East Africa*, Longman Group Limited, 1965.

O'Meara, Dan, *Volks Kapitalisme: Class, Capital and Ideology in the Development of Afrikaner Nationalism*, 1934-1948, Cambridge: Cambridge University Press, 1983.

Omer-Cooper, J. D. *The Zulu Aftermath: A Nineteenth-Century Revolution in Bantu Africa*, Evanston: Northwestern University Press, 1969.

Padmore, George. *Pan-Africanism or Communism?* Garden City, New York: Anchor Books, 1972.

Palmer, Mabel. *The History of Indians in Nata*, Cape Town: Oxford University Press, 1976.

Palmer, Robin & Neil Parsons (eds.). *The Roots of Rural Poverty in Central and Southern Africa*, Berkeley: University of California Press, 1977.

Parrillo, Vincent N. *Strangers To These Shore: Race and Ethnic Relations in the United States (fourth edition)*, New York: McMillian Publishing Company, 1994.

Pettifer, Julian and Richard Bradley. *Missionaries,* London: BBC Books, 1990.

Pelzer, A.N. *Verwoerd Speaks: Speeches 1948-1966,* Johannesburg: APB Publishers, 1966.

Pienaar, S.W. *Believe in Your People: D.F. Malan as Orator*, 1908-1954, Cape Town: Tafelberg, 1964.

Plaatje, T. Sol. *Native Life In South Africa, Before and Since The European War and The Boer Rebellion*, New York: Negro Universities Press, 1969.

Pobee, John S. *Toward An African Theology*, Nashville: Abingdon, 1979.

Poel, Jean Vander. *The Jameson Raid*, Cape Town: Oxford University Press, 1951.

Pre, Roy Hdu. *Separate But Unequal: The "Coloured" People of South Africa – A Political History*, Johannesburg: Jonathan Ball Publishers, 1994.

Price, Robert M. and Carl G. Rosberg, (eds.). *The Apartheid Regime: Political Power and Racial Domination*, Berkeley: Institute of International Studies, University of California, 1980.

Reader, D. H. *The Black Man's Portion: History, Demography and Living Conditions in the Native Locations of East London, Cape Province*, Cape Town: Oxford University Press, 1961.

Regehr, Ernie. *Perceptions of Apartheid: The Churches and Political Change in South Africa*, Scottdale, Pennsylvania: Herald Press, 1979.

Rhoodie, N. J. & H. J. Venter. *The Apartheid Idea: A Sociohistorical Explanation of its Origin and Development*, Pretoria: University of Pretoria, 1960.

Roberts, Brian. *Kimberley: Turbulent City*, Cape Town: David Philip Publisher, 1976.

Robinson, Cedric J. *Black Marxism: The Making of the Black Radical Tradition*, London: Zed Books, 1983.

Rodney, Walter. *How Europe Underdeveloped Africa*, Dar-es-Salaam, Tanzania Publishing House, 1972; Washington, D.C.: Howard University Press, 1982.

Rotberg, Robert I. and Ali Mazyui (eds.). *Protest and Power in Black Africa*, New York: Oxford University Press, 1970.

Roux, Edward. *Time Longer Than Hope: A History of the Black Man's Struggle for Freedom in South Africa*, 2nd ed. Madison: University of Wisconsin Press, 1964.

Sachs, Albie. *Justice in South Africa*, Berkeley and Los Angeles: University of California Press, 1973.

Salamanca, Bonifacio S. *The Filipino Reaction to American Rule, 1901-1913*, Hamden, Conn.: Shoe String Press, 1969.

Sandbrook, Richard and Robin Cohen (eds.). *The Development of an African Working Class*, London: Longman, 1975.

Setiloane, Gabriel. *The Image of God Among the Sotho – Tswana*, Rotterdam: A.A. Balkma, 1976.

Schapera, I. *The Khoisan Peoples of South Africa: Bushmen and Hottentots*, London: Routledge, 1930.

Schrire, Robert (ed). *Malan to De Klerk: Leadership in the Apartheid State*, London: Hurst & Company, 1994.

Shain, Milton. *The Roots of Antisemitism in South Africa*, Charlottesville and London: University of Virginia Press, 1994.

Shorter, Aylward. *African Christian Theology-Adaptation or Incarnation?*, Maryknoll, New York: Orbis Books, 1977.

Simons, H. J. and R. E. *Class and Colour in South Africa, 1850-1950*, Baltimore: Penguin Books, 1969.

Sithole, Ndabaningi. *African Nationalism*, London: Oxford University Press, 1968.

Smith, Edwin W. *The Golden Stool: Some Aspects of the Conflict of Cultures in Modern Africa*, London: Holborn Publishing House, 1926.

Smuts, Jan C. *The Basis of Trusteeship in African Native Policy*, Cape Town: Institute of Race Relations, 1942.

Stetler, Nico. *The Freedom Charter and Beyond: Founding Principles for a Democratic South African Legal Order*. Cape Town: Wyvern, 1991.

Stultz, Newell M. *Afrikaner Politics in South Africa 1934-1948*, Berkeley: University of California Press, 1974.

Sundkler, Bengt G. M. *Zulu Zion and Some Swazi Zionists*, Oxford: Oxford University Press, 1976.

_____ *Bantu Prophets in South Africa*, London: Oxford University Press, 1961.

Sweets, Leonard I. Black Images of America, 1784-1870, New York: W. W. Norton & Company, 1976.

Takaki, Ronald. *A Different Mirror: A History of Multicultural America*, New York: Back Bay Books, Little Brown and Company, 1993.

Taylor, Dexter J. *Christianity and the Natives of South Africa: A Yearbook of South African Mission*, Lovedale: General Missionary Conference of South Africa, 1928.

Temu, Arnold and Bonaventure, Swai. *Historians and Africanist History: A Critique, post-Colonial Historiography Examined*, London: Zed Press, 1981.

Thompson-Terry, C. A. *The History of the African Orthodox Church*, New York: Privately printed, 1956.

Thompson, Leonard. *The Political Mythology of Apartheid*, New Have: Yale University Press, 1985.

_____ *The Unification of South Africa, 1902-1910*, Oxford: Clarendon Press, 1960.

Thompson, Leonard. *Survival in Two Worlds: Misheshe Lesotho, 1786-1870*, Oxford: Oxford University Press, 1975.
_____ Jeffrey Butler. *Change in Contemporary South Africa*, Berkeley and Los Angeles: University of California Press, 1975.

Turner, Harold W. *Religious Innovation In Africa*, Boston: G. K. Hall & Co., 1979.

Underhill, Ruth M. *Red Man's America: A History of Indians in the United States*, Chicago: University of Chicago Press, 1971.

Uya, Edet O. *Black Brotherhood: Afro-Americans and Africa*, Lexington, Massachusetts: D. C. Heath and Company, 1971.

Van den Berghe, Pierre. *South Africa, A Study in Conflict*, Berkeley: University of California Press, 1970.

Van der Horst, S. T. *Native Labour in South Africa*, Cape Town, 1942 or London: Cass, 1971.

Van Onselen, Charles. *Chibaro: African Mine Labour in Southern Rhodesia, 1900-1933*, London: Pluto Press, 1976.

Vincent, Theodore. *Black Power and the Garvey Movement*, San Francisco: Ramparts, 1972.

Walker, Eric A. *A History of Southern Africa* (3rd Edition), London: Longman, 1964.

Warwick, Peter. *Black People and the South African War, 1899-1902*, Cambridge: Cambridge University Press, 1983.

Weisbord, Robert G. *Ebony Kinship: Africa, Africans, and the Afro-American*, Westport: Connecticut, Greenwood Press: 1973.

West, Martin. *Bishops and Prophets in a Black City: African Independent Churches in Soweto*, Johannesburg, Cape Town: David Philip, 1975.

Wilkins, Ivor and Hons Strydom. *The Super-Afrikaners: Inside the Afrikaner Broederbond*, Johannesburg: Jonathan Ball Publishers, paperback edition, 1980.

William, Brian. *Sol Plaatje, South African Nationalist 1876-1932*, Berkeley: University of California Press, 1984.

Williams, Gardner F. *The Diamond Mines of South Africa*, London: MacMillan & Company, 1902.

Williams, Donovan. *Umfundisi: A Biography of Tiyo Soga 1829-1871*, Lovedale: Lovedale Press, 1978.

Williamson, Joel. *New People: Miscegenation and Mulattoes in the United States*, New York: Free Press, 1980.

Willis, David W. and Richard Newman. *Black Apostles at Home and Abroad, Afro-Americans from the Revolution to Reconstruction*, Boston: G. K. Hall & Co., 1982.

Wilmore, Gayraud S. *Black Religion and Black Radicalism*, Garden City, New York: Anchor Press/Doubleday, 1973.

Wilson, Francis. *Migrant Labour: Report to the South African Council of Churches*, Johannesburg: South African Council of Churches and SPRO-CAS, 1972.

Wilson, Monica. *Reaction to Conquest: Effects of Contact with Europeans on the Pondo of South Africa*, London: Milford, 1936.

Wood, Forrest G. *Black Scare: The Racist Response to Emancipation and Reconstruction*, Berkeley and Los Angeles: University of California Press, 1970.

Woodson, Carter G. *The Mis-Education of the Negro*, New York: AMS Press, Inc., 1977.

Worden, Nigel. *Slavery in Dutch South Africa*, Cambridge: Cambridge University Press, 1985.

Wright, Louis B. *Religion and Empire: The Alliance Between Piety and Commerce in English Expansion, 1558-1625*, Chapel Hill: University of North Carolina Press, 1943.

Zulu, Alphaeu. *The Dilemma of the Black South African*, Cape Town: University of Cape Town, 1972.